I0124569

Cross-Border Solidarities in Twenty-First Century Contexts

Cross-Border Solidarities in Twenty-First Century Contexts

Feminist Perspectives and Activist Practices

Edited by
Janet M. Conway, Pascale Dufour, and
Dominique Masson

ROWMAN & LITTLEFIELD
Lanham • Boulder • New York • London

Published by Rowman & Littlefield
An imprint of The Rowman & Littlefield Publishing Group, Inc.
4501 Forbes Boulevard, Suite 200, Lanham, Maryland 20706
www.rowman.com

6 Tinworth Street, London SE11 5AL, United Kingdom

Copyright © 2021 by The Rowman & Littlefield Publishing Group, Inc.

All rights reserved. No part of this book may be reproduced in any form or by any electronic or mechanical means, including information storage and retrieval systems, without written permission from the publisher, except by a reviewer who may quote passages in a review.

British Library Cataloguing in Publication Information Available

Library of Congress Cataloging-in-Publication Data

Names: Conway, Janet M., 1963- editor. I Dufour, Pascale, 1971- editor. I
  Masson, Dominique, editor.
Title: Cross-border solidarities in twenty-first century contexts : feminist perspectives
  and activist practices / edited by Janet M. Conway, Pascale Dufour, and Dominique
  Masson.
Description: Lanham, Maryland : Rowman and Littlefield, 2021. I Includes
  bibliographical references and index. I Summary: "Grounded in empirical studies of
  activist practices, this international and interdisciplinary collection employs feminist
  analytics to interrogate the possibility of emancipatory cross-border solidarities in
  contemporary contexts"–Provided by publisher.
Identifiers: LCCN 2021020678 (print) I LCCN 2021020679 (ebook) I
  ISBN 9781538157695 (cloth) I ISBN 9781538157701 (paperback) I
  ISBN 9781538157718 (ebook)
Subjects: LCSH: Feminism–Case studies. I Feminist theory–Case studies. I
  Women's rights–Case studies. I Solidarity–Case studies.
Classification: LCC HQ1154 .C76 2021 (print) I LCC HQ1154 (ebook) I
  DDC 305.4201–dc23
LC record available at https://lccn.loc.gov/2021020678
LC ebook record available at https://lccn.loc.gov/2021020679

Contents

Introduction

Transnational Solidarities Reconsidered: Crossing Borders in the Twenty-First Century

Janet M. Conway, Dominique Masson, Khalil Habrih, and Pascale Dufour

Since the last wave of scholarship on the subject in the 1990s and early 2000s, transnational solidarities have been destabilized by a series of epochal shifts. The decline in frequency and influence of the UN conferences of the 1990s, which represented the apogee of international human rights and global feminism regimes, poses the question of where, with whom, at which scales, and around which visions, discourses, or issues should cross-border feminist solidarities be built. The emergence of post–Cold War geographies and geo-political categories and of post-socialist feminisms has created conditions for a reconfiguration of the global politics of feminisms and their solidarities across borders. Post-9/11 and U.S. wars in the Middle East and West Asia, the global war on terrorism and criminalization of oppositional social movements undermines their capacity to protest on a significant scale. After two decades, the alter-globalization movement and World Social Forum process are declining, and the vacuum has created conditions both for reactionary movements against globalization and the elaboration of different visions for "other possible worlds" from a range of other actors and sites.

In the wake of the 2008 financial meltdown, deepening inequalities, and austerity measures, there have been new waves of protest globally (Ancelovici, Dufour, and Nez 2016). The mobilizations of the Arab Spring, the Indignados, Occupy Wall Street, and student strikes in Chile and Quebec appeared to many analysts to augur a "return of the national" in the wake of the global justice movement (della Porta 2015). Although more intensely localized, we contend that these and the subsequent twenty-first-century movements continue to display significant transnational connectivity. Idle No More, which began as a Canada-wide Indigenous uprising provoked immediate mobilization of international solidarity and made visible again a globalized Indigenous Peoples' movement. The same happened in the 2020 Wet'suwet'en resistance to the Coastal Gaslink pipeline in British Columbia. Black Lives Matter, which erupted in 2014 as a protest against police violence in a number of North American cities, by 2020 became a worldwide rebellion against anti-Black racism and white supremacy as the ongoing afterlife of European empire-building—and this is in the midst of a global pandemic that closed borders, restricted travel, and limited public gatherings. Conditions, forms, and processes of transnationalization of solidarities are mutating—the "transnational object" appears to have changed and the way transnationalization operates has also changed (Dufour 2016)—but transnationalization, in variable and uneven ways, continues to be a defining feature of the twenty-first-century contexts and movements.

The intensifying crisis of neoliberal globalization, which is also a crisis of liberal democracy, has also seen the appearance of neo-populisms, neo-racisms, and new authoritarianisms that are eroding the foundation of the post–World War II liberal world order. This epochal transition underway in the "geoculture" (Wallerstein 1991) is also marked by intersectional feminisms, decolonial critique, and the "rights of Mother Earth" which have problematized the emancipatory traditions of the modern left as a shared framework of resistance among social justice movements. In short, we are in a new global political economy of solidarities that urgently calls for transnational, cross-cultural, and transdisciplinary analyses and invites reconsideration of the question of solidarity under these new conditions.

In its focus on cross-border solidarities, this book engages the question of organizing across political borders and across spatialized differences, in a variety of places, and at a range of scales. Informed by critical concepts in geography, it addresses conceptual debates about solidarities as socio-spatial praxes constructed as global, international, transnational, or translocal, as well as those arising from different kinds of difference experienced in particular places.

Our long-standing interest in the social construction of space as central to cross-border solidarities has heretofore oriented us to the study of transnationalization. In Conway (2008), Masson (2010), and Dufour et al. (2010), we contend that geographical concepts of place and scale powerfully contribute to further feminist inquiries into transnational solidarity-building in directing our attention to solidarities across space and difference as actively produced and grounded in concrete socio-spatial praxes (see chapters 3 and 4).

Geographer Doreen Massey theorizes "place" as both a locus and a moment at which "economic, political and cultural relations, each full of power and with internal structures of domination" intersect "in a distinct mixture of wider and more local social relations" (1994, 154, 156). Place, it is important to note, is a unit of analysis, and can be set by the analyst at various scales. "Scale" we understand as the extension and stretching of political, economic, and cultural processes over variable expanses of space (Masson 2010; see also Swyngedouw 1997a, 1997b; Agnew 1997). In this perspective, the transnational is understood as a socially constructed scale of immense variability, the political import and content of which remains contingent on specific historical praxes and calls for their empirical analyses. Because transnational movement activity involves many scales of organizing on a continuum from the local to the global, processes of solidarity-building may well unfold distinctly at different scales. These concepts enable analysis of cross-border solidarities as socio-spatial practices that are also enacting processes of transnationalization.

In retrospect, our insight that the building of solidarity involves the making, deepening, and stretching of linkages between previously unconnected struggles appears to be important, but insufficient. Even as processes of transnationalization have been a critically important feature of cross-border solidarities since the 1990s, the two should not be conflated. With this collection, we turn our attention to *solidarity* as a variable, contradictory, and contingent practice meriting conceptualization and analysis in its own right. Given how frequently and naturalistically solidarity is invoked by activists and researchers alike, we argue that the concept calls for deconstruction and re-articulation as a problematique—a task that we initiate here.

As critics have remarked, mainstream social movement studies offer remarkably little for investigating the construction of solidarities in collective action (Gill 2009, 667; Featherstone 2012, 5; Brown and Yaffe 2014, 37–38). Classical social movement theory models its understanding of solidarity on the classical sociology of Weber and Durkheim. Solidarity is viewed as the social ties that bind a constituency—a factor of movement cohesion. These ties may be understood in relation to "people's social location—for example, as worker or as black women" (Gamson 1991, 40). Here, solidarity is conceptualized as a preexisting resource, which can be harnessed and cultivated by movement actors (Fireman and Gamson 1979) or as a resource for stable governance (Krunke et al. 2020). Alternately, ties of solidarity are seen as deriving from identification with the group, producing feelings of a bond with others, and fostering loyalty and commitment (Melucci 1988, 1995; Gamson 1991). Although some recent scholarship is grappling with the limitations of these formulations in relation to contemporary developments (e.g., della Porta 2015, 2019), work on cross-border solidarities inspired by the classical social movement literature does not focus on solidarity as itself a problematic for study.

Yet, calls for solidarity remain central to transnational movement struggles, as well as to the work of many INGOs and in international campaigns (Giugni and Passy 2001; Reitan 2007). Noting the increased proliferation of references to solidarity in the scholarly work in this field, Siméant points to the uncritical appropriation of the term by scholars, who "rarely interrogate it, and take for granted what ought to be questioned" (2003, 76). In the literature on transnational social movements, solidarity usually is undefined and untheorized. These mobilizations are often treated "as if they expressed, by definition, forms of transnational solidarity" (2003, 77). In many cases, and although the vocabulary of solidarity may appear in the title of the works, transnationalization is the true conceptual focus of studies and solidarity remains unattended as a category of analysis (see, for instance, Smith, Chatfield, and Pagnucco 1997). In other cases, as in our 2010 book *Solidarities beyond Borders: Transnationalizing Women's Movements* (Dufour et al. 2010), the establishment of transnational connections is implicitly equated with the construction of solidarities.

In contradistinction, this collection explicitly interrogates how solidarities are being understood and constructed in a variety of cross-border struggles, and for what ends, under twenty-first-century conditions. Employing intersectional and transnational feminist analytics, we investigate the praxes of cross-border solidarities in a variety of contexts. *Intersectional feminism* invites critical attention to gender, race, class, sexuality, nation, religion, and/or other axes of difference and inequality as mutually constituted. *Transnational feminism* is intersectional in this sense but is further attentive to how these dynamics are situated in a global field of power shaped by histories of colonialism, imperialism, and nation building. The latter also provides a critique of modernity essential to problematizing the concept of solidarity itself.

In this book, there is no pretense of being exhaustive of struggles nor geographies. The studies here arise from a variety of places and occur at different scales. Cross-border solidarity invokes relations not only across the juridical-political borders of nation-states but also across myriad other demarcations of difference between groups within putatively shared sociopolitical spaces. What it means to cross borders is therefore always simultaneously political and analytic. What is key for transnational feminists is coalition building across borders without reifying the binaries or reinforcing the hierarchies that operate in demarcating difference through borders in the first place (Hyun Sook Kim 2007; Naples and Mendez 2014).

In this conception of cross-border solidarities, we are drawing on transnational feminism as a body of knowledge whose critical perspectives we seek to bring into dialogue with empirical study of cross-border social movements and activist practices. By transnational feminism, we are referring to a capacious literature that has consolidated since the 1990s to articulate a normative analytic for the production of transnational feminist knowledge (Mohanty et al. 1991; Alexander and Mohanty 1997; Mohanty 2003; Grewal and

Kaplan 1994; Kaplan and Grewal 1999). This is distinct from transnational feminism understood more descriptively as a social movement engaged in cross-border relations and initiatives, such as those of transnational feminist networks (TFNs). The latter is the subject of sociologically oriented scholarship, often in dialogue with the subfield of social movement studies (e.g., Moghadam 2000, 2005; see Conway 2017a for discussion).

Although we insist on and seek to demonstrate the value of transnational and intersectional feminist analytics for the study of contemporary cross-border solidarities, the literatures on transnational feminisms and the sociological study of feminist movements are also limited and problematic for our inquiry. Despite its origins in debates about global feminist solidarities, the former increasingly treats solidarity as a normative vision or aspiration of transnational feminist praxes rather than its object of inquiry. Where praxis is studied, it is increasingly that of the feminist researcher rather than that of activist collectivities. The latter treats solidarity as a taken-for-granted virtue of the activities it documents. In neither case is solidarity itself conceptualized or grounded empirically in the study of activist praxes.

In what follows, we seek to problematize and conceptualize solidarity as an object of inquiry in a way that both situates our project in relation to transnational feminist critique and specifies both the contributions and the limitations of that critique for apprehending the practices we have been studying. In so doing, we aim both to attest to the contribution and relevance of transnational and intersectional feminist analytics to the sociological study of social movements and their solidarities and push the field of transnational feminism to return to its grounding in feminist movement praxes.

We begin with a critical genealogy of the notion of solidarity, locating and problematizing it within Euro-modernist thought, and drawing some insights for the contemporary study of solidarities. Then, we turn to intersectional and transnational feminist critiques of Western feminisms and their elaboration of solidarities across difference as an alternative to the Euro-modernist conceptions. In a move that unsettles both the Euro-modernist and transnational feminist genealogies and exposes the uncomfortable tensions of attending to messy practices in situ, we introduce our empirical reference point, the World March of Women (WMW). This serves to open up other vectors of discussion and analysis to which the chapters of the book attest.

A GENEALOGY OF SOLIDARITY

Solidarity as an object of sociopolitical inquiry is beset by a number of problems that stem from the politico-normative nature of the concept as well as from its European historicity. It is a notoriously polysemous and polymorphous term that has its origins in the French Revolution and early modern European political and scientific thought, as industrialization, social and political upheaval, and the founding of the nation-state made the question of reinventing social ties a central concern of political and moral thinkers. Extrapolating from the historical inquiries of Bayertz (1999) and Scholz (2008), four different conceptions of solidarity took shape in European thought over the long nineteenth century—human solidarity, civic solidarity, social solidarity, and emancipatory solidarity, which understand solidarity as a type of sociopolitical relation between individuals, groups, and society as a whole, to which are attached positive moral obligations. This history of the concept is embedded within Euro-centric modernity, that is, an understanding of modernity as arising endogenously within Europe, without reference to Europe's transregional entanglements, notably its histories of empire building (Bhambra 2007). All the foregoing conceptions are linked to political projects in which solidarity plays the role of cementing or uniting political communities in the service of consolidating European nation-states and abstracted from their imperial relations. This points to the complicities between invoking solidarity and drawing the boundaries of the political community: who is included or excluded from its promises, and on what bases. Even though these variants of solidarity emerged from different schools of thought and metaphors (Hunt-Hendrix 2014, 40), their histories are intertwined with Euro-modernity, and this continues to condition current understandings.

Early modern Republican thought gave rise to a universalistic elaboration of human solidarity. From Ancient Greek philosophy, it drew upon the idea of political friendship, "an orientation of reciprocal concern towards one's fellow citizen" and for their well-being (Hunt-Hendrix 2014, 17). From the Christian notion of *caritas* (charity), it borrowed the universalizing idea that all human beings are equal by virtue of a shared essence. Solidarity was envisioned as a relation of reciprocity between citizens of equal status within a political community, in the context of the affirmation of their shared, secularized humanness (Bayertz 1999; Stjernø 2005; Hoelzl 2004). Yet, the conception of what was universal and what was human was suffused with the understandings and exclusions of Euro-modernity at the height of empire building. It was gendered and racialized in particular ways, privileging men over women, and defined, whether explicitly or implicitly, along the lines of race and civilization proper to European imperial-colonialist projects. Solidarity can thus be seen as a device of modern power to secure its hegemony, operating through selective inclusion and exclusion, both within nation-states and in relation to colonized populations.

Also woven into the modern European genealogy of the concept of solidarity is the resignification, under socialist and Republican influence, of Roman law terms *obligatio in solidum*. Civic solidarity expressed the natural interdependency of the members of society, from which followed the existence of a mutual debt owed by each member to all others (Hayward 1959; Blais 2008). Solidarity, that is, the responsibility of each person for all, and the moral obligation to repay one's debt to society were to be guaranteed by the state through fiscal redistribution, labor contract regulation, insurance schemes, and social services, that is, through what would become the modern welfare state (Blais 2008; Hunt-Hendrix 2014, 49–55). The discourse of interdependence as a natural state and the figure of the abstract citizen, however, masked the unequal relations of power attached to gender, race, and coloniality that would prevent many from being considered equal beneficiaries of civic solidarity.

In early European scientific thought, the nascent field of sociology showed a keen interest in understanding social solidarity, that is, the bonds that held together societies and groups in a context of political instability and rapid social change. Although along different lines, Comte, Durkheim, and Weber understood solidarity as a mechanism of social integration linked to the division of labor (Stjernø 2005; Hunt-Hendrix 2014). For Durkheim, while mechanical solidarity in premodern societies linked people through sameness, in modern societies organic solidarity reconciled differences through complex interdependence. He worried, though, that organic solidarity would not occur automatically and offered prescriptions for that to happen, among which were the development of shared moral orientations superseding individual egoism and a more just social order (Stjernø 2005, 34–35). Social solidarity was thus seen as a mechanism of social cohesion—not only a fact to be studied but also one that needed to be normatively engineered.

In all three strands of thought reviewed above, solidarity appears as a moral/sociopolitical problem to be solved in/for Euro-modernity, this within political or scientific projects that aim at restoring stability and harmony and largely eschew questions of social conflict. Such understandings of solidarity continue to underpin much scholarship in mainstream social movement studies.[1] In contrast, and important for our genealogy, also elaborated during the long nineteenth century is a conception of solidarity centering societal conflict and valorizing the struggles of the marginalized: emancipatory solidarity.

In Marxist thought, solidarity is a specific type of relationship established among workers who share, objectively and subjectively, similar conditions of exploitation and alienation. "Solidarity refers to a horizontal, class-based relationship that extends beyond workers of one neighborhood or one nationality to other working people who may be total strangers" (Gill 2009, 667).

Yet solidarity among the marginalized is not a given. Rather, it is treated as a strategic problem to be solved in order to ensure sociopolitical cohesion at the level of the aggrieved group. Marx and his followers offer a processual account of the building of such strategic relationships and of its constituent elements. Solidarity does not follow automatically from sharing a social position within capitalist relations of production. Part of the relationship of solidarity is the workers' consciousness of their common situation. This consciousness needs to be developed, that is, it requires a transformation of workers' subjectivities leading to the recognition of a common adversary and of common interests and to the practical joining together of workers in a common fight. The establishment and cultivation of relationships of solidarity are crucial to the political project of "uniting the working class and constituting it as a subject in the struggle" against capitalism (Stjernø 2005, 42). Marxism also fostered the idea that the relationship of solidarity is to be shaped by an ethics of means and ends: current relations of solidarity are to be prefigurative of the fully democratic and socialist future envisioned. Thus, the process of solidarity-building is that of constituting, subjectively and materially, forms of political community oriented toward emancipation from capitalist relations. Solidarity is enacted through praxis. In Gramsci, such praxis involves developing "an alternative culture based upon attitudes and values" that not only embodies working-class solidarity but is also aimed at striking broader cross-class political alliances around shared interests and a shared political project, in the creation of a counter-hegemonic block (Stjernø 2005, 57). Marxist conceptions of solidarity have had internationalist ambitions, as exemplified in the call, "Workers of the World Unite!" as well as explicitly anti-imperialist and decolonizing variants as in the Tricontinental initiative of the mid-twentieth century.[2]

Because of its subsequent influence on the discourses and practices of critical social movements into the present, the language of Marxism (or, more largely, historical materialism) provides some valuable entry points into the empirical analysis of solidarity-building as a praxis and process. Yet, it largely ignores gender as an axis of subalternity, difference, or conflict. As well, although Marxism condemns colonialism as an expression of capitalist imperialism, racialized oppression is largely considered epiphenomenal or, in the case of Indigeneity, an artifact of primitive accumulation destined to be subsumed under class or anti-capitalist solidarity.

There are a number of interrelated insights to be drawn from this Euro-modernist genealogy of solidarity, to problematize the concept and to bring it to bear on sociopolitical inquiry.

First, all four conceptions of solidarity are political and do political work. For this reason, we avoid juxtaposing "political" solidarity to human, civic, or social solidarity as many other scholars do. We opt instead for "emancipatory" solidarity, not to uncritically valorize it, rather to denote the variants arising from Marxist thought, which have a politicized dimension and an egalitarian impulse. We pluralize and problematize this further below.[3]

The elaboration of solidarity's different variants in the long nineteenth century is intimately linked to political projects of various natures, which different understandings of solidarity are meant to actualize. All, it follows, are also normative: solidarity in its different guises is imbued with moral or ethical prescriptions about the shaping of specific types of sociopolitical relations which mean to bring about the political imaginaries of which these political projects speak.

Second, these visions of solidarity are all anchored in Euro-modernist conceptions of political community that are complicit in relations of power and domination. From the recognition of shared humanness to that of the mutual responsibility of citizens, from the reciprocal concern of members of the social body to the joining together of workers and other exploited classes in struggle, when solidarity is construed as a positive moral obligation among individuals (mis)represented as equals, it silently excludes, among others, feminine/feminized bodies, racialized bodies, and colonized bodies as bodies that matter for politics and for conceptualizing solidarities. The Euro-centric, gendered, racialized, and colonial underbelly of these conceptions makes it particularly problematic for the study of transnational solidarities.

Juliet Hooker (2009) has argued that Western liberal democratic polities are, in fact, racial polities. Constituted by the inheritances of Euro-modernity and the afterlife of European colonialism, "The contours of political solidarity continue to be indelibly shaped by race." So, third, because of its lineage in modern European thought, and the imbrication of Euro-modernity with relations of coloniality within and across the borders of nation-states, solidarity in all its variants is characterized by a particular social ontology of race. This conditions the social relations imagined and enacted by various solidarity projects.

The visuality of race as a marker of social difference and the ongoing meaning of this difference, rooted in coloniality, as signifying radical Otherness means that nonwhite, particularly Black, people are still positioned as outsiders to the political community. Due to the material effects of discrimination, their lives are lived substantially differently and often spatially segregated from politically dominant groups. Hooker argues that this renders their suffering less visible and, when visible, less deserving of empathy or redress. She terms this the racialization of solidarity and argues that it actively impedes the realization of racial justice. Despite rhetorics of equality and inclusion in the political community, solidarity is imprinted with whiteness, reflecting only the ethical self-understanding of dominant groups (Hooker

2009; see also Ahmed 2004; Gaztambide-Fernández 2012; Mahrouse 2014).
We can see this operating in some of the practices studied here (see chapters
3, 5, and 7).

Fourth, as with other aspects of Euro-modernist thought, the exclusions
effected by solidarity are achieved through assertions of universalism. Euro-
modernist understandings of solidarity are steeped in universalisms and
invested in the goal of social order or political cohesion, which makes difference difficult to contemplate other than through assimilation or as absolute
alterity. Euro-modernist elaborations of solidarity presume abstract equality
(of humanity, of the citizenry) and/or on organic interdependence, similarity
(of position, of condition), and/or commonality (of adversary, interests, goals,
and struggles). They thus elide questions of dissimilarity, marginalization,
and power within the political community that (supposedly) coalesces in,
around, or thanks to solidarity.

Writing about Indigenous peoples of the Andes, Marisol de la Cadena
(2010) observes the colonizing effects of European-centered understandings
of solidarity in the face of radical difference. She attests that Andean
Indigenous peoples inhabit worlds of different ontological natures and engage
in life-forming relationships with both humans and "other-than-human"
"sentient earth-beings" (2010, 336, 341). That these relationships are partly
unintelligible to their allies imposes on Indigenous mobilizations the task
of translating their claims in the former's language. As long as they remain
unacknowledged, Euro-modernist legacies and the relations of power they
index continue to inscribe gendering, racializing, and colonizing conceptions
of solidarity in both activist efforts at solidarity-building and in the academic
work that seeks to understand them.

Fifth, solidarity is a concept steeped in normativity, which makes it an
unwieldy object for empirical analysis. One approach to making solidarity
more useful as an analytical concept is to objectivize its very normativity. By
this, we mean to clearly identify the different political projects that give the
term its various meanings, the particular relationships "solidarity" is set up to
represent, and the distinct moral/ethical prescriptions that are at stake.

Finally, in a more poststructuralist vein, we could say that solidarity is
inherently performative. It cannot be studied apart from the practices that
are performed in its name. Solidarity practices are historically and contextu-
ally contingent. They, therefore, need to be situated in specific time-spaces
in order to be analyzed. Solidarity needs to be actively produced and reproduced and, as an activist practice, involves political will, desire, and agency.
Activist solidarities always involve power relations and invoke political
imaginaries, whether implicitly or explicitly, but they also have the potential
for critical reflexivity. For these reasons, we approach solidarities as praxes
which can be analyzed as such.

SOLIDARITIES OF DIFFERENCE:
INTERSECTIONAL AND TRANSNATIONAL
FEMINIST REFORMULATIONS

The question of solidarity has been of long-standing interest to feminist histories, theories, and political practices, especially those involving relations across borders of nation-states. Feminist cross-border solidarities have been indelibly marked by the Euro-modernist genealogy of solidarity and by resistance to it. The intersectional discourse of transnational feminism, its tributaries in postcolonial and U.S.-based Third World and women-of-color feminisms, and their convergent critique of white, Western feminisms is central in this regard. These overlapping fields share an anti-racist and anti-colonial critique of white, liberal feminism and its preconceptions of solidarity, which some transnational feminists also rooted in an explicit critique of Euro-modernity (e.g., Grewal and Kaplan 1994). Rather than evading it, these feminist reformulations of solidarity center the problem of difference, especially racialized and spatialized difference, within and across the borders of nation-states.

Historically, the discourse of transnational feminism emerged in U.S. academia against the historical canvas of the transnationalization of feminism through the late twentieth century, a process facilitated largely (although not exclusively) by the United Nations. From the Declaration of International Women's Year in 1975 to the Fourth World Conference on Women in Beijing in 1995, the UN conferences and the resources for organizing that they made available helped propel the proliferation of women's groups around the world, the global circulation of feminist discourses, and the transnationalization of feminist organizing (see chapter 1).

As a perspective addressing cross-border solidarities, transnational feminism emerged in response to political conflicts in and among women's movements both within the United States and appearing in UN venues. Regarding the latter, one important fault-line was that drawn between "Western" and "Third World" feminisms. Western feminism, meaning the liberal feminism predominating in white middle-class women's movements, emanated primarily from the United States and was influencing the aid and development institutions and their policy prescriptions for Third World societies. This dominant form of feminism was increasingly being confronted by women's movements from the Global South on two counts: as ethnocentric in its assumption that all women shared a similar condition of oppression under patriarchy, and as imperialistic in its project for global sisterhood based on women's putatively common identity.

In her seminal essay "Under Western Eyes" (1991b), Chandra Talpade Mohanty argued that hegemonic feminism reduced the explanation of women's oppression globally to gender hierarchies within the family. It projected a false homogeneity about women's diverse realities and erased the specificity of Third World contexts and the agency of Third World women. She further argued that feminists needed to critically situate themselves and their critiques in geopolitical power relations, particularly in the histories and legacies of colonialism in order to avoid reproducing oppressive power relations in the name of feminist solidarity.

Grewal and Kaplan wed the Third World feminist rejection of global sisterhood to a thoroughgoing postcolonial critique of modernity, including of Western humanism and Enlightenment traditions more broadly. They were concerned that feminisms be reflexive vis-à-vis their imbrication with various modernist projects in order to avoid reproducing their hegemonies and exclusions. They sought to conceptualize transnational feminist solidarities as links among diverse, localized feminist practices confronting "scattered hegemonies" (Grewal and Kaplan, 1994, 17–19; see Desai 2015 for discussion).

In a parallel fashion, movements of racialized women, particularly in the Americas, challenged the hegemonic feminism of middle-class, white-dominated women's movements and forged anti-racist feminist politics premised on a multiplicity of oppressions and the intersections of race, class, and gender, among other axes of social differentiation and inequality. Intersectionality as both an analytic and a praxis of the politics of difference crystallized at this time, particularly through the work of Black feminists addressing the U.S. context. Through the 1980s, "US Third World feminism" was the site of groundbreaking political and theoretical work on coalition-building across difference, on epistemologies for coalition politics, and the new subjectivities produced in and through these politics (Collins [1990] 2000; Sandoval 2000; Yuval-Davis 1993).

Where these perspectives converge, concrete struggles for survival rather than putatively common oppression or shared identity were seen as the more reliable basis for solidarity, and "coalition" rather than "unity" as the preferred political goal (Mohanty 2003, 117, citing Reagon 1983). For marginalized communities struggling for survival, a tactical "politics of identity," grounded in a common historical experience of oppression and struggle, was central to consolidating those movements. Crucially, it was also seen as a precondition for coalition politics with others around broader agendas. The two were seen as interdependent and complementary forms of activism (Collins 2000, 67).

Such coalitions demand "transversal dialogue . . . based on the principles of rooting and shifting—that is—being centered in one's own experience while being empathetic to the differential positioning of the partners" (Collins 2000, 245; citing Yuval-Davis 1997, 88). Coalition partners remain rooted in their own particular group histories but, through deep listening and dialogue, may shift or expand out from their immediate experience and viewpoints.

Such coalition politics is by necessity grounded in an epistemology of partial, positional, and situated knowledges and represents a rupture with the search for hegemonic knowledge in oppositional politics, and with Euro-modernist conceptions of solidarity premised on abstract universalisms, organic sociality, or class struggle.

According to Sandoval (2000, 63), this mode of resistance exemplifies a new form of historical consciousness that is itself the product of recent decolonizing historical events in which the search for a hegemonic oppositional knowledge has given way to what she calls "differential consciousness." Differential consciousness is the basis for "differential social movement." Sandoval names this process the "methodology of the oppressed." She suggests that decolonizing processes of the late twentieth century have destabilized Western subjectivities such that they also have been rendered more porous to others and are thus also more capable of differential consciousness.

Conditions for dialogical solidarity must be painstakingly constructed and continually and reflexively deepened. In order to craft non-colonizing dialogues across varieties of difference and inequality, Mohanty (2003, 125) argues that activists must grapple with "genealogies of difference." This requires fluency in one another's histories of oppression and struggle that goes beyond simple affirmations of diversity and pluralism. The point of analyzing difference is that differences can be historically specified and understood as part of larger political processes and systems. The central issue, then, is not one of merely "acknowledging" difference. Rather, the most difficult question concerns the kind of difference that is acknowledged and engaged. Difference seen as benign variation (diversity), for instance, rather than as conflict, struggle, or the threat of disruption, bypasses power as well as history to suggest a harmonious, empty pluralism (Mohanty 2003, 193).

Mohanty's critiques of Western hegemony and of liberal universalist or pluralist projects for "global sisterhood" as well as the persistence of unequal power relations related to different social and geographical positionings have become sine qua non for feminist discussions of solidarity. Among activists, they have also provoked reflexive processes and significant organizational change based on "an awareness of the dangers of downplaying the many differences constituting women globally" (Dempsey et al. 2011, 207).

Solidarity in this view is a political and ethical horizon that has to be struggled for. For Mohanty, solidarity is grounded in "mutuality, accountability, and the recognition of common interests" (2003, 7), which make relationships among diverse communities and groups possible. It draws clearly on traditions of historical materialism, but it has been refracted through awareness of differentiation among women, particularly through racialization under conditions of globalized coloniality. Instead of presuming an "enforced commonality of oppression," Mohanty's notion of solidarity stresses the volitional and ethical choice that groups make to struggle together. Thus, understanding and respecting diversity and difference are central undertakings that cannot be circumvented in the rush to forge strategic alliances.

Intersectional and transnational feminist reformulations of solidarity foreground projects for racial and gender justice within an anti-colonial frame. These reformulations were generated by women of color in response to the effacement of their experiences in women's and feminist movements claiming to represent them, and they yielded alternative imaginaries of struggle, change, and ways of being in movement together (see chapter 6). Their philosophical and practical embrace of difference and the injunctions to coalition, differential consciousness, transversal dialogue, and the like suggest non-totalizing, coexisting political projects in the plural that are coproduced through open-ended construction. Although there are some continuities and affinities with emancipatory solidarity, intersectional and transnational feminist reformulations signal a significant rupture with the Euro-modernist genealogy of solidarity.[4]

UNSETTLING TRANSNATIONAL FEMINIST THEORIZATIONS OF SOLIDARITY: CONSIDERING THE WORLD MARCH OF WOMEN AND SOLIDARITIES ON THE GLOBAL LEFT

Concretely, our collaborative study of cross-border solidarities has been grounded in the World March of Women. Separately and together, we have been studying this transnational feminist network (TFN) for over a decade. Considering the World March of Women has sharpened our sense of the limitations of the literatures on social movements, transnational feminism, and on transnational feminist activism in approaching the study of cross-border solidarities—and specifically the kind of solidarities enacted by the WMW (see Giraud and Dufour 2010; Conway 2017a; chapters 3 and 7).

In many respects, the WMW instantiates the kind of transnational feminist praxis imagined by Mohanty and Grewal and Kaplan. It is a North-South network with strong South-South links and Southern leadership, grounded in concrete, survival struggles of poor women, committed to grassroots mobilization, and acutely conscious of place-based difference. It foregrounds issues of land, water, food, and work, but is explicitly feminist in so doing, and it attends to body politics of violence against women, sexuality, and reproduction while critiquing feminist politics that would automatically prioritize body politics over the former set of concerns. In its trenchant critique of neoliberal globalization and its activism in the anti-globalization mobilizations, the March's praxis anticipated Mohanty's widely cited 2003 work calling for the same.

In 2013, informed by intersectional and transnational feminist analytics, we set out to study transnational feminist solidarity-building around food sovereignty, which by 2010 had been affirmed as a priority for international action in the March (Masson, Paulos, and Beaulieu-Bastien 2017; Masson and Conway 2017; Conway 2018; Conway and Paulos 2020). Over the course of our study, the centrality of the March's politics of alliance with mixed-gender movements became evident, particularly with La Via Campesina and its Latin American member groups organized in CLOC and the intersecting memberships of these regional and global anti-globalization networks (Dufour, Masson, and Diaz 2019). It also foregrounded the agency of rural, peasant, and Indigenous women who bridged these networks (Masson and Beaulieu-Bastien 2021; chapter 4). The dynamics and strategies, practices and discourses, power relations and concrete dilemmas of transnational feminist coalition-building in this context and with nonfeminist others were decidedly distinct from anything that appeared in the literatures we were relying upon. The specificities of the WMW as a transnational feminist network, of food sovereignty as a feminist concern, of Latin American popular feminism as an important genealogy in understanding the feminism of the WMW, and WMW's politics of alliance with mixed-gender and nonfeminist movements against neoliberal globalization all presented puzzles about the feminist cross-border solidarities we were observing. In particular, we did not detect a critique of nations and nationalisms, nor the centrality of race and colonialism, nor the intersectional understandings of difference as essential to transnational feminist coalition-building that we had expected to find.[5]

Amid the evident newness of the March's practices, it took us some time to recognize the powerful ongoing presence of older traditions of emancipatory solidarity, namely those of socialist feminism and left internationalism. These are apparent, for example, in their gender-class analytic, federative structure, global aspirations, and strong discursive unity. Many analysts had assumed these traditions had been eclipsed after 1989, rendered obsolete by world events. Indeed, they had fallen out of view in much feminist/sociological scholarship of the era of neoliberal globalization (chapter 1). However, appreciating their ongoing afterlife and how they are being re-mixed and remade is key to understanding significant social movement developments of the twenty-first century, prominently the World Social Forum, but also of anti-capitalist feminist networks like the World March of Women.

These specifics of the WMW's practice of cross-border solidarities appear at odds with some central underlying commitments of the field of transnational feminism. We make these observations not to uncritically valorize the March's praxis vis-à-vis the scholarship, or vice versa, but to outline the analytic conundrum we encountered and which has set the agenda of this book.

To begin to understand this, it is illuminating to follow Herr's (2014) commentary. She observes that Mohanty's work bridges "Third World feminist" and "transnational feminist" fields and demonstrates how the former has given way to the latter in many ways. Herr argues that Third World feminism has been focused on activisms in their particular local and national contexts. As outlined above, an important current within transnational feminism problematizes nations and nationalisms as modernist, statist, and exclusionary constructs and proposes the transnational as an alternative imaginary for feminist cross-border solidarities. In its attention to the transnational as involving relations and processes across borders of many kinds, Herr contends that transnational feminism as a body of scholarship has lost its grounding in localized struggles. In our review of works in the field published over the past decade, we largely concur with this conclusion.[6]

Transnational feminism also sharply critiques and differentiates itself from international(ist) feminisms, critiquing the latter for its reification of nation-states, national identities, and the national scale. While the transnational feminist critique of nations and nationalisms is critically important, feminist historian Francisca de Haan (2010) has argued that its dismissal of all internationalist feminisms is deeply problematic. It has contributed to constructing U.S.-led liberal feminist internationalism and its gender-centric perspective as falsely hegemonic. De Haan argues that transnational feminist historiography has participated in effacing the historical presence and significance in the post-1945 period of multi-issue socialist feminist internationalism, such as that of the Women's International Democratic Federation and, in this, has unwittingly colluded with Cold War agendas to marginalize such alternative perspectives.

On several fronts, these observations are very pertinent to the studies collected here. Feminist scholars of (post-)socialist societies (Cerwonka 2008; Suchland 2011) have noted the persistent effects of the three worlds' metageography in the analytic paradigm of transnational feminism, with its emphasis on "Third World" women and the Global South versus Western (First World) hegemonic feminism. This construct effectively erases the existence of (post-)socialist societies (Second World) from consideration of the global. Further, they argue, discourses of difference in U.S.-based transnational feminism foreground racial and ethnic difference and therefore do not read Eastern Europe and its feminisms as "difference" to be engaged as such. In that these critical discourses of transnational feminism now help define the terms of hegemonic feminist knowledge internationally, scholars from such other worlds are reduced to being transmitters of these discourses, rather than producers of knowledge about their own historically specific realities (Cerwonka 2008). Cîrstocea and Chetaille (chapters 1 and 2) build on these insights.

As mentioned, our own empirical studies of cross-border solidarities grounded in the World March of Women have consistently presented us with a misfit in relation to attempts to use intersectional/transnational feminist analytics to understand the practices of what we now see as a contemporary form of socialist (or popular) feminist internationalism. When we began to see that the solidarities enacted by the World March had to be understood in the context of a historic recomposition of the global left following the collapse of the Berlin Wall, the end of the Cold War, and the triumph of neoliberalism, the contours of the problem of conceptualizing and theorizing contemporary solidarities also sharpened. This recomposition of the left under conditions of globalization and global network society has cemented critiques of vanguardism, armed struggle, the singular focus on the state as the locus of power, and the drive for ideological orthodoxy underway since the "new social movements" of the 1960s, including the second wave of feminism. This new "global left" which has consolidated over the last twenty years through the World Social Forum and similar processes defends democracy, diversity, and pluralism, and seeks to build convergence across difference in the construction of anti-capitalist counter-hegemony (Leite 2005; Santos 2006; Conway 2013).[7] Situating the World March of Women in this context helped us specify the modalities of solidarity-building we perceived in its praxis (chapters 3 and 7).

SAMENESS—DIFFERENCE—ALTERITY: MODALITIES OF SOLIDARITY FROM EURO-MODERNITY TO THE PLURIVERSE

Through the genealogy of solidarity in Euro-modernity outlined above, we observed that solidarity has operated to naturalize and so to depoliticize inequality and difference, and to secure and maintain social order. Through its regulation of inclusion and exclusion in the political community, it secured hegemony within the nation-state and in relations with colonial others. This is solidarity as an instrument of hegemonic power.

Although operating within the same "logic of hegemony" (Day 2005), the Marxist re-signification of solidarity as the bonds forged among the exploited and oppressed *against* hegemonic power in the service of their emancipation politicized inequality and proposed the transformative potential of solidarity. This has proven to have great powers of attraction. This conception of solidarity as having emancipatory potential, rooted in "an understanding of the structural sources of grievances" (Eterovic and Smith 2001), continues to animate many contemporary movements, although its Marxist lineage is often obscured. Yet, even as it has proven potent and appears durable, emancipatory solidarity has also been continually subject to critique and reformulation. Dialectics of sameness, difference, and alterity operate in constructing solidarity, both in the service of and in opposition to hegemonic power and call for more careful and critical analysis.

In a recent survey of contemporary critical and oppositional movements, Conway (2019) proposed three modalities through which cross-border solidarities are currently being imagined and undertaken: counter-hegemonic, intersectional-feminist, and pluriversal. While often entangled and overlapping in practice, with intertwined genealogies, they are also distinct and contesting modalities. We present these here as a heuristic scheme to help situate the practices documented in this collection in relation to each other and to the genealogies of solidarity presented above. Several contributions attest to the tense and ambivalent copresence of these modalities, their hybridization, as well as instances of their productive interplay in contemporary cross-border solidarities. We see variations of these modalities at work where solidarity is being invoked to contest inequality, oppression, and exclusion in their myriad forms.

In brief, counter-hegemonic solidarities aim to build a common front against a common enemy. In its left-wing versions, this is often understood as capitalism secured by the modern state, in favor of an alternative hegemony and an alternative societal project, usually imagined as some version of democratic socialism. Its lineages are in Marxian thought, particularly Gramsci. Built on a socio-material logic of solidarity in which capitalism is understood as structuring a common context of suffering and struggle, counter-hegemonic solidarities are premised on sameness, commonality, and aggregation. They are mass, popular, and assimilative as, for example, in Occupy Wall Street's invocation of the (undifferentiated) 99% against the 1%. The emancipatory solidarities of Euro-modernity continue to appear in many forms across and beyond the Global South. Notably, counter-hegemonic solidarities are invoked by many forms of democratic and/or populist politics beyond those with identifiably leftist pedigrees.

Cohering with the discussion above, intersectional-feminist solidarities are premised on a multiplicity of systems of oppression, subjectivities, and their intersections. They aim to build coalitions across difference to redress conditions of inequality and injustice, particularly those arising from racialized gender. As discussed, their lineages are in postcolonial, anti-racist, and transnational feminisms and their challenge to the Western liberal feminist project of global sisterhood. Power is understood to be both concentrated and diffused, and complicities within oppositional movements themselves are objects of critique and resistance. Intersectional-feminist solidarities are pursued in all domains of social life, including in the everyday and inter-personal. They suggest non-totalizing, coexisting political projects in the plural that are coproduced through open-ended construction. They have variable, often tense, relations with color-blind and majoritarian projects of the left, even as anti-capitalist critique is foundational to intersectionality (Collins and Bilge 2020).

Pluriversal solidarities are premised on a world of many worlds. They are expressed in the Zapatista vision of building a world where many worlds fit. They demand negotiating cosmological, even ontological, difference (de la Cadena 2010; Blaser 2010) in a politics of coexistence and shared or overlapping sovereignties. Their lineages are in Indigenous defense of place-based life projects in the face of the colonizing projects of settler societies and modern states, and Indigenous diplomacies vis-à-vis other Indigenous peoples. Indigenous worlds exist in partial connection to modern-colonial societies but retain their own specificities and are the site of decolonial alternatives to neoliberal capitalism understood as modernity-coloniality. In the context of settler-colonial states of the Americas and elsewhere, pluriversal solidarities between Indigenous and non-Indigenous peoples demand a reckoning with the colonial character of "the modern political" on which emancipatory solidarities have rested, and on the stolen lands and resources on which modern societies the world over have been built (Conway 2013, 154–55). They also proceed in considerable tension with feminisms of all kinds, as the gender binary itself is being critiqued as a colonial construct.

As we have attested, transnational feminism has consolidated into a normative analytic often removed from consideration of concrete praxes of activist collectivities. The studies here continue to raise new questions and insights about the inevitable particularity and limitations of any one framework, including one as evidently productive as transnational feminism. Despite some evident limitations, it continues to be a critically important touchstone in consideration of cross-border solidarities, feminist, and otherwise. In centering issues of race, colonialism, and geopolitics in solidarity encounters, transnational feminism has contested the afterlife of empire in contemporary liberal internationalisms of states, international institutions, and social movements alike. Coloniality as a present condition finds expression in neo-Orientalist narratives of rescue and uplift of downtrodden others and assimilation into the norms of Western modernity (DuBois and Oliviera 2009). In problematizing the solidarity relation enacted by Western liberalism, transnational feminism displaces the taken-for-granted whiteness of the subject of most theorizations of solidarity. It extends its critique of race blindness, class, and capital-centrism to historical materialist modes of analysis and practice. As a critique, transnational feminism has also pushed us, scholars and activists alike, to contemplate why race and colonialism are *not* more central to praxes like that of the World March of Women, whether they should be, how they might be, and what these absences tell us both about the analytic and the praxes under consideration.

These three modalities of solidarity—counter-hegemonic, intersectional-feminist, and pluriversal—coexist in uneasy, unstable but increasingly undeniable relation in the world of transnational social movements and their dynamic practices and projects for cross-border solidarities. Their copresence produces tension and contradiction. These modalities come in and out of view throughout this collection. Seeing, analyzing, and making sense of this plurality of solidarity-building practices in twenty-first-century contexts, their tensions and contradictions, conflicts and convergences, has been a fruit of this collection. In the process, we have discovered the need to think anew about solidarity itself.

CONTRIBUTIONS TO THE BOOK

Part I addresses the transnationalization of solidarities. The two contributions here attest to the ongoing salience of West–East geopolitics for understanding twenty-first-century solidarities. We start with a study of transnational feminist mobilizations in a historical and geopolitical perspective. Ioana Cîrstocea's chapter, "Studying 'Global Feminism' as a Transnational Assemblage: Geopolitics of Women's Rights in the (Post)Cold War (1975–1995)," considers how the Cold War and its ending conditioned the consolidation of "global feminism," and how such solidarities were "both a tool and arena" of hegemonic power, pacifying real geopolitical conflicts among women's movements, and complicit in "disciplining the Second World." Through close study of a key figure, U.S.-based activist Charlotte Bunch, a major organizational instantiation of Third World or Southern feminism, the Development of Alternatives for Women in a New Era (DAWN), and the "women's rights as human rights" initiative in the 1980s and 1990s, the author argues that these instantiations of global feminism were interpolated with U.S. policy in the late–Cold War period and the post-1989 triumphalism of liberal internationalism. This scholarship demonstrates how the history of interactions between Second and Third World feminisms, and this variant of transnational feminism, has been elided, with important implications both for the historiography and contemporary understandings and practice of transnational feminist solidarities. We see in this chapter a modality of solidarity as an instrument of the global hegemonic power of the U.S.-led West, operating through the orchestration of inclusion and exclusion in the UN women's conferences.

Agnès Chetaille's chapter "European Solidarities across the East/West Divide: Power and Difference in Lesbian and Gay Transnational Cooperation with Poland in the Mid-2000s" analyzes the asymmetries of transnationalization of solidarities in post–Cold War Europe. Situated in the twenty-first-century context of right-wing resurgence, aggressive heteronationalism, and a powerful Catholic church reasserting its influence over public culture, Polish LGBT activists seek the protection and resources that come with transnational solidarity relationships with West European activists. However, these solidarities are paradoxical. Through a complex interplay of discourses of sameness and difference, they function to "other" the East. Chetaille documents how Western European activists and organizations presume sameness in LGBT positionalities across European contexts, but where Central and Eastern Europe are positioned as backward (i.e., different) and catching up to the modern and progressive West. This tradition-to-modernity framing, and the knowledge hierarchies it presumes, enables the West European activists to claim to know best how Polish activists should advance LGBT rights agendas, in the name of a common struggle. This epistemic hierarchy is imbricated with the Westerners' power to allocate resources to Polish partners and to include/exclude them from political networks. Chetaille sees Orientalist tropes at work in West/East activist relations despite considerable political and organizational diversity among various actors: between formal and informal forms of organization, between vertical and horizontal approaches to decision-making, and between liberal-institutionalist and "radical intersectional" orientations to social change. Chetaille also troubles a common distinction in the social movement literature between "altruistic" and "political" modes of solidarity that argue that the latter is more reciprocal. In contrast, Chetaille sees in both underlying political projects characterized by hierarchies of power and knowledge coupled with material inequalities that reproduce Polish dependency. Despite this, Chetaille also insists that Polish activists are active agents in cultivating different kinds of solidarity relationships for their own ends and that transnational solidarity relationships remain mutable and open-ended.

Part II is composed of three chapters addressing cross-border solidarity-building in movement organizations and encounters in Latin American contexts, all engaging "colonial difference" (Mignolo 2012). In "Solidarity-Building as Praxis: Anti-Extractivism and the World March of Women in the Macro-Norte Region of Peru," Dominique Masson and Anabel Paulos argue that transnational feminist critique must be combined with fine-grained analysis of why and how, concretely, solidarities are constructed by feminist collectivities. They combine the normative insights of transnational feminism with critical concepts in geography to conceptualize solidarity as a strategic organizational praxis in the service of particular political visions and goals. The authors argue for attention to the discursive, material, and spatial practices that build links between heterogenous actors, places, and mobilizations—a framework that is deployed by many of our contributors. The World March of Women, discussed above, is analyzed here as a feminist actor building linkages in strategic and calculated ways with nonfeminist women-led movements against extractivism. This includes painstaking relationship-building by the self-identified feminists—urban, educated *mestizas*—with Indigenous women involved in community-based mobilization. This effort proceeds from providing concrete forms of logistical support, to political assistance, to transnational linkages, to feminist political training and results in the formation of an Indigenous women's group that formally joins the March. The authors situate this praxis of solidarity within the March's mass movement-building political project of popular and socialist feminism aligned with other popular movements of the global left. We see here feminists enacting a counter-hegemonic modality of solidarity, and constructing linkages with Indigenous women on that basis, in ways that discursively subsume ontological difference (de la Cadena 2010) into the universalizing and race-blind categories of capital and class, but also involve a transnational feminist network assuming anti-extractivist struggles as its own. In this process, despite the unequal power relations and evident eliding of Indigenous difference, Masson and Paulos stress the processual and co-constituted character of this praxis that keeps it open and unsettled in terms of the difference Indigeneity might effect on the popular feminist subjectivity of the March.

In their chapter, "Allowing Rural Difference to Make a Difference: The Brazilian *Marcha das Margaridas*," Renata Motta and Marco Antonio Teixeira contend that the problematic relationship between transnational feminist theory and contemporary praxis is neither only about fit (as per Conway 2017a) nor about the limits of normative theory for empirical analysis (as per chapter 3) but also about the geopolitics of knowledge. Following Giraldo (2016), they argue for the importance of theorizing from categories of difference that arise endogenously from struggles in situ, and especially so in contexts not steeped in histories and legacies of Anglophone intersectional and postcolonial feminist theories. Proceeding both deductively and inductively, they argue for the salience of rurality as an intersectional category of difference that has emerged within the *Marcha das Margaridas* in Brazil. Rurality emerges as an internally differentiated category of difference that intersects with class and gender, generation, and ethnicity to produce the political subject of the *Marcha*, "women from the field, the forest and the waters." Rurality is seen by the authors as a vector of coloniality, the site of colonial difference, as well as of socio-spatial difference. In this study, we see a complex interplay of modalities of solidarity-building: intersectional-feminist that includes socio-spatial and socio-ecological axes of difference, pluriversal, in engaging rurality as Other and exposing the Euro-modern (and feminist) subject of solidarity as urban, and counter-hegemonic, as solidarity-building in the *Marcha* is situated within a praxis of popular feminism embedded in a trade union movement.

In "The Cosmopolitical Challenge of Building Border-Crossing Feminist Solidarities," Johanna Leinius centers her analysis on *how* difference is engaged, and the difference this makes, to the possibility of non-colonizing border-crossing solidarities. Focusing on the conceptual and organizational practices that structured how difference would be engaged by participants, she compares two social movement encounters, both of which were oriented to counter-hegemony in the name of emancipation. In the first, informed by inter-sectional-feminist understandings of difference—as embodied and produced through conflictual relations of inequality, organizers structured an encounter among Latin American women's groups to engage such differences, hoping that this would enable deliberation across divides of race, culture, sexuality, and disability that had long beset the region's feminist meetings. But, as Leinius notes, structuring discussions by relegating participants to a series of fixed categories functioned to assign difference to specific bodies. It left others unmarked as different, thus allowing hegemonic feminism and its associated bodies and concerns to remain normative. In the second example, organizers viewed difference as arising from distinct socio-ecological contexts, constituting different worlds that could not be assumed to be wholly intelligible to each other. Here, organizers fostered a range of affective and expressive modes of communication between territorially based struggles but ultimately sought to order their relation through preestablished analytic categories. Leinius characterizes these encounters as, respectively, intersectional-feminist and pluriversal in their modalities of constructing cross-border solidarities. Both approaches recognized the centrality of difference as a resource for resistance and its interpellation with power and inequality, and sought to redress asymmetries of power and knowledge in solidarity-building encounters. Nevertheless, as forms of "cosmopolitics"—politics across worlds—both instances were limited by organizers' own drive for knowledge outcomes ordered according to their own preconceived categories. Solidarity as a "problem of relation rather than a problem of knowledge" (Spivak 2000) comes starkly into view.

As the problem of difference grows in intensity, confronting all movements and modalities of solidarity-building, translation has gained traction as a problematique in social movement politics. Part III focuses on translation across cultural and linguistic borders as an essential operation in solidarity-building across difference. Translation studies presents resources for approaching difference as a problem both of communicability of language and intelligibility of meaning across cultural worlds, of the possibilities and limits of that endeavor, and of the politics of attempting it. Pagé and Lebon, along with Leinius, contribute to an emerging field addressing the feminist politics and practice of translation, which has myriad implications for studies

of transnational and translocal connectivities, including those of social movements (e.g., Alvarez et al. 2014; Blackwell 2014; Costa and Alvarez 2014;
Ergun and Castro 2017).

In "Power, Translation, and Localized Transnational Feminism," Geneviève
Pagé develops an approach to the study of conceptual travel and translation
attuned to the power imbalances between differently positioned languages and
theoretical traditions in an asymmetrical global political economy of knowledge. Her study is situated in Montreal, conceptualized as a transnational
space constituted by flows, operating at multiple scales, of people, practices,
and discourses. As a space of encounter between different cultural and linguistic communities, Montreal is also a "contact zone" characterized by conflictive and asymmetrical power relations structured by histories of colonialism:
between English and French, and between both of these and diverse racialized
communities. In this context, Pagé tracks the conflictive reception of the discourse of intersectionality in the Francophone feminist community, and links
it both to anti-colonial nationalist resistance to English-language theoretical
traditions and historic inattention to the concerns of racialized and Indigenous
feminists by hegemonic Quebec feminism. In analyzing this complex process of translation, Pagé identifies several factors conditioning the reception
of intersectionality, including a felt need for new thinking to address a real
problem, bridge actors who could render the new thinking compatible with
existing core commitments, and an openness to reconfigure the borders of the
movement. Pagé adds that the politics of translation must also pay attention
to the power asymmetries between languages themselves, in this case between
French and English. Pagé concludes that conceptual translation across feminist communities involves not just the crossing but also the reconfiguration, of
borders, re-drawing who is considered inside/outside feminist communities,
and on what basis. Translation comes into view as a fraught, power-laden but
essential operation in cross-border solidarity-building. Acknowledging that
translation is neither inherently democratic nor neutral and that it is embedded
in multidirectional, crisscrossing power relations between languages and cultures is essential to assessing whether and how it redresses and/or reinforces
different power inequalities in cross-border solidarities.

In efforts at conceptual translation, power is moving in multiple directions at once, and missteps and failures are not uncommon, with significant
effects on democratic deliberation in social movement networks. In "(Mis)
translations in Translocal Solidarity-Building and the Need for Controlled
Equivocation: *Cuerpo-territorio* in the World March of Women," Nathalie
Lebon asks which practices are relatively more effective at facilitating
conceptual translation and negotiating power imbalances. She identifies the
March's use of language caucuses, its lengthy face-to-face encounters, and
its ways of articulating regional and national difference. However, she also

notes that political differences attributable to language also cut across North-South, minority nationalisms, and Indigenous-non-Indigenous positionalities in myriad and complicated ways. Lebon argues that, in different contexts, intersectional power dynamics are constituted differently and along different axes, and that this creates "unaligned geographies of difference" that the March was ill-equipped to navigate.

Lebon analyzes the failure of translation of the concept of *territorio* and the resulting inability of the March to agree on a unifying slogan for its 2015 global action. Employing the concept of "controlled equivocation" (Viveiros de Castro 2004), Lebon demonstrates that translation across linguistic worlds always involves a level of incommensurability. Controlling the equivocation means making clear that seemingly identical terms can carry very different connotations in their respective worlds. *Territorio*, in Spanish, was associated with Indigenous claims for autonomy in Latin America and was received by the *mestiza* popular feminists of the March as compatible with their anti-capitalist opposition to extractivism; however, the French translation, *territoire*, was associated with right-wing ethno-nationalism, and was rejected by European and Quebec activists as politically reactionary in their contexts. What got elided in both positions was the more ample understanding of *territorio* in Indigenous cosmovisions, which Indigenous women of Quebec did embrace. Lebon observes that the prevailing counter-hegemonic modality of solidarity in the March, in its seeking commonality, is here seen as unable to appreciate the need for, or possibility of, an alternative pluriversal logic. Lebon concludes that while sense-making is essential to fostering relations of trust and the possibility of collaboration, so too is recognizing a multiplicity of worlds and the impossibility of perfect commensurability across them. Finding practical ways to control equivocation is therefore central to cultivating non-colonizing solidarities across borders.

We are honored that Manisha Desai, social movements scholar and leading voice in the articulation and critique of transnational feminism as a body of knowledge, has contributed an Afterword. In her abiding concerns with feminist and activist praxis, and her sensitivity to spatial and epistemic difference, she makes for a wonderful interlocutor in this discussion of cross-border solidarities.

As we bring this book project and our multiyear collaboration to a close, we are acutely aware of the escalating crises of an unravelling civilization that are planetary in scope. In this context of political and economic polarization, heightened violence and oppression, and the threat to continuance confronting many species including our own, there has perhaps never been greater need for collaboration across difference for sustainable, just, and democratic futures. We still contend that intersectional and transnational feminisms are an indispensable resource in that undertaking. In this poignant moment of ending and beginning, we are grateful for the joy we have had, Janet, Dominique, and Pascale, in learning together, and with our students and with the activists of the World March of Women. This book, the product of many hands besides our own, is an offering to a necessarily permanently open-ended conversation about cross-border solidarities that we make in the spirit of peace, hope, and friendship.

NOTES

1. For a discussion of the modernist underpinnings of social movement studies and their implications, see Conway (2017b).

2. See Mahler (2018) for consideration of the Tricontinental, its relationship with Black internationalism, and its recurrence in contemporary movements in the Americas. Her study suggests an alternative genealogy of Marxist-inflected solidarity that could fruitfully dialogue with that of transnational feminism presented below.

3. We note that solidarity is invoked by oppositional groups across the political spectrum, not only those on the political left or with egalitarian or democratic impulses. This taxonomy of solidarities does not exhaust the range of contemporary variations of discourses of solidarity. Rather, it is an attempt to name major philosophical commitments that continue to underpin contemporary practices and analyses.

4. For an expanded discussion of the significance of transnational feminist knowledges for the politics of global justice, see Conway (2011).

5. Elsewhere, we have debated how to characterize the WMW in light of these observations. See Conway (2017a).

6. Key theoretical and conceptual developments in transnational feminism and their implications for understanding transnational feminist solidarity have recently been taken up by McLaren (2017), but largely in philosophical terms rather than in concert with empirical studies of concrete practices of activist collectivities (but see contributions to her edited collection by Bueno-Hansen and Falcón, and Gallegos). Although exhortations to coalition-building remain ubiquitous in the transnational feminism literature, anchorage in activist initiatives, organizations, or movements has waned. In its stead, attention has turned to the feminist classroom, women's study programs, and universities as sites of transnational feminist knowledge production (e.g., Alexander and Mohanty 2010; Burton and Allman 2008; Branfman 2019; Mohanty 2013; Vaz and Lemons 2013). Beyond the university but still preoccupied with academic knowledge production, discussions of transnational feminist solidarity, coalition-building, and praxis are proceeding around the conduct of activist scholarship (Sudbury and Okazawa-Rey 2009; Perry 2013) and collaborative research (Swarr and Nagar 2010; Nagar 2014; Quick Hall 2019). Long-standing concerns about the production of emancipatory subjectivities have morphed into preoccupations with affect, interpersonal dynamics, and "dissident friendship" (Chowdury and Philipose 2016), mostly remote from considerations of movement-based activist praxis (but see

Daskalaki and Fotaki 2017 for an exception). Notwithstanding this characterization of the field, we draw attention to the following counterexamples: Chowdhury (2009), Conway (2010, 2012), Estrada-Claudio (2010), Dempsey et al. (2011), Hewitt (2011), Naples and Bickham (2014), Tellez and Sanidad (2014), van den Brandt (2015), Lim (2015), Desai (2016, 2020), Mikkonen (2020), Anderl (2020), as well as important interventions by Perry (2016) and Quick Hall (2019) who articulate a transnational *Black* feminist framework in relation to empirical studies of grassroots mobilizations.

7. For trenchant observations about how the global left as seen through anti-globalization movements elides race, see Mahler (2018).

Part I

TRANSNATIONALIZATION

1

Studying "Global Feminism" as a Transnational Assemblage

Geopolitics of Women's Rights in the (Post)Cold War (1975–1995)

Ioana Cîrstocea

FORGING INTERNATIONAL AGENDAS: TWO DECADES OF UN-LED WOMEN'S ENCOUNTERS BEYOND BORDERS

Research in the history of feminism and the sociology of social movements has revealed that, during the last decades of the twentieth century, transnational feminist mobilizations were instrumental in advancing women's rights on the agendas of multilateral organizations and in integrating gender issues into international politics. An increasing body of literature tackles the events organized by the United Nations (UN) between the mid-1970s and the mid-1990s, namely the International Women's Year (IWY), the Mexico City first women's conference (1975), the UN Women's Decade (1976–85), the world women's governmental meetings, and NGO forums in Copenhagen (1980), Nairobi (1985), and Beijing (1995).[1] In their wake, "women's human rights" were consecrated in the early 1990s as an area of international politics, and the "gender mainstreaming" principle became a consensual transversal policy tool recommended by the Beijing Platform for Action (Walby 2005). A progressive narrative of "women's global movement" or "global feminism" was therefore set up in the literature (Naples and Desai 2002; Antrobus 2004; Moghadam 2005; Ferree and Tripp 2006; Hawkesworth 2006; Desai 2007, 2009; Basu 2010; Joachim 2013; Quataert 2014; Baksh and Harcourt 2015). It stages the timespan ranging from 1975 to 1995 as a continuum of mobilizations legitimizing, within multilateral institutions, the expertise of women's rights activists connected "beyond borders" (Keck and Sikkink 1998).

Yet, this same interval includes a major political hiatus: the end of the Cold War. Indeed, the "women's global movement" emerged under the conditions of the encompassing confrontation between the capitalist and socialist "blocs" (namely, the USA and the USSR, with their strategic allies) that shaped the international relations system for over forty years (1947–1991). This chapter looks at understanding how making a universal ("global") activist framework was possible in a divided geopolitical context, knowing that multiple ideological trends have shaped the history of international feminism (Stienstra 1994).

By taking a sociological perspective and building on archival records and publications produced by political activists and institutional donors involved in events acknowledged as the landmarks of the "global women's movement,"[2] this chapter studies actors, encounters, and discourses pertaining to this referent. I will first sketch a literature review and discuss the methodology and analytic tools that I have found useful for framing "global feminism" as a sui generis transnational assemblage structured by mechanisms to be deciphered using the sociologist's toolbox. Then, I will take a closer look at one of the leading figures of the movement. I will also consider the establishment of an activist organization featured in the scholarship as the epitome of "global feminism." I will then examine the collusion between "global feminism" and the "human rights" frame of reference, which was one of the main ideological streams of the late Cold War and a privileged area of U.S. foreign policy in the 1980s and 1990s.

Considering the material and symbolic resources allowing for the structuring and the international circulation of the framework of "global feminism," this chapter investigates the professional, bureaucratic, and geopolitical dynamics that shaped the international agendas on women's issues during the period under study. Previously overlooked by scholarship, the complex entanglements of women's activism, international development cooperation programs, and "cultural diplomacy" initiatives will be tackled here in an attempt to shed light on the practical and ideological role that "global feminism" played in the Cold War geopolitics and in the globalization processes subsequent to the end of the "East-West" confrontation.

DESIGNING A SOCIOLOGICAL RESEARCH OBJECT

"Women's Global Movement" versus Contending International Framings of Women's Rights

The dissemination of feminist concerns within the international bodies was described in institutional documents as well as in the writings of the participants in the UN-organized women's events of the 1975–1995 period (Papanek 1975, 1977; Tinker 1982; Fraser 1984; Henry 1985; Bunch et al. 1985; Çağatay et al. 1986; O'Barr et al. 1986; Moghadam 1995; Friedman 2003; Fraser and Tinker 2004). Informed by archival evidence and interviews, other works were published starting in the 2000s (Quataert and Roth 2012; Michel 2014; Baksh and Harcourt 2015; Olcott 2017). A large part of this scholarship focuses on women's solidarity across borders and on their successful strategies aimed at sensitizing bureaucratic agencies to feminist ideas (Antrobus 2004; Jain 2005; Moghadam 2005). Scholars also studied earlier liberal internationalist women's associations showing that their leaders, coopted in the UN system during the 1960s, could later participate in formulating the bureaucratic agendas on gender issues (Stienstra 1994; Garner 2010). According to the existing literature, the aggregation of transnational women's groups around multilateral venues since the mid-1970s allowed for a systematic inclusion of their concerns in the UN framework (Stienstra 1994) and therefore for a double-stream globalization ("bottom-up" and "top-down") of women's rights politics (Moghadam 2005). Subsequently, the activism of "transnational advocacy networks" (Keck and Sikkink 1998) triggered considerable evolution in women's rights law in various national settings.

Recent scholarship has criticized the "mainstream" literature on transnational and global feminisms showing that the events organized by the UN in the 1970s and 1980s were shaped by the Cold War geopolitical context (Ghodsee 2010; De Haan 2010, 2014; Fidelis et al. 2014; De Haan et al. 2016; Olcott 2017; Ghodsee 2019). Particularly, Kristen Ghodsee and Francisca de Haan exposed the ideological biases and blind spots of the works studying the international women's rights movements of the 1970s to 1990s based on the sole perspective of the Cold War "winners." For instance, they shed light on the activities of the Women's International Democratic Federation (WIDF), an organization set up with the Soviet Union's support in the aftermath of World War II. Sponsored by the socialist governments and established in dozens of states, it maintained active political networks in the decolonized countries, organized regular international gatherings, published multilingual materials circulating worldwide, and offered political training to the women of the "Third World." Despite its decades-long life, the WIDF has been curiously marginalized in the historiography of the "women's global movement."[3] Revealing the importance of this "other" women's rights internationalism, the critical scholarship published in the late 2010s maintains that the "global feminism" narrative is one-sided.[4]

Indeed, the issues dealt with in multilateral settings were subject to controversies opposing the socialist and capitalist visions of the world as well as the subsequent hegemonic ambitions of the two superpowers. The postcolonial countries were often the theater of violent conflicts between the "blocs" and their governments oscillated between adopting elements of one of the political systems or the other, while making strategic use of the material, technical, and knowledge resources coming from both (Westad 2005; Kwon 2010; McMahon 2013; Engerman 2018). Besides, critical scholars made the case for women's rights as a Cold War concern and for the UN as a privileged site for political confrontation.

The women's events organized by the multilateral body staged considerable tensions rooted in the geopolitical situation of the time. Issues such as "imperialism," "racism," "international debt," and "nuclear arms race" structure the speeches of the official delegates participating in the governmental meetings, they stand out in the final papers of the conferences and they overhang the commitment to or the rejection by the states of international normative documents. Specifically, the accounts of the first (Mexico City 1975) and second (Copenhagen 1980) world women's conferences picture vivid debates focusing on world economics and geopolitics. Supported by the socialist "bloc," the representatives of a coalition assembling decolonized states (the "Group of the 77," established in the early 1960s) launched a declaration at the Mexico City world conference on women in 1975. Referring to ideas formulated by the UN Conference on Trade and Development in 1972 and included in a declaration of the UN General Assembly in 1974, this document appealed to a "new international economic order" (NIEO) and denounced the neocolonial dimension of the development aid programs and the inequalities in wealth and voice between states (Olcott 2017; Michel 2014).

"Mainstream" liberal feminists coming from the industrialized countries considered such debates as a way of "confiscating" the women's gatherings, while radical activists took the opportunity of criticizing the politics of their own governments and of the multilateral bodies altogether. Therefore, "global feminism" did not exist by 1980. On the contrary, ideological visions and geopolitical divisions underpinned international women's rights politics at that time, while the very reference to "feminism" was contested or even rejected by a wide share of the participants in the UN encounters (Olcott 2017).

Still, the idea of a "global women's movement" became dominant in the political imaginaries of the years to come, summarizing a consensual agenda made of "women's human rights," "preventing and combating violence against women," "the empowerment of women," and "gender mainstreaming" embraced as the privileged tool of late twentieth-century feminism. The "gender mainstreaming" principle was included in the UN Platform for Action adopted in Beijing in 1995, then entered the European Union treaty (1997), and is being now carried forward by the majority of the states and shaping equality policy programs worldwide. Such universal references may function as astounding globalizing vectors casting a shadow on the local political histories of women's emancipation experiences. In the countries of Central and Eastern Europe, for instance, the watchwords promoted by the international bureaucracies during the 1990s waved off the ideological references related to the "woman question" and to the "women-and-family-friendly" policies set up by the socialist states since their establishment (Cîrstocea 2019). The globalized and globalizing "gender mainstreaming" agendas (Cîrstocea et al. 2019) appear therefore as privileged tools participating in "disciplining the Second World" (Fábián 2014) and in aligning it with (neo)liberal practical and ideological agendas (Cîrstocea 2019).

Mapping "Global Feminism"

Before detailing the concrete methodological operations my work is based on, a few precisions are needed to situate my understanding of "global feminism" vis-à-vis a classical argument in the feminist theory literature. The scholarship dedicated to transnational feminisms showcases a theoretical and political debate opposing, on the one hand, universal or global "sisterhood" understood as a form of (early) universal and utopian feminist politics carrying imperial assumptions or "*impensés*," and, on the other hand, "transnational feminist solidarities" as an intersectional political framework, aware of postcolonial criticisms and overcoming them by means of strategic alliances and transversal reflexive projects (Conway 2017a; Hundle et al. 2019). Partly produced during the timespan analyzed in the present chapter (1975–1995) and also discussing some of the transnational dynamics observed within the UN venues, the scholarship developing such arguments includes works by Third World-identified feminists. Still, it emerged in Western or Northern academic spaces (especially in the United States) and it became part of the internationalized disciplinary canon of gender studies (Wöhrer 2016). Moreover, this debate is mainly a conceptual one, while the social composition and the day-by-day practice of the activist groups it refers to is rarely considered in the light of empirically grounded data (Ferree and Tripp 2006; Conway 2017a; chapter 3).

Aware of the arguments involved in the discussion mentioned above, I nevertheless choose to adopt an external position in my work. This means that I take "global feminism" as a "watchword" whose analytical role is that of a tool helping to locate and to map those social groups that mobilized across borders and produced such a referent in a given historical and geopolitical context. Therefore "global feminism" is not understood in this paper as a theoretical or analytical category, but as an endogenous notion used by locally rooted groups and theorized by various individual activists in reference to their specific political projects. Two principles underline

my analysis: the transnational feminist activist networks allowing for the
"global feminism" referent to occur and to spread (1) were actively constructed, and (2) they were historically and geopolitically situated. This
means that they belong to particular political settings and that they were
framed under both material contingencies and ideological circumstances
underpinned by the Cold War rivalry between the two "blocs" and political
systems.

Scholars studying UN-organized events and UN-centered political dynamics often depict the emergence of women's "global" agendas as a "spontaneous" phenomenon produced by "institutional opportunities," the new
communication technologies, the availability and the democratization of
air transportation services, and even "globalization" itself. Departing from
such perspectives and focusing on the practical circumstances allowing for
transnational feminist encounters and common activist repertories to occur,
I envision "global feminism" as the ideological product and the tagline of
a geographically and historically situated transnational "praxis" (chapter 3,
61–62). According to Masson and Paulos, a "transnational feminist praxis"
is a specific form of solidarity-building, meaning an "active linking together
of hitherto geographically and/or socially distant and disparate place-based
struggles, through the construction of connections between actors, places,
and mobilizations." This produces "new political imaginaries" and "new
forms of political identification," connecting actors and their struggles on the
basis of "interrelated discursive, material, and spatial practices" (chapter 3).
Such an approach also echoes the critical perspective adopted by Inderpal
Grewal when framing "global feminism" as a discourse. Circulating through
"transnational connectivities" which are "never quite global" (in the sense of
reaching the whole world), it involves networks of knowledge and power and
it shapes communities across various geopolitical differentials and locations
(Grewal 2005).

In order to shed light on the social mechanisms that gave birth to the
"global feminism" framework during the 1980s and the early 1990s, connections and connecting practices will be investigated here. The starting
points for doing so are both the actors formulating and circulating the
idea of "global feminism" and the circumstances in which this idea was
expressed. For mapping out the groups referring to "global feminism"
in their practice, I also chose to pay attention to the material means that
allowed for traveling, meeting, exchanging ideas, and building women's
networks in the divided late Cold War world. Inspired by my previous
research on the international production and circulation of discourses
about "gender" and of the expertise on "gender" issues in post-socialist
Eastern Europe (Cîrstocea 2019), as well as by Keck and Sikkink's work
which underlined the extent of the U.S. philanthropic aid in the formation

of transnational advocacy coalitions, I included the donors supporting women's rights agendas internationally in the scope of my empirical inquiry. The social profiles of those women who elaborated the discourses of "global feminism" and who considered themselves participants in building a "global women's movement" are the main focus of my bibliographic and archival research. Studying the political and professional trajectories as well as the internationalization paths of such individuals, I am also interested in the activist productions that received credit for having "de-Westernized" "global feminism," progressively asserting a "Southern" women's leadership in the arenas opened and structured by the UN Women's Decade events and encounters (Antrobus 2004; Jain 2005; Baksh and Harcourt 2015).

A Landmark in the "Global Movement for Women's Rights"

In order to untangle the social and political mechanisms involved in the emergence of "global feminism" as a mobilization framework, I first reviewed the literature dedicated to this topic. For starting fieldwork, I then chose a moment that the scholarship acknowledges as an emblematic one in the history of the "global movement for women's rights." This is an international campaign undertaken in the early 1990s by the Center for Women's Global Leadership (CWGL, Rutgers University), targeting the UN and coordinated by U.S. feminist activist and scholar Charlotte Bunch. Denouncing violence against women, the campaign successfully substantiated the claim that "women's rights are human rights."[5] After a moment of intensive awareness-raising toward this concern during the 1993 UN Human Rights Conference in Vienna, the mobilization led to the adoption of the Declaration on the Elimination of Violence against Women by the UN in December that same year. The theme is also among the twelve "critical areas" listed in the Platform for Action adopted at the UN fourth Women's World Conference in Beijing in 1995.

Seen from an activist's perspective as a momentous victory of feminism in multilateral venues, the "women's rights are human rights" campaign can also be considered as a "transnational assemblage" made of activist circulations and encounters "beyond borders" (Keck and Sikkink 1998; Joachim 2007; see also Siméant 2010; Dufour et al. 2010; Saunier 2013). From a sociologist's point of view, the deployment of the campaign reveals some of the activist nodes of "global feminism" and provides an insight into the social configurations structuring the movement. On the one hand, it sheds light on the actors who devised and endorsed this mobilization framework. On the other hand, it uncovers historically built resources that were instrumental in the process.

OBSERVING THE MAKING OF "GLOBAL FEMINISM" AT AN INDIVIDUAL'S SCALE

"A Network in One Package"[6]

In order to fathom the social mechanisms of the "transnational praxis" involved in producing the ideological references of the "global women's movement," let us now consider the trajectory of the leader of the "women's rights are human rights" campaign, Charlotte Bunch. She was born in 1944 in a North Carolina middle-class educated family. She became politically active in the United States left during her student years at Duke University and she was also early internationalized as a Young Women's Christian Association and Methodist youth leader, then as a participant and organizer of civil rights, anti-Vietnam War, feminist, and lesbian mobilizations.

In her writings and speeches from the late 1960s and early 1970s, Bunch combined feminist analysis and anti-imperialist critique before focusing, from 1972 onwards, mainly on "developing a women's ideology, program, culture and movement." She explained this shift in the journal *The Furies* issued by the lesbian separatist homonymous group:

> Of course, being anti-imperialist and antisexist go hand in hand: both are evils created by white male domination of the world. . . . [W]omen who remain enslaved are drawn into these battles of men over race, nation, and class and have never succeeded in putting our interests first. Few of these battles between men have significantly altered the oppression of women . . . This time we must build a movement that brings these together from a feminist viewpoint—that doesn't sacrifice women and is ultimately strong enough to challenge imperialism. Feminists must concentrate on developing a women's ideology, program, culture and movement. . . . We must develop a world view and strategy for change that deals with the other forms of imperialism, but we must do so from a feminist perspective. . . . We must choose to win this time. (reprinted in Bunch 1987, 275–77)

Yet, in the late 1970s, she resumed her involvement in international feminist issues. Moreover, networking and "global" women's rights became her main activist focus after a meeting in preparation of the 1980 Copenhagen UN women's conference. Organized in 1979 in Bangkok by the Asian and Pacific Center for Women and Development (APCWD),[7] the gathering assembled bureaucrats, researchers, and activists. Second on the alphabetical list of participants, thirty-five-year-old Charlotte Bunch was then the coeditor of the U.S. radical journal *Quest. A Feminist Quarterly*. Earlier activities explain her presence in Bangkok: in the fall of 1975, she had participated in Canberra in a feminist conference organized by Elizabeth Reid—the future director of the APCWD. At that time counselor on women's policy to the Australian prime minister and formerly responsible for organizing the Australian IWY manifestations, Reid was acknowledged by the activist press as "the only feminist speaker at the governmental conference in Mexico City 1975."[8] Introduced by Charlotte Bunch, an issue of *Quest* published in winter 1978 was dedicated to the topic of "international feminism," and included contributions from activists, scholars, and artists who referred to geographic and political contexts as diverse as India, the Netherlands, Indonesia, Guinea Bissau, Israel, Brazil, France, Italy, Japan, and Cuba. It also included a selection of texts by Elizabeth Reid, edited, compiled, and presented by Charlotte Bunch under the title "Women, Economic Development and the UN," together with two contributions echoing international feminist encounters organized in the aftermath of the IWY conference in the United States and in Europe.

The 1979 Bangkok meeting appears as an early encounter of people who would collaborate in building "global feminism" for the years to come. Beyond the APCWD hosts and organizers, the fourteen workshop participants also counted Shirley Castley, an Australian civil servant from the Social Welfare department in Sydney and one of Elizabeth Reid's close collaborators, a representative of the Sweden development aid agency, a British economist, and guests from Tanzania, the Philippines, China, India, and Barbados. Among the latter were Vina Mazumdar, an Indian political scientist and pioneering figure of women's and gender studies in her country, and Peggy Antrobus, an economist and social worker trained in the United Kingdom, adviser on Women's Affairs to the government of Jamaica.[9] In spring 1980, the group met again for a follow-up gathering in Stony Point (New York), whose participants included Adrienne Germain, a U.S. sociologist trained at Wellesley, member of the Ford Foundation's staff, and one of the individuals praised for building the foundation's "feminist" orientation (Korey 2007; Hartmann 1998; Caulier 2010; Coogan-Gehr 2011). The Ford Foundation was one of the meeting's founders, together with the Carnegie Corporation.[10]

Aimed at exploring "the possibility of formulating an international perspective on feminism while respecting differences of background and ideology," this second meeting led to the publication of a platform document including a basic definition of women's politics that was to be found in future writings relating to "global feminism" as well.[11] According to it, feminism was understood as a "transformational politics that addresses every aspect of life." Its goals were:

> [F]reedom of choice, power to control our own lives within and outside the home; removal of all forms of inequity and oppression, through the creation of a more just social and economic order, nationally and internationally; involvement of women in national liberation struggles, in plans for national development, in local and global struggles for change. (reprinted in Bunch 1987, 302)

In the aftermath of these two encounters, Bunch and Castley were hired by the International Women's Tribune Center (IWTC) to organize and animate workshops on "international feminist networking" to be held during the Copenhagen UN women's conference. Set up in New York in 1976 by the IWY conference secretariat, this body was involved in organizing the NGO forums accompanying all the subsequent UN world women's gatherings and it acted over several decades as a "North-South" communication and networking hub (Walker 2004; Olcott 2017). In that same context, Charlotte Bunch was also assigned the production of a video about "world feminists" that would be screened during the 1980 Copenhagen NGO Forum. From that point on, she focused her militant and professional activities on developing her understanding of international women's activism while closely working with the IWTC as a consultant for several projects.

During the 1980s, in addition to activist, expert, and teaching activities in the United States, she began traveling to Latin America and Asia, encountering women's groups and giving conferences and lectures on feminist issues. Coupled with "human rights," the topic of "global feminism" was her main research focus when she obtained a chair in women's and gender studies at Rutgers University in 1987. Starting in 1990 and building on previous activist and institutional connections, Bunch (then professor at Rutgers and head of the CWGL) organized the "global" campaign that ended up putting "women's human rights" in the UN documents.

From a "Feminist Utopia" to Organizing "on a Larger Scale"

According to Charlotte Bunch, "global feminism" is a critical perspective on all types of power and domination, encompassing the sense of a worldview intended to specifically challenge the geopolitical structures and inequalities affecting women's lives. In her introduction to the 1978 thematic issue of *Quest* mentioned above, she was already foreseeing such a perspective: "Can we talk about the global oppression of women—its causes and cures—in any universal terms? . . . What theoretical, strategic, and programmatic developments are taking place that are vital to an international audience?" (reprinted in Bunch 1987, 280).

In a text written in the aftermath of the 1980 Copenhagen UN conference, in reaction to claims expressed in conservative circles against "politicizing" the women's gathering, she advocates the idea of a "global and not international feminism," that is, a "movement of people working for change across and despite national boundaries." For her, feminism is a "transformational politics that addresses every aspect of life, not simply a laundry list of so-called women's issues." Still, in the early 1980s, she saw "global feminism" merely as a project for the future: "[D]eveloping a feminist political perspective on NIEO

(New International Economic Order), the nuclear arms race, or the international slave traffic in women is still work in progress. . . . We have much to do in order to demonstrate the potential of feminism for providing new ways of viewing the world that can help build a just future" (reprinted in Bunch 1987, 301–05).[12]

A few years later, when assembling and animating a panel at the UN women's conference in Nairobi (1985), Bunch pictured feminism as a "transformational perspective that grows from women's experiences, women's lives, women's view of the world and questions of power and domination in all of its aspects in all spheres of life, for women, for men, for the globe."[13] A practical dimension would complement this theoretical perspective, illustrated by the accomplishments of what Charlotte Bunch already considered to be an existing worldwide political movement:

> One of the most exciting world developments is the emergence of feminism all over the globe. Women of almost every culture, color, and class are claiming feminism for themselves.
>
> Global feminism exists. Feminist activity and thought are happening all over the world.
>
> In a world where global forces affect us daily, it is neither possible nor conscionable to achieve a feminist utopia in one country alone.
>
> My visions of global feminism are grand, perhaps even grandiose. But the state of the world today demands that women become less modest and dream/plan/act/risk on a larger scale. (reprinted in Bunch 1987, 328–45)[14]

Similar ideas are featured in Bunch's inaugural speech as Laurie Chair in women's and gender studies, delivered at Rutgers University on November 4, 1987, when she mentioned the "expansion and diversification of women's movement in the world" together with examples of networks and mobilizations in the "Third World post-Nairobi." Availing herself of the slogan "think globally, act locally," she states that feminism is a "global," "integral worldview," a "transformative politics," and not a narrow focus on "women's issues" (or "kitchenization").[15]

"DE-WESTERNIZING" FEMINISM DURING THE UN WOMEN'S DECADE

Establishing a "Southern" Feminist Network[16]

In order to shed light on the geopolitical mechanisms channeling the emergence and the spreading of the references to "global feminism," I will now consider an organization which was an important actor of the "women's global movement" since the mid-1980s. Launched in Nairobi at the Third World Women's Conference in 1985, Development Alternatives with Women for a New Era (DAWN) has been since known as one of the main incarnations of "Third World" or "Southern" feminism. Literature on transnational feminist solidarities refers to it as the typical example illustrating the worldwide ("global") expansion of the scope and scale of feminism in the wake of the IWY and during the UN Women's Decade (Antrobus 2004; Jain 2005; Moghadam 2005; Fraser and Tinker 2004; Baksh and Harcourt 2015; Olcott 2017).[17] Having a closer look at it, and especially at the structuring work done in its early years, allows me to discuss the wider geopolitical dynamics underlying transnational women's solidarities during the Cold War.

Assembling locally rooted and internationally connected feminist activists, bureaucrats, academics, and experts, DAWN announced its birth at the end of the UN Women's Decade. Its membership and its activist identity seemingly capitalize on a series of previous initiatives, some of which harshly criticized international development aid programs. For instance, a position paper signed by a "Third World women's caucus" was produced and circulated during the Copenhagen UN women's conference in 1980. It denounced the unfair global order, assessing the neo-colonizing dimension of development cooperation programs. The text also deconstructed the "Third World" label, considering it patronizing and homogenizing.[18] Connected or not to this, a seminar on the theme "Another Development with Women" was organized in Dakar in June 1982 by Senegalese sociologist Marie-Angélique Savané of the Association of African Women for Research and Development (AAWORD/ AFARD), with support from the Swedish Dag Hammarskjöld Foundation.[19] According to a published statement, the participants[20] appraised the "increasing inequalities within nations" and the "constant intensification of both overt and covert efforts to further entrench international capitalism under the guise of development . . . worsening women's condition in the Third World." "Another development with women," was therefore to be envisioned that would be shaped by the "fundamental principle of structural transformation." In that framework, rethinking the status of women was seen as belonging to the "new consciousness and cultural resistance to domination."[21] In January 1983, the Indian economist Devaki Jain[22] presented a paper on the topic "Development as If Women Mattered. Can Women Build a New Paradigm?" in a Paris meeting of the Development Assistance Committee (DAC) of the Organisation for Economic Cooperation and Development (OECD). Produced in preparation of the Nairobi Conference,[23] the text was based on the review of several dozen evaluations of development projects, and it criticized the international aid policies, expressing the idea that development should be a "route for justice" and that women had to resist "international economic arrangements which are exploitation."

Eventually, in 1985, the idea of an "alternative development with women" would be taken on by DAWN, a transnational group displaying it in its own name and assembling some of the people involved in the earlier critical efforts mentioned above.[24] DAWN's launch was announced during the Nairobi UN women's conference, where workshops and debates were set up to discuss a text expressing "Third World's women's view" on the geopolitics of the time. Partly contradicting the "Southern" label boldly showcased by the group, several of the twenty-two founders of DAWN were based in the "North." Others, who can be described as "professional-class cosmopolitans" (Olcott 2017, 155), were steady interlocutors of "Northern" institutions in the "South," such as Peggy Antrobus (Jamaica, WAND), Devaki Jain (India, Institute for Social Studies Trust),[25] and Carmen Barroso and Neuma Aguyar (Brazil, Carlos Chagas Foundation).[26] Moreover, numerous "Northern" experts as well as employees of development cooperation agencies and women's rights activists (including Charlotte Bunch) offered feedback on DAWN's manifesto before its official launch.

Authored by Caren Grown (a U.S. expert, at that time a postgraduate student in economics at the New School for Social Research [NSSR] in New York) and Gita Sen (an Indian economist, visiting scholar at the NSSR), the document had been prepared over the previous couple of years through transnational exchanges facilitated by institutions based in the hegemonic liberal countries. Via the Christian Michelson Institute in Norway, the Ford Foundation financially supported the organization of two DAWN preparatory meetings in Bangalore and Bergen. The U.S. Population Council granted office space to the two scholars working on the manifesto draft. The Rockefeller Foundation helped the preparation and circulation of the paper for feedback and, later on, the production of a book based on it.[27]

Building Consensus

As for its contents, the document launched by DAWN negatively assesses the UN Women's Decade's achievements and recommends departing from the dominant development ideological framework. It criticizes the limits and the harmful effects of the international aid, calling for women's further participation and for their "vision" and "experiences" to be included in the conception and the implementation of the cooperation programs.[28] Aimed at "contributing to ongoing debate about the commonalities and differences in the oppression of women," the manifesto endorses "sisterhood" as a goal to be achieved through dialogue and collaboration.[29] The first pages of the text refer to documents produced in the frame of the earlier Bangkok and Stony

Point feminist transnational encounters[30] and indicate that it was building on those initiatives to sharpen the political analysis and strengthen the attempts to change.

As for the "Third World perspective," it is referred to, in a rather ironic manner, as "includ[ing] all who share our vision, whether from South countries, or from oppressed and disadvantaged groups within the North." After discussing world crises of the time—the food shortages, the poverty, the international debt, the structural adjustment policies, the militarization, the religious fundamentalism, the sexual objectification of women, the discriminatory traditions and laws—the document outlines "alternative visions, strategies and methods." According to it, feminism is a political movement "potentially global in scope," to be flexibly built upon women's shared commitment to put an end to their subordination. Macro-objectives, such as supporting a "just and equitable international order," "liberation from colonial and neocolonial domination," "reduction of military expenditures," and "control of multinational companies," are stated along practical aims such as developing popular education, research on gender issues and women's study programs, and institutional reforms. DAWN also declared encouraging networking and "supporting women in countries under repressive regimes or in which states attacked women's social and economic status."

Therefore, in between the Copenhagen and Nairobi UN women's forums, political concerns expressed first in the form of radical anti-capitalist criticisms were melted in the rhetoric of a quite pacified "global" feminism, as DAWN recommends itself as a transnational initiative allying women across postcolonial and Cold War dividing geopolitical lines. Its establishment embodies this metamorphosis and the group discursively occupies the space opened by the critical anti-capitalist voices at the conferences in Mexico City and Copenhagen a few years before. Carefully prepared, its political program combines concerns of women from the "South" and from the "North" under the federating banner of struggling against "domination," which is understood as being a common women's issue. Divergences in the political orientations of the postcolonial governments, as well as the radical challenge to development aid understood as an apparatus based on capitalist neo-imperial assumptions and ambitions disappeared under the unifying label of "patriarchy" expressing oppression as a general phenomenon.

Northern donors supported the building of DAWN and its raising visibility in the years to come. The hypothesis of an active consensus construction can be formulated at this point, especially knowing that certain radical activists mocked "networking" as the "current rage" at the Nairobi Conference and denounced "money [channeled by] funding agencies to produce and maintain international networks" (Henry 1985, 2–3). Indeed, Northern donor organizations selected the participants from the "South" in the Nairobi UN Forum, for instance opting for funding the traveling costs of women with no previous experience of international events. This might appear as an attempt to smooth the exchanges by erasing the memory of tensions and conflicting debates that previously occupied the front stage of the international encounters.[31] For instance, when preparing the workshops for the launch of DAWN's manifesto in Nairobi, the organizers were anticipating confrontation and hired consultants with professional experience in conflict resolution and cross-cultural communication, which were specifically mandated to "facilitate dialogue on controversial issues."

In the following years, DAWN proceeded toward institutionalization with funding from various private and public institutional bodies, such as the U.S. private foundations Ford and Rockefeller, the Dutch government, UNIFEM, and it further explored ways of imagining "transversal" feminist issues and practice. Its first three-year program drawn up in early 1986 focused on two main themes, namely the research on women and the economic crisis. The advisory board discussed the direction to take in the aftermath of the Cold War; for instance, the sense of DAWN's politics in a world freed of the bipolarity was questioned during a meeting in spring 1990.

To sum up, the feminist solidarity, the organizing practice, and the symbolic representations of an emblematic "Southern" or "Third World" women's network involved extra- or para-militant dynamics far more complex than currently assumed. Actors from economically and politically dominating countries, such as the United States, were closely working with individuals and institutions based in the decolonized "Global South." Presented in the literature as the epitome of a "de-Westernized" feminism, DAWN embodies the results of a complex transnational solidarity-building process, benefiting from material resources as well as political inputs and theoretical insights from activists and bureaucrats in the "Global North." Not only genuine feminist mobilizations but also professional, political, and geopolitical dynamics shaped its emergence, connecting actors from various locations through the circulation of funds and know-how aimed at supporting women's international cooperation in regions of the world that were disputed scenes of influence during the Cold War.

PERFORMING "WOMEN'S RIGHTS AS HUMAN RIGHTS"

Converging Agendas of Human Rights and Women's Rights in the 1980s

In order to further discuss the emergence and the institutional recognition of "global" concerns for women's rights, I will now consider the convergence of feminist liberal internationalism with the ideological frame of "human rights," which was an important theme of the U.S. foreign policy in the late Cold War (Guilhot 2005; also, Dezalay and Garth 2002; Snyder 2011, 2018).

According to the evidence I was able to gather to date, one of the earliest attempts at shaping women's rights as a concern for international human rights lies in a 1981 thematic issue (Hosken 1981) of the journal *Human Rights Quarterly*.[32] Editor Fran P. Hosken[33] explains in her introduction that the collection of articles ("symposium") was assembled in the aftermath of the Copenhagen 1980 UN women's conference and aimed to "define women's human rights, to develop priorities, and to evaluate if and how existing human rights initiatives affect women." Invited contributors—mainly law scholars and practitioners active in U.S. institutions or working for international bodies—tackle subjects in the areas of health and reproductive rights, economic rights, and international instruments protecting women. Hosken also mentions several "enforcement mechanisms" for the new UN Convention on the Elimination of All Forms of Discrimination against Women (CEDAW),[34] namely "fact-finding, political organizing and complaint filing," and she refers especially to U.S. government instruments such as the U.S. Foreign Aid Act and the Country Reports on Rights Practices submitted annually by the Department of State to the Congress.[35]

Coming back to Charlotte Bunch, one of the leading figures of "global feminism," whose activist work provided the main guiding lines of the analysis developed in the present chapter, she was aware of that early attempt to frame women's rights in the international human rights repertoire. Documents in her archives show that she had read and annotated a paper published in the 1981 *Human Rights Quarterly* Symposium discussed above by law scholar Catherine Tinker under the title "Human Rights for Women: the CEDAW."[36] Bunch also made direct references to human rights treaties in her correspondence with the funders of a project on international trafficking of women that she had coordinated at the IWTC in 1980–1983.[37] Dormant after the end of that project (which Bunch retrospectively considered with a critical eye because of its focus on women mainly as "victims"), the human rights framework would be reactivated for feminist political ends in the context of its becoming a highly visible political theme in the United States during the second half of the 1980s.

Complementing earlier activities developed under the policy area of "women in development," the U.S. international cooperation actors considered gender issues through the lens of human rights after the end of the UN Decade on Women. For instance, the International Women's Rights Action Watch (IWRAW), an organization structured during the UN women's conference in Nairobi in 1985 and operational in spring 1986, was aimed at monitoring the reporting to the CEDAW committee and at gathering data about women's status country by country, to be published in a periodical titled *The Women's Watch* launched in 1987. Based at the University of Minnesota, the IWRAW was founded and chaired by Arvonne Fraser (1925–2018), an activist and political campaigner, lifetime partner of Mayor and Congressman Donald Fraser (Dem.), who is recognized as one of the early promoters of human rights as a policy area in U.S. foreign affairs (Snyder 2018). A member of the U.S. delegations to the first two UN women's conferences, Arvonne Fraser was the director of the USAID's "Women in Development" office set up during the Carter administration. She also headed the "Women in Development" group established in 1978 on the U.S. representative's initiative within the OECD's DAC, and she represented the United States to the UN Commission on the Status of Women (Fraser 2004, 2007; Ghodsee 2019). The IWRAW's work benefited from the Carnegie Corporation's material support and from the collaboration of prominent law scholars based at Columbia University. Together with organizations such as the Association for Women's Rights in Development (AWID) established in 1982, which assembled professionals of international cooperation concerned with women's issues in development programs,[38] and with Human Rights Watch, which opened a women's rights project in the late 1980s (Neier 2012, 585–86), IWRAW embodies what could be characterized as a facet of U.S. foreign policy activism dealing with human rights themes and taking a gender-issues orientation in the late Cold War.

As for Charlotte Bunch, when appointed to the Rutgers Laurie Chair in women's and gender studies in 1987, she gave an inaugural speech displaying in its title "Global Feminism, Human Rights and Sexual Violence." She also organized a seminar on the theme "global feminism and human rights," composing and disseminating a narrative oriented by the overarching goal of inflecting the international norms concerning human rights so that they included feminist ideas allowing the politicization of intimate issues and especially of sexual violence.[39] Bunch also attended various academic events debating international law, international human rights, and women's rights issues together, such as, for instance, a 1988 conference at Harvard on "women's rights and human rights." According to an archived interview, she was opposed to a superficial "add-women-and-stir" approach; rather, she aimed for an authentic cross-fertilization of the two ideological streams and for a new, comprehensive conceptualization of human rights. So, she advocated for expanding the definition of the latter according to the feminist critique of the "public/private divide" and for subsequently politicizing domestic matters in international venues.[40] Prepared concurrently, her paper "Women's Rights Are Human Rights" was published in a 1990 issue of *Human Rights Quarterly* (Bunch 1990) and is nowadays widely acknowledged as a turning point in scholarship in both international human rights law and feminism.[41]

When entering her academic career as a professor at Rutgers University in 1987, Charlotte Bunch seemed to align her feminist politics on the ideologies shaping U.S. politics of the late Cold War. Yet, as she stated later, she did not fully share the mainstream understanding of human rights of that time and she endorsed that political framework without reservations only after 1990:

> Before (the 1990s) human rights were so much a part of the Cold War, it was hard to bring a real feminist interpretation into it. . . . Then that really made a huge difference in the possibility for feminism: because it was no longer one block against the other and we were starting to talk about human rights in a new way. . . . At the Vienna Conference (UN 1993) the first came a global recognition that the right to food and shelter are human rights, and not just socialist countries rights. . . . Also, development for the global South, all these issues that had been worked on but have been blocked by the ideological Cold War mentality.[42]
>
> That decade the 1990s was a high point of international cooperation post-Cold War, with talk of a "peace dividend" as many thought less money and attention would be expended on war and militaries. As such, it was a period of opening up when human rights was gaining credence as a global vision and expanding in scope. (Bunch and Reilly 2019, 25)

After the end of the Cold War, the full merging of the "human rights" ideological reference with feminism under the motto "women's rights are human rights" was to confer a sudden and enduring visibility to Charlotte Bunch and lastingly reframe the discourses and the understanding of "global feminism."

Toward the Universal Consecration of "Women's Human Rights" in the Early 1990s

Partly contradicting radical activists' expectations for a new political horizon, the socialist regimes' collapse and the end of bipolar confrontation paved the way for liberal representations to dominate the international scene. Indeed, after the end of the Cold War, "rights," "human rights," "women's human rights," and "gender mainstreaming" became the common language of a "one-size-fits-all" (Ghodsee 2010, 10) global politics on gender equality endorsed and promoted by international and multilateral bodies.

In order to make clear the tremendous disruption that took place in the early 1990s, let me note that, during the two previous decades, the multilateral venues debating women's rights politics had not often been dominated by liberal voices. Erased from the history of international women's emancipation struggles and almost forgotten today, the WIDF (a socialist organization established in 1945 and having a global reach) together with its national branches' representatives were vocal actors during the UN Women's Decade. Only in recent years have researchers started to consider the international programs—in women's rights matters but not exclusively—that were promoted by the Soviet-bloc states and their allies, be they officially "aligned" or not. This new research shows the depth and breadth of the exchanges and collaborative projects involving women's organizations from the "Second World" and the postcolonial states. Allowing for a genuine, transnational process of political learning, socialist internationalism in women's rights matters included various strategies, such as the production of multilingual publications circulated worldwide, the setting up of meetings in preparation of the UN world conferences, the political training of numerous "Third World" fellow internationalist women by means of well-organized "experience exchanges," and study visits in the socialist countries (Ghodsee 2019). This forgotten activism "beyond borders" closely entangled women's rights politics with counter-hegemonic and anti-capitalist claims. Built on considerable material resources and benefiting of high-level political support, it carried weight in the UN venues of the 1970s and 1980s and it significantly marked the language and the contents of the international documents pertaining to women's rights. For instance, both the initiatives of the IWY (1975) and of the CEDAW (1979) involved significant input from representatives of the socialist "bloc" organizations and their allies within the UN.

Coming back to "global feminism" as considered in this paper, the idea was formulated by liberal feminist activists and framed through transnational, bureaucratically supported encounters involving, on the one hand, women based in the "Global North" hegemonic countries and, on the other hand, "subaltern cosmopolitans" (Olcott 2017) who were their selected counterparts in the "Third World." Discretely but constantly sponsored by institutions operating in the corridors of "cultural diplomacy" such as the big philanthropic U.S. foundations, this political program provided an ideological alternative to the women's rights internationalism promoted by "Second World" organizations. Successively reshaped since the early 1980s, the referent of the "global women's movement" was an instrumental resource in effacing the achievements and the memory of competing "other" internationalisms in women's rights matters after the end of the Cold War.

Between the 1980s and the 1990s, the constituency of "global feminism" itself shifted. Referring to "North-South" and "South-South" alliances, the "global" of the 1980s left aside the "Soviet bloc," while the "global" of the 1990s included this geopolitical region as well.[43] When Eastern European women took part in the activist forums set up around the post–Cold War UN conferences,[44] transnational networks supported by U.S.-based public and private institutions as well as by international bodies encouraged their adopting the liberal "gender equality" vocabularies and practices. Featured as universal, the repertory and the ideological references of the bureaucratically supported "women's human rights" and "gender mainstreaming" paved the way for dismissing the political traditions of women's emancipation structured in the "Second World" and carried by the socialist "bloc" actors and their geopolitical allies in the decolonized world. In the meantime, under the effect of post-authoritarian political and economic restructuring processes, the agendas previously promoted by the now collapsed socialist states were discarded and the institutional mechanisms supporting them were swiftly disbanded in the countries of Central and Eastern Europe.[45]

In light of the analysis presented above, "global feminism" can be understood not only as a successful activist solidarity-building project, as it is commonly understood, but also as one of the privileged settings for producing the (post)Cold War ideological order. Under the header of democracy-building and therefore more openly than in the previous decades, considerable resources were allocated in the early 1990s to international activist networks structured around the all-encompassing framework of "women's human rights" and "global feminism." Based in the United States, these networks served at assessing the new, "leadership [of the U.S.] in the global community with regard to women's rights."[46] Both the U.S. government and private funding sponsored the CWGL campaign, the Vienna 1993 Tribunal on Violations of Women's Rights, and the 1995 UN world women's conference in Beijing.[47] Moreover, the White House itself advanced the idea of "global feminism," while the credo of "women's (human) rights" was a central piece in the U.S. government international policy of the 1990s (Horn 2010; Garner 2013; Suchland 2015): "If there is one message that echoes forth from this conference, let it be that human rights are women's rights and women's rights are human rights, once and for all," First Lady Hillary Clinton proclaimed in Beijing 1995.[48] In 1996, Charlotte Bunch was inducted into the National Women's Hall of Fame "for her substantial, ongoing contributions to the global empowerment of women." She also received the Eleanor Roosevelt Award for Human Rights from President Bill Clinton in 1999.

"GLOBAL FEMINISM" AS "GLOBALIZING POLITICS"

Considering the emergence and expanding references to "global feminism" in a sociological perspective—namely focusing, on the one hand, on the very actors who endorsed such discourse, and, on the other hand, on their practices and on the material and symbolic resources allowing their activism—this chapter shows how the "global" was produced as a scale of mobilization under particular geopolitical circumstances. In the context under study, translocal and transregional links connected individuals based in the "Global North" (the United States especially) with individuals from the "Global South," that is, groups and individuals who were partners of institutions based in the "Western bloc" and operating in the "Third World." Through carefully orchestrated and visibly staged discursive work, new political identities were produced and displayed as "global" in multilateral venues. According to the analytical frame adopted in the present chapter, the building of "global feminism" is a process of ideological "scaling" of women's rights activism (Masson 2006, 2009; Conway 2008; Dufour et al. 2010; Dufour 2016). It is also a (geo)political "performance" (Rai and Waylen 2008), in the sense of a dynamic production of common understandings and feelings of belonging. In particular places and during the given historical moment of the late Cold War and especially of the 1980s decade, the references and political objectives of the struggles for women's rights were performed as universal (here "global"), and women's identities were discursively constructed as "shared." Besides genuine activist reflexivity on the possibilities and pitfalls of international feminist activism, these processes involved institutional strategies of consensus making through encounters "beyond borders" shaped and run according to norms of preventing controversies and effacing opposing ideologies and political allegiances. As it conceals competing internationalist repertories and contains political dissent, the "global feminism" framework is a transnational assemblage deeply shaped by geopolitics. Its geographical references (the "North," the "South," the "Third World," and the "global" itself) euphemize tense geopolitical situations, unequal distribution of power and resources, as well as sharp political cleavages always present under the neat surface of final documents adopted in international venues.

Counterbalancing the women's rights internationalism carried out by the "Soviet-bloc" organizations during the Cold War, "global feminism" appears in the light of research rendered in the present chapter as a "globalizing politics," or a situated process of building universal references. Endorsed by multiple agents and taking various discursive forms, such a political process assembles distinct performances allowing for peculiar ideas to become uncontested and to look like being the "only possible and imaginable at a moment in time" (Bourdieu 2002). Political solidarities between women based in liberal hegemonic states and women from decolonized societies were discursively and organizationally structured, and they were featured in the multilateral venues with support from the international aid agencies and from various international cooperation actors. Governments' international alliances as well as U.S. private donors' policies for funding operations overseas framed the map and the "activist praxis" (Conway 2017a; chapter 3) of the "worldwide" mobilizations for women's rights in the 1980s and the early 1990s. They certainly allowed feminists to meet, networks to be formed, transnational references to crystallize, and "global" agendas to unfold and to be implemented at the institutional level. Yet, more or less explicit selection criteria, inclusion and exclusion rules, as well as unevenly-distributed politically- and strategically-oriented material resources account for the make-up, the configurations, the outreach, the extent, and the ideological contents embedded in the transnational feminist repertories framed as "global feminism" in the late Cold War.

Thus, the activist side of the story is merely the tip of the iceberg. The ambiguous role endorsed by U.S.-based institutions in the entanglements of the networks and discursive productions pertaining to "global feminism" invites further analysis of the promotion of women's rights "across borders" after the IWY conference and especially during the 1980s. There is no doubt that, through multileveled and contested processes of circulation and adaptation, ideas as well as actors of grassroots radical feminist movements eventually succeeded in accessing the international bureaucracies and contributed to a sound reframing of their agendas. Capturing the political imagination[49] of critical actors, these processes—only partly documented here—entangle genuine activism with national and international power games using women's rights politics as both a tool and an arena in the Cold War "cultural diplomacy" complex.[50]

NOTES

1. The UN-organized women's events combined governmental conferences and parallel gatherings of civil society representatives known as "NGO forums." Attendance numbers rose from six thousand people in Mexico City to thirty thousand in Beijing (Olcott 2017, 248).

2. The primary sources of my work include archival evidence produced by U.S.-based activist groups and donor organizations involved in the preparation of the four UN women's conferences (see details below). This chapter is part of work in progress for an intended book-length project on "global feminism." My research has been conducted since December 2017 with funding from the LabEx TEPSIS, Ecole des Hautes Etudes en Sciences Sociales EHESS (School of Advanced Studies in Social Sciences), Paris, "Fonds de préfiguration" Program. I am grateful to Sébastien Le Pipec (EHESS) for editorial help, to the three coordinators of this edited volume for insightful feedback on the first drafts of my text, to my colleagues and students for stimulating questions and remarks.

3. Disbanded in 1991, the WIDF was re-established in 1994 (De Haan, 2010). I have recorded sixteen references to the historical activities of this organization in Stienstra, 1994 (a 218-page book published before the Beijing 1995 consensus was

established), compared to only four references in Baksh and Harcourt, 2015 (a 977-page handbook dedicated to transnational women's movements and published in celebration of the "40th anniversary of the IWY, the 30th anniversary of the World Conference in Nairobi, the 20th anniversary of the Beijing Declaration and Platform for Action, and the 15th anniversary of the Millennium Development Goals and of the UN Security Council Resolution 1325 on 'women, peace and security,'" 1).

4. The "post-Cold War turn" criticizing the Western/Northern and liberal-focused approaches goes well beyond the historiography of women's rights politics. See Grosescu and Richardson-Little (2019) on the production of international criminal and humanitarian law; Sikkink (2017) on the genesis of international human rights norms; Falcón (2016) on the history of UN anti-racism norms. Written and published long before the "turn" and based on a critical sociological approach, Guilhot (2005) provides a thorough analysis of the emergence and legitimation of human rights and democracy promotion as U.S. foreign policy themes deeply shaped by Cold War politics.

5. See http://cwgl.rutgers.edu for details of those activities and archived publications. See Reilly (2019) and Herr (2019) for recent works on the later "career" of the "women's human rights" international norm set at the beginning of the 1990s.

6. Empirical evidence used in this section comes from the following sources: Charlotte Bunch's CV retrieved on March 20, 2013, on the Rutgers University website (http://www.cwgl.rutgers.edu); Bunch 1987 (collection of writings and speeches from the late 1960s on); Evans 2003; Gold 2011; Trigg and Soderling 2016. I also did extensive research on the archival collection "Additional Papers of Charlotte Bunch, 1944–2010, MC 708" ("MC 708" below) at the Schlesinger Library (Radcliffe Institute, Harvard University) and I interviewed Charlotte Bunch on November 12, 2014, in New York. For the section subtitle, I refer to a letter kept in MC 708, box 23, folder 4.

7. This regional UN body established in 1977 in Tehran moved to Bangkok in 1978. See *APCWD Women's Resource Book 1978* available in the digital collection *Women and Social Movements, International: 1840 to Present* (K. K. Sklar and T. Dublin, eds., Alexander Street, http://wasi.alexanderstreet.com/).

8. For more details on her profile and activities, see Olcott 2017. A copy of Reid's Mexico discourse is kept in Bunch's archives (MC 708, box 42, folder 4).

9. Appointed in 1974, she participated in the 1975 IWY conference as an official delegate. Later, she established the Women and Development Unit (WAND) at the University of the West Indies (1978), which she directed until her retirement in 1991. Antrobus has been a steady counterpart to U.S. international cooperation programs in the Caribbean region: She worked with Adrienne Germain of the Ford Foundation and with Joan Dunlop of the Rockefeller Foundation. At the Copenhagen conference in 1980, she co-organized a series of USAID-supported workshops on "women in development" in collaboration with a Carnegie Corporation's officer (MC 708, box 42, folder 8). In retrospective accounts of her activities, she credits Charlotte Bunch with igniting her very commitment to feminism (Olcott 2017, 244).

10. See *Developing Strategies for the Future. Feminist Perspectives. Report of the International Feminist Workshop Held at Stony Point, New York, April 20–25, 1980; Feminist Ideologies and Structures in the First Decade for Women. Report from the Bangkok Workshop Held June 23–30, 1979*, edited by the International Women's

Tribune Centre, 1980 (available in *Women and Social Movements, International: 1840 to Present*).

11. According to Stienstra, these workshops provided "a firm conceptual basis upon which women's international organizing could be built," as well as "articulations of feminism in the global context [that] remain at the foundation of much contemporary feminist organizing at the international level" (Stienstra 1994, 108–09).

12. "Prospects for Global Feminism" (1981–1982), notes and drafts in MC 708, box 42, folder 9.

13. Transcription: "What Is Feminism?—A Global Perspective," Nairobi, 1985 (MC 708, box 43, folder 7).

14. Fragment from a piece of writing which was first published in 1985.

15. MC 708, box 24, folder 7 and MC 708, box 25, folder 1.

16. This section includes arguments previously developed in my presentations given at the international conference "Fabriques du genre dans le Sud global" (EHESS, Paris, February 28, 2019 to March 1, 2019) and at the international workshop "International Mobilizations on Women's Rights Issues during the Cold War" (EHESS, Paris, June 28, 2019).

17. In a recent contribution, Peggy Antrobus provides an account by one founding member of the organization's three-decade-long activity and tremendous contribution to building the "global feminist movement." According to this author, in DAWN's view, the "global" is an "analytical concept" attempting "to theorize the practice of women's organizing for participation in global conferences on global issues and their ability to formulate and agree upon common perspectives" (Antrobus 2015, 177).

18. MC 708, box 40, folder 10.

19. MC 708, box 34, folders 6 and 8. Established in 1977 in Dakar, this association of African researchers in social sciences is mentioned in various publications as a vocal critic of the neocolonial assumptions involved in the international cooperation mechanisms and processes (Stienstra 1994, 128; Antrobus 2015, 185).

20. Among them were Vina Mazumdar (India), Lourdes Arizpe (Mexico), Fatima Mernissi (Morocco), and Nawal el Saadawi (Egypt).

21. In the Cold War context, such language, alluding to Marxist theories, amounts to vivid anti-capitalist criticism.

22. Editor of *Women in India* (Publication Division, Government of India, New Delhi 1975) and participant in the Mexico City IWY conference (see Olcott 2017 for details), she also contributed a piece titled "Can Feminism Be a Global Ideology?" to the 1978 *Quest* issue on "international feminism" mentioned above in "A Network in One Package."

23. Discussed in Antrobus 2015, the document is available in the collection *Women and Social Movements, International: 1840 to Present* (*cit.*). As an outcome of the IWY conference, the Development Assistance Committee (DAC, unit of OECD) had established a "Women in Development" group in 1978, at the initiative of the USAID representative. Arvonne Fraser (see above in "Converging Agendas of Human Rights and Women's Rights in the 1980s") headed this group who channeled Western states' money toward Southern actors involved in preparing the UN women's conferences (Fraser 2007, 195–96; Ghodsee 2019, 167–68).

24. Both Devaki Jain and Marie-Angélique Savané are founding members of DAWN, together with Lourdes Arizpe and Fatima Mernissi mentioned in note 20.

25. Established in 1980, this New Delhi NGO was supported by international programs (among others of the Ford Foundation). Devaki Jain headed it between 1975 and 1994.

26. Instrumental to the institutionalization of research in social sciences in Brazil, it was supported by the Ford Foundation.

27. Evidence in this section comes from the MC 708 (box 32, folder 5; box 44, folder 3; box 46, folder 9) corroborated with documents in the Rockefeller Archive Center (Rockefeller Foundation Records, Projects SG 1.9–1.15, R2437, SIE 8530 and Rockefeller Foundation Records, Projects SG 1.16–1.19, R2707, SIE 8716) and with the "Proceedings from DAWN's Bergen Meeting," DERAP Working Papers A343, Chr. Michelson Institute, Bergen, 1985 (available in the collection *Women and Social Movements, International: 1840 to Present*).

28. An Indian left-leaning journal referred to DAWN and its manifesto in the following terms: "[addressing] mainly international aid agencies and governments"; "soft funding from the first world flowing for using leverages within the existing system"; "peddling staff of pedantic radicalism"; "paternalism of all sorts" (cf. *Economical and Political Weekly*, April 5, 1986, press clipping in Charlotte Bunch's archives).

29. During the same post-Copenhagen years, U.S. feminist journalist members of the *Ms.* Foundation assembled and published a collective book titled "*Sisterhood Is Global*" (Morgan 1984). The Ford Foundation was one of the funders of the project and the editor thanked Charlotte Bunch, Shirley Castley, Elizabeth Reid (among others) "for networking" (Morgan, 1984, p. 809).

30. Mentioned in this paper in the sections "A Network in One Package" and "From a 'Feminist Utopia' to Organizing 'on a Larger Scale.'"

31. Besides, as put by Kristen Ghodsee, "it is rather unlikely that US diplomats working in overseas missions would select [for funding] Third World women critical of US foreign policy" (Ghodsee 2019, 167–68).

32. Launched in 1979 as *Universal Human Rights*, this Johns Hopkins University Press publication changed its title in 1981.

33. 1920–2006. An architect and designer trained at Harvard, she was also a feminist journalist, writer, and activist. She consulted with the World Bank in several projects in the "Global South" in the early 1970s, founded the International Women's Network in 1975, and edited for many years a publication titled *WIN News*. She was famously involved in early debates attempting to frame female genital mutilation as an international policy concern.

34. Adopted by the General Assembly of the United Nations in 1979 and known today as the first "international treaty on women's rights." After being one of its first signatories, the U.S. government has not yet ratified the document.

35. In the framework of new foreign policy orientations adopted as a result of congressional activism since the early 1970s and reinforced by the Carter administration, a "human rights amendment" was included in 1976 in the U.S. Foreign Assistance Act. A paragraph about women was added in 1979, referring to the legal status of women, their employment, the number of women in high government positions, and women's participation in social, economic, and political life.

36. *Human Rights Quarterly* 1981 (kept in MC 708, box 43, folder 10).

37. "Female Sexual Slavery Project," MC 708, box 38, folder 1; see also Barry 1984. Charlotte Bunch worked on the project with Shirley Castley (introduced in "A Network in One Package") and Kathleen Barry, author of a homonymous paper contributed to the *Human Rights Quarterly* 1981 symposium on "women's human rights."

38. On the "WID" programs within the USAID, see Tinker 1990 and Fraser and Tinker (eds.) 2004 (especially the contributions by Jane S. Jaquette, Irene Tinker, and Arvonne Fraser). See also Moghadam 1995. See https://www.awid.org/ for details on AWID's historical and current activities.

39. Cf. documents in MC 708, box 24, folder 10, and MC 708, box 25, folder 1.

40. Cf. documents in MC 708, box 25, folder 1.

41. At the moment of writing, 1,077 quotations of this paper were recorded by JSTOR (last check November 3, 2020). See Bunch and Reilly (2019) for a "twenty-five years on" follow-up review by Charlotte Bunch.

42. Interview with Charlotte Bunch (2014). The critique of the Cold War human rights understanding appears already in her late 1980s papers (MC 708, box 25, folder 1).

43. It is worth mentioning here that, with few exceptions and until very recently, the theoretical debates on "transnational feminism" left aside the ex-Soviet "bloc," as underlined by post-socialist critical scholars (Cerwonka 2008; Suchland 2011; Grabowska 2012; Tlostanova et al. 2019; Bonfiglioli and Ghodsee 2020; Kulawik and Kravchenko 2020). See Ghodsee (2019) and Cîrstocea (2019) for recent works closely studying transnational political solidarities involving women from that region during the Cold War and in its aftermath, respectively.

44. Several such events took place in the early 1990s: on environmental issues in Rio de Janeiro in 1992; on human rights in Vienna in 1993; on population issues in Cairo in 1994; on women's issues in Beijing in 1995; on human settlements in Istanbul in 1996.

45. Charlotte Bunch and DAWN member Mariama Williams were sporadically involved in the early activities of a group called the Network of East-West Women (NEWW) established in 1990. Connecting U.S. feminists with women from Central and Eastern Europe, the network animated transatlantic militant and scholarly exchanges that shaped the directions of new women's rights activism and policy-making, contributing also to establishing gender studies as a new academic field in the post-socialist countries; see Cîrstocea (2019) and Cîrstocea (2020) for details.

46. Letter by Charlotte Bunch to President Clinton, September 2, 1993 (MC 708, box 55, folder 1).

47. Which triggered the suspicion of various activist groups, especially in Latin America, who denounced the cooptation of women's rights politics by hegemonic actors (Falquet 1999; Alvarez 2000).

48. H. R. Clinton, "Remarks to the U.N. 4th World Conference on Women Plenary Session," Beijing, September 5, 1995, https://americanrhetoric.com/speeches/hillary clintonbeijingspeech.htm, accessed May 27, 2019.

49. I borrow this formula from Stone (1996).

50. Laville (2002), Coogan-Gehr (2011), and Caulier (2009) also follow this interpretive path.

2

European Solidarities across the East/West Divide

Power and Difference in Lesbian and Gay Transnational Cooperation with Poland in the Mid-2000s

Agnès Chetaille[1]

Between 2004 and 2007, the Polish lesbian and gay (LG)[2] movement, facing intense political attacks from a constellation of local right-wing actors in the name of nationalism and Catholicism, became the center of a large wave of transnational solidarity. This mobilization had worldwide manifestations but was mostly deployed at the European scale. Lesbian and gay/LGBT[3] organizations and various other "progressive" actors (such as the European Green Party, some trade unions, political foundations, and queer feminist collectives) demonstrated their support to the Polish movement in both symbolic and material ways. This resulted in multiple initiatives, actions, interactions, and encounters. The level to which the Polish movement found itself connected to transnational actors during this period became one of its distinctive characteristics (Chetaille 2013; Ayoub 2016). Since then, much literature has been written on the specificity of sexual politics in Central and Eastern Europe (CEE) (most recent edited volumes include Slootmaeckers, Touquet, and Vermeersch 2016; see also Buyantueva and Shevtsova 2020). In particular, the seminal book edited by Robert Kulpa and Joanna Mizielińska on "de-centring Western sexuality" (Kulpa and Mizielińska 2011) was an important step of the growing effort to conceptualize the place of the region in the world-system with tools inspired from postcolonial and decolonial theories. It paved the way for systematic analysis of how material and symbolic relations between "East" and "West"[4] come to play in mobilization and countermobilization around sexual politics in Europe. Specifically, representations of the East as *backward, traditional, over-religious*, and *sexually and morally conservative* as opposed to an unquestionably *modern, progressive, secular,* and *sexually liberated* West have been circulating widely and are particularly acute in Western European *homonationalist* (Puar 2007) politics and Eastern European *heteronationalist* ones. The question of transnational cooperation and solidarities across these oppositions and representations has initiated fruitful research (Woodcock 2011; Binnie and Klesse 2011, 2013; Wiedlack and Neufeld 2014; Kulpa 2014; Neufeld 2018; Wiedlack, Shoshanova, and Godovannaya 2020; Smirnova 2020), once again inspired by critical theories from the South (in particular Mohanty 2003).

However, there is still much to say about transnational solidarity of sexual minorities in Europe across the East/West divide. In particular, on the issue of activist cooperation, rare are the studies that are not trying to look for forms of solidarities able to overcome the opposition and inequality between West and East—usually endorsing a normative definition of what solidarity *should be* in this context (Wiedlack, Shoshanova, and Godovannaya 2020, 23–25). I believe that to overcome hierarchies and "the unequal division of labor between Western and Eastern allies" (Wiedlack, Shoshanova, and Godovannaya 2020, 8), the first step is rather to describe and analyze group dynamics and the way Western domination over CEE activists come into practice in their interactions. This is what I intend to do in this chapter, while focusing on the level of activist encounters and East/West relations in practice within transnational projects. I develop a critical exploration of two inter-related cases of transnational cooperation with Polish lesbian and gay groups in the mid-2000s and their ramifications through time. My goal is to revisit these experiences, assuming neither a necessary and fixed power structure between the Western European groups and the Polish ones nor an idealized solidarity that would be subversive in itself. In the background of my analysis is Gayatri Spivak's (1988) infamous question, "Can the subaltern speak?" or, in this case, "Can Polish lesbian and gay activists speak?" This question, in turn, spawns many more: Who has the power to *describe the situation*? To *define* the (common) political project? Who can decide to initiate or prolong cooperation? Who can choose their partners? And who can express criticism?

This chapter draws on ethnographic fieldwork started in 2004 with the Polish groups described here. Over time, the transnational dimension became central to this work. The first reason was that transnational experiences were frequent for these groups. More importantly, though, it also directly resulted from my own position as a young French anthropologist and activist in these Polish groups, which gave me a privileged access to transnational exchanges. As an observer participant, and both as a social scientist and an activist myself, I took an active part in the dynamics described below, especially the ones around the Krakow Festival. The tensions that I observed and participated in, in turn, profoundly questioned and influenced my own practice as they also informed my own position as a knowledge producer about the Polish LGBT movement and an insider/outsider ally/member. In 2005, the encounter between the Krakow-based group, which was welcoming me, and a group located in Paris, which I had never heard of before, was especially enlightening and transformative for me. For many reasons, I was in a vantage position to perceive the relations of power between the two groups. On the one hand, born and socialized in France, I initially shared with the French activists many culturalist assumptions about Polish reality, as well as a sense of entitlement about what progressive/radical politics are, or should be. On the other hand, integrated in the Polish group already for a few months, I had started to learn its strategies, modes of action, and organizing. I was welcomed in informal moments between its members and could understand most of their conversations in Polish. The tensions between these groups that I observed, and to a certain extent took part in—if only as a translator and cultural mediator—reflected highly on the tensions structural to my own positionality. In the following years, while the contacts between the two groups faded away, I remained in touch both with the Polish group[5] and the French one, with whom I became politically active in Paris for a few years. I count people from both groups among my friends to this day. This chapter results, to a large degree, from the desire to revisit this period while turning my analytical efforts back onto the Western European "radical" activists of which I am one. Although I did not have the space to include in-depth methodological analysis of my own role as an activist researcher in the analyzed dynamics, I perceive the critiques that I put forward in this chapter as, above all, a (self-) reflexive exercise.

I focused my analysis on the level of group interactions and decided to compare and contrast two interconnected cases of transnational cooperation across the East/West divide.[6] My intention is to show how geopolitical tensions deploy across different types of activism, although power relations take a different form in each specific case. The examples thus cut across the lines of Liberal rights-based vs. radical intersectional activisms, of vertical vs. horizontal organizing, all mixing elements of political solidarity and altruistic action. In the first section, I will present these two cases of transnational cooperation with the Polish lesbian and gay movement and the way they are interconnected and unfold at different levels. In the second section, I will explore the tension around the meanings and practice of solidarity in the context of these experiences. Finally, in the third section, I will show how the latter often created opportunities to *reproduce* East/West difference rather than build common identities.

VERTICAL AND HORIZONTAL TRANSNATIONAL NETWORKS: THE MULTILEVEL GEOGRAPHY OF LESBIAN AND GAY ACTIVISM

Central to the cases of transnational cooperation presented here is an organization created in Warsaw in 2001, *Kampania Przeciw Homofobii* (KPH) (the Campaign against Homophobia). Soon after its creation, KPH started to focus on lobbying, political activities, and public activism, and became the largest and only nationwide organization.[7] KPH was organized with a central board consisting mostly of Warsaw-based activists, and local branches in a number of cities and towns throughout Poland. It is difficult to assess the number of members of the organization in that period since logs were not thoroughly kept and turnover was high. However, the Warsaw Branch quickly diversified its activities (harboring a youth group, a legal group, an international group, free psychological counseling, etc.) and was able to rent a space, where dozens of activists would meet weekly, as early as 2004. The organization developed expertise in applying for grants to international donors and some of its members started to get employed, at first occasionally. It was well integrated on a national scale, with activists from different locations regularly visiting each other for workshops and strategic meetings. However, the orientation toward advocacy work and the progressive professionalization of the Warsaw central group often clashed with the grassroots local ones, whose size rarely exceeded ten to fifteen active members at a given time, and who were usually more oriented toward social and cultural activities.[8] These differences, as I will show, gave rise to different transnational experiences.

Structuring Top-Down Transfers: ILGA-Europe and KPH's Central Board

KPH, and especially its central board and Warsaw Branch, developed in close cooperation with a transnational partner, ILGA-Europe.[9] Founded in 1996 as the European branch of the *International Lesbian and Gay Association*, this organization is a transnational advocacy network (Keck and Sikkink 1998) which gained core funding from the European Commission in 2001. This event marked a turning point in its history: ILGA-Europe underwent a process of rapid NGOization (Paternotte 2016) and became a professionalized expert group working mostly—although not only—at the EU level. Among KPH's numerous transnational experiences, the collaboration with this European advocacy network has been, to this day, the most stable and influential for the Polish organization.

Immediately following its creation in 2001, KPH became a member organization of ILGA-Europe and was associated with its strategy regarding the

EU's fifth enlargement process. In the late 1990s, ILGA-Europe started to develop an interest in the process of integration of CEE countries into the EU. Its advocates intended to use conditionality at the heart of the accession process as leverage to influence the situation in the region. They worked to push lesbian and gay issues on the negotiation agenda, with the goal to get EU institutions to recognize discrimination on the grounds of sexual orientation in CEE countries. However, systematic, standardized data corresponding to bureaucratic norms in use in these institutions were lacking on the subject. As one of the main activists behind this campaign recalls: "I thought . . . what we have to do is to really work hard to get LGB issues into the accession reports, in detail. *And to do that, we've got to prove the existence of discrimination. . . .* We picked four countries: Romania, Slovenia, Poland, and Hungary, devised the questionnaire to identify discrimination and organized for them that they do surveys, and produce a report."[10] These reports were published by ILGA-Europe in 2001 and used to lobby members of the European Parliament and representatives of the European Commission. The Warsaw-based organization *Lambda-Warszawa*, which was ILGA-Europe's Polish partner until the creation of KPH, produced the first report on Poland. However, as soon as 2001, KPH joined the production of the second report (published in 2002) and was in charge of the following ones (2005–2006 and 2010–2011). In this context, the initial structure of ILGA-Europe and KPH's cooperation was entirely vertical, with a top-down transfer of knowledge from the transnational to the national level. This transfer notably included categories in which to conceptualize and describe social experiences of homophobic stigmatization and violence, and know-how connected to advocacy work and lobbying as a mode of action.

The process of becoming ILGA-Europe's privileged partner in the production of standardized knowledge and its use to lobby EU institutions awarded KPH with a high degree of legitimacy. It singled it out as a valid collaborator for the prestigious EU institutions and other potential Western organizations, as a reliable producer of information, and also as a possible partner for Polish domestic state institutions. Adopting the language of *anti-discrimination* and a position of expertise on EU policy, KPH managed to initiate close collaboration with the *Government Plenipotentiary for Equal Status of Women and Men*, a body in charge of implementing EU policies against discriminations.[11] More generally, the Warsaw-based group embraced a strategy of political lobbying and advocacy similar to ILGA-Europe's own action. Although this orientation did not result solely from the collaboration with ILGA-Europe,[12] the influence of the European network on the Polish organization is undeniable. During those years, almost all KPH regular members attended training workshops organized by ILGA-Europe, and the Polish activists frequently consulted with their transnational partner regarding their lobbying strategy.

They also acquired specific skills such as the production of standardized knowledge for advocacy and the extensive use of the legal language of EU regulation. This collaboration was *vertical* in nature, as ILGA-Europe works as a federation and KPH is one of its member organizations. Moreover, the top-down structure of the dynamics was clear during this period. It was reflected in knowledge transfer—ILGA-Europe *providing* the local organization with conceptual and practical frames to be implemented, and then *retrieving* standardized knowledge to be used in their lobbying effort at the European level—in the access to material and symbolic resources—distributed by ILGA-Europe downward to its local members[13]—and ultimately in the relation of power between both organizations—ILGA-Europe being consulted to give their opinion on KPH's development and strategy, and not the other way around, especially during the initial phase. This does in no way imply, however, that Polish activists remained passive in this process. On the contrary, KPH members' agency was high in using this transnational collaboration and combining it with local resources and opportunities—when other Polish organizations followed another trajectory.

Consequently, vertical collaboration with ILGA-Europe created undeniable opportunities for KPH, under the condition that the organization aligned, at least partially, with the strategies and language of the transnational network. Especially for the core members of the organization, based in Warsaw, it provided Polish activists with tools to address the domestic institutions and with legitimacy for potential (international) donors, while at the same time impressing a profound mark on the shape of their activism—most importantly on the type of frames and action repertoire used by the organization.

Horizontal, Transient Solidarity: Krakow Cultural Festival's Transnational Network

In spring 2004, activists from the Krakow Branch of KPH organized a festival named *Kultura dla Tolerancji* (KdT) (Culture for Tolerance), which was meant to present "gay and lesbian culture" to the Polish public through various cultural events (film screenings, exhibitions, discussions, academic conference, etc.) and a "March for Tolerance" in the streets of the city. This program, although developed in close collaboration with the activists from Warsaw, reflected both the reluctance to engage in purely political action and the willingness to address the prominence of culture in the city's local identity. Krakow, the third Polish city in size with an urban area of approximately 1.2 million inhabitants, is renowned for its university and historical and contemporary role in Polish literature and theater, among other things. It also harbors many Catholic institutions and groups, some of whom are active as a conservative force. This specificity became obvious with the many outraged reactions to the public advertisement of the festival from a variety of actors, including local chapters of political parties and Catholic ultraconservative organizations. The March, although successful with over a thousand participants, was violently attacked by counterdemonstrators (Kubica 2006). The images of this attack provoked a national discussion about LG rights and activism and circulated widely in Europe and beyond. Over the following years, the festival was repeated every spring, bringing together a constellation of local actors around the main organizing group.

This event became the epicenter of another transnational experience, which took the form of a loose transnational network convening heterogeneous organizations, from various countries, on a temporary basis. Based on informality, flexibility, and individual connections, this network was both less structured and less stable than the cooperation described in the previous section. Besides the Polish organizers of the festival, three main groups with very different profiles took part in this experience between 2005 and 2008. The first group was composed of leading members of an initiative including a café and lesbian and gay center in Antwerp, Belgium. They were in the position of entrepreneurs looking for cultural events to sponsor. The second group was an aggregation of activists from diverse organizations from the region of North Rhine-Westphalia, Germany, who were not used to working together in their own local context. Some represented institutionalized organizations, linked either to advocacy or to HIV/AIDS support and prevention, whereas others were part of less formal ones, such as a migrant lesbian and gay group or a lesbian collective. The third group was a small organization of about twenty active members, created in Paris in 2003. It specialized in radical and intersectional claims against homophobia, sexism, racism, capitalism, and militarism. Its members insisted on developing politicized identities, such as "dykes" and "fags," as a critique of respectable identity politics often conveyed, according to them, by the words "lesbians" and "gays." That is why I decided to call them here *Gouines et Pédés Politiques* (GPP) (Political Dykes and Fags), as they often presented themselves.[14]

Created as a result of partly coincidental circumstances, this transnational network functioned only episodically (primarily around the yearly festival in Krakow and invitations of Polish activists to Antwerp and Cologne, where French and Belgian activists joined them once). For both the German and French groups, the role of an activist of Polish descent, who established the first contact with the group in Krakow and then maintained communication, was crucial. The relations between the groups were never formalized over time, despite several attempts resting mostly with individuals. Ultimately, most contacts faded away, especially between Krakow activists and their Western European partners.[15] The network enacted some relations of material support. All three Western partners did, at some point, financially aid Polish organizations: in 2005, GPP brought money that they had raised in Paris, the Belgian entrepreneurs helped to find important private donors from Antwerp for the 2007 edition of the festival. Financial donations were made from NRW organizations to *Lambda-Kraków* for HIV/AIDS prevention programs. However, these donations remained exceptional, and this experience did not introduce KdT organizers into a network of transnational donors that could secure their financial situation for the following years—unlike KPH's integration within ILGA-Europe.

What Should We Do When the Pope Dies? A Multilevel Space of Strategic Positionalities

The network around the festival came into being at a time of acute strategical tensions between the organizing group in Krakow and KPH's central board. A short account of these events will show how the four sets of actors—KPH's national board, ILGA-Europe, the Krakow Festival organizers, and their Western European partners—were positioned in relation to one another. In 2005, shortly before the second edition of the Krakow Festival, Catholic Pope John Paul II died. In the context of a prolonged period of national mourning and heated public demonstrations of collective sorrow, discussions emerged on whether to maintain the March for Tolerance and other events of the festival. The organizers feared to be accused, as they had already been the previous year, of "provoking" Catholic believers—which was considered an issue both for the event's public image and for the safety of the participants. The Krakow group and the board of KPH both agreed on canceling the public march. However, the question of whether to cancel other planned events, or the whole festival, caused significant conflict within the organization.

This crisis highlights how different positions influence the choice of strategies. On the one hand, a majority of KPH's national board members, engaged in a dialogue with both domestic and international institutions, advocated for canceling the March as well as the whole festival. In the end, they imposed changing the word "festival" into "days," considered less festive, and to remove terms such as "sex" and "vagina" from the event's program. Their arguments included the protection of the organization's reputation—especially regarding their official status as "public benefit organization" (*organizacja pożytku publicznego*)—and of their collaboration with the Government Plenipotentiary. During informal conversations, it was brought to my attention that ILGA-Europe's then executive director had advised KPH's board to be as prudent as possible, especially concerning the March.[16] Retrospectively, I can only propose a hypothesis as to the motivation behind ILGA-Europe's advice. At that time, and following attacks on Krakow's 2004 March for Tolerance and other

Pride Parades in Central and South-Eastern European contexts, ILGA-Europe was trying to develop systematic monitoring of LGBT public events in the region and report on cases of violence and/or absence of protection from the police. The organization was preparing *Handbook on Observations of Pride Marches*.[17] Similarly to their earlier strategies, the objective was to develop standardized knowledge throughout Europe and especially the CEE region, while at the same time gaining recognition at the European level as reliable producers of data on discrimination. ILGA-Europe had planned to hold an international training seminar on the issue in Krakow at the time of the festival. Their call for prudence was most probably informed by the responsibility to ensure safety for their seminar's participants, but also to issue clear, consistent guidelines to all activists throughout the region, including "waiting for the right time and place" (Loudes 2006, 15).

On the other hand, after an intense exchange of opposing opinions, local KPH activists from Krakow also agreed on canceling the March that they had been working hard to organize. Most of them identifying as atheists, they converged around the idea that they were to respect the Catholics' feelings of grief *just as they would respect their roommate's feelings and not organize a party, would they live with someone who had just lost their father*.[18] However, they strongly resisted the idea of canceling the whole festival and perceived the conditions imposed by the central board as an unfair external intervention. Interestingly, the Krakow group was in no way upholding a more critical stance toward the Catholic Church than the Warsaw one, neither were they intending to be more "radical" or provocative. I argue that this difference of perspective was due to their greater distance from the domestic and international polity and especially from institutional partners calling for prudence. This resulted in the fact that, as one activist who was part of both groups put it: "Some things look different from Warsaw than they do from Krakow."[19]

Finally, in this conflict between local and national levels, Western partners who had expressed support to the festival, and especially the GPP from Paris, played a specific role. Prior to the festival, a Leftist, anti-clerical Polish newspaper pictured them as radically anti-Church and praised them for an action they had co-organized with an anarcha-feminist group a few months before, in Notre-Dame Cathedral in Paris, as a protest against John Paul II's latest book. In the context of the Pope's death, they started to be embarrassing allies and became a topic of concern for Polish organizers and one of the stakes of the conflict. KPH's national board demanded that the group's presence not be announced on the official program of the festival whereas Krakow activists, while being slightly worried about the French group's intentions and methods, defended their right to come and take part in the event officially. In the end, the board's demands were met, but the conflict stirred outrage among Krakow activists. During the festival, the French group, who had heard about the local clash, requested some clarification from local activists. They met with the Krakow-based organizers, who were asked to tell them about the conflict. It was immediately reinterpreted by Paris activists in categories opposing respectability and radicalism:

> What you're going through is exactly the same everywhere. . . . More and more there are people saying: "Don't talk about sex, don't call things by their names, don't be too extravagant." . . . What you're going through, from what we've understood, with KPH Warsaw is what we're going through with our main mainstream organizations in France and I think, all around Europe.[20]

These meetings also were the first platform where, before the festival was over and in front of their French partners, Krakow activists had an opportunity to exchange about the conflictual events and talk about the future. With Paris activists advising them to do so,[21] most of them decided to quit KPH after the festival. In the following weeks, it was decided to establish an independent organization called the *Foundation Culture for Tolerance*. Money collected in Paris during a fundraising event and brought to Krakow by the GPP served as structural funds to create this new organization.

This mapping of multilevel strategic positioning in a time of political crisis reveals that the two cases are interconnected[22] and that they share more structural features than it appeared at first glance. The contrast between them is clear. Unlike the relationship between KPH and ILGA-Europe, the network around the Krakow Festival brought together Western groups with divergent strategies, none of which was a federative organization with the power to include or exclude the Polish group, which makes it an experience of *horizontal* cooperation. Additionally, it met mostly in Poland and functioned around an event that was organized by Polish activists according to their own agenda. However, the analysis of group interactions in a time of conflict shows that it did not necessarily develop a more balanced structure than the vertical, integrative collaboration pattern of the first cooperation case. The following sections will explore this apparent paradox further.

SUPPORTING POLISH GAYS AND LESBIANS OR ADVANCING LG RIGHTS IN EUROPE? TENSIONS IN TRANSNATIONAL SOLIDARITY

Transnational cooperation appears to be infused with and structured by relations of difference and power, and to harbor friction along the lines of resources, strategies, and identities (for a fruitful synthesis of the way transnational feminism(s) have been conceptualizing these processes, see

Introduction). Previous studies have shown that not everybody has the same chance to organize transnationally. This "uneven geography" of transnational activism (Smith and Wiest 2005) is reflected in the composition of transnational networks, especially in the representation of different regions or types of organizations, but also in the (im)possible reciprocity in relations between transnational partners (Eterovic and Smith 2001). What has mostly been analyzed in terms of a North/South divide also appears, at the European scale, between West and East. The reasons behind the decision to resort to transnational mobilization, for all partners involved, is as telling as the position and type of relation that they hold in the given cooperation. Why do we decide to "go transnational"? And how do we meet potential transnational partners for collective action? Who chooses whom, and for what reasons? These questions can help us have a better view of the dynamics at stake behind transnational cooperation and understand the various meanings of "solidarity."

A Solidarity Market: When Western Groups Pick and Choose

One element common to all examples described here is the position of Western European groups looking for their favored partner in the Polish context. Just as ILGA-Europe identified one local partner organization for privileged cooperation, collectives involved in the Krakow network often demonstrated reluctance to work with the first organization they met, all of whom were trying to get a more extensive picture of the local activist scene.[23] The GPP, initially invited in 2005 by the organizing group of the festival, chose to meet with other competing local groups as well—especially those who disagreed with the decision to cancel the March for Tolerance and had decided to organize another public event in its place. Similarly, the group from Cologne and Düsseldorf, already heterogeneous in itself, established contact with several local organizations and, although always revolving around KdT festival, set up a cooperation with an association involved only marginally with the festival and specialized in HIV/AIDS prevention and community building, *Lambda-Kraków*. As cultural entrepreneurs, the representatives from Antwerp were the only ones to establish more stable collaboration with activists from the festival itself, which involved both financial support and curatorial exchanges.

Polish groups, on the contrary, did not expect to choose their Western partners. After the first edition in 2004, the Krakow Festival published a broad, international invitation to support and join the second edition. The aim of this call was twofold, as explicitly stated in the invitation letter:[24] accessing material and symbolic resources, and counting on the official presence of foreigners from Western Europe at the March to result in better police protection against counterdemonstrators.[25] KdT organizers never *chose* to initiate collaboration with the GPP, the LG center from Antwerp, or the German groups. They welcomingly responded to whomever showed interest. Neither could they select their partners beforehand, nor, after meeting them, could they clearly voice a collective choice made for explicit reasons. Over time, selection rather took the form of passive tactics like disinterest or break of communication with certain groups while maintaining connection with others, as I will show in the last section.

Why Do We Go Transnational? The Reasons behind Transnational Cooperation

In the mid-2000s, the motivations of Polish groups resorting to West-East transnational cooperation were primarily, as stated, to gain protection from local repression and to access material and symbolic resources lacking on the local and national levels. These reasons appeal to "solidarity" in the traditional sense of unilateral support flowing from more privileged groups and places to less privileged ones. However, this did not prevent the same groups from deploying other types of solidarity at the same time. Jon Binnie and Christian Klesse (2011) have shown, in a study carried out with the same Krakow-based group, that Polish LG activists perceived and practiced solidarity in a different, more reciprocal and political way when it came to other local, non-lesbian and gay groups (be they feminist, anarchist, or ecologist). Additionally, in the same year that the Belgian, German, and French groups visited the festival for the first time, the organizers had chosen to showcase three other foreign groups in the program, from Belarus, the Balkans, and Israel. To a certain extent, it is as if the Polish activists distinguished between the groups that they intended to organize or exchange with on an equal level,[26] and those they mostly turned to for support. This tactic, not necessarily conscious, of resorting to "Western aid" as a resource at their disposal almost taken for granted, while developing more reciprocal solidarity in other relations, could result from a mixture of internalization of West/East inequality and a strategic, instrumental use of this power structure.

On the other side of these power dynamics, for those with more power and privilege, the decision to "go transnational" involves different rationales, unrelated to receiving support. In the first example of cooperation, ILGA-Europe's advocates, while reporting on homophobia in CEE countries, did not only intend to help local communities get more protection and rights. They used the EU enlargement process as a platform to advance LG rights recognition by EU institutions, so much so that political scientist and former chair of the European Parliament Intergroup for Gay and Lesbian Rights Joke Swiebel writes that it is in the context of the accession process that "gay and lesbian rights were for the first time formally and practically conceived as human rights in the EU" (Swiebel 2009, 24). The process was also extremely important in ILGA-Europe's history, especially for its recognition as an expert partner by the EU. Among all CEE countries, the "Polish case" came to take particular importance in 2006, when the term "homophobia" appeared for the first time in a resolution of the European Parliament under the influence of ILGA-Europe's lobbying efforts—as a reaction to the growing politicization of homophobia by then Polish government, targeted by this resolution. This was a major achievement on ILGA-Europe's general agenda.

Vocally opposed to ILGA-Europe and to its liberal, rights-based politics, the GPP also had their own agenda when coming to Krakow. The GPP's visit to Poland coincided with their campaign against the 2005 project of EU Constitution. This draft provoked passionate discussions in France, with people at both the Right and Left ends of the political spectrum raising critiques (the text ended up being rejected in a referendum vote, much to the surprise of the majority of political and media elites). Poland was somehow very present in this debate, through the figure of the "Polish plumber" which was abundantly used to symbolize threats to French workers' rights.[27] A few weeks before their trip to Krakow, the GPP had issued a petition calling to reject the EU Constitution project, criticizing the little progress regarding LGBT rights in the draft, as well as the lack of social rights and the status given to religious lobbies. They had already expressed their critique of the link between the EU and the Catholic Church in relation to Poland in June 2004, when they installed a European flag picturing black crosses instead of yellow stars in front of the Polish embassy in Paris. What better place than Poland for criticizing both the limited action of the EU in the field of LGBT rights (as well as women's rights and workers' rights) and the influence of the Catholic Church? For many in the European Left, the Polish (social democrat) government's endorsement, in 2003, of the Catholic Church's position on the addition of a reference to Christianity in the Constitution's project, as a means to win over support of the Polish Church for the referendum on EU accession, had turned Poland into the symbol of the Vatican's attempts to influence EU politics.[28] GPP activists clearly stated this political critique to their counterparts from Krakow, "We are on the same, the same . . . land, no? . . . The political situation is very concerning, in France, and at the European level. And about this, we need to have common strategies, beyond the particularly difficult situation here [in Poland]. So, what we could discuss now is how much the Catholic Church is leading an offensive [at the EU level]."[29] However, their voice was not heard—or maybe it was intentionally ignored by Krakow activists. At that time, and as demonstrated by the consensus on canceling the March after the Pope's death, Polish activists were trying not to attack the Catholic Church frontally. Additionally, they usually evaluated the EU very positively. The transnational cooperation envisioned by the GPP, in the end, never happened.

Selfless Altruism or Political Solidarity?
On Interests and Political Projects

Contrasting motivations to enter transnational cooperation shed light on the question of the very nature of "solidarity" (for a convincing analysis of the tensions between the traditional conceptions of solidarity and the critique put forward by transnational, Third World Indigenous and intersectional feminisms, see Introduction). As many authors have emphasized, this notion is itself a social construct, always subject to negotiation, and it should be studied as such rather than as a normative feature of given social actions (see, for instance, Fillieule 2001, 54). The distinction made by Ivana Eterovic and Jackie Smith (2001), regarding transnational activism, between "altruistic patterns of association" and "political solidarity" can be helpful here. The first notion describes types of cooperation "in which constituencies do not overlap with the beneficiaries of collective action" and that "presume that relations between more economically privileged areas (e.g., the global North) and the later-industrializing, poorer countries of the global South are characterized by one-way dependency" (Eterovic and Smith 2001, 198). It is a pattern in which "more economically privileged activists [are] working on behalf of their relatively deprived counterparts in other countries" (197). The second notion, "political solidarity" (that the authors identify at the time with the "new transnationalism") is rooted in "an understanding of the structural sources of grievances" (200) and of their transnational nature influencing the situation of all partners in the interaction. "Based on mutual solidarity between movements in different countries, it seeks to reorient the direction of development in the North as well as the South" (198).[30] The authors assume this pattern of cooperation, which has "greater potential to challenge the global structural sources of grievances," as necessarily more collaborative and reciprocal than the first one. They associate a larger representation and participation of organizations from the South in networks endorsing the second model as compared to those following the older model of the Northern "aid to the Third World."

The cases studied here, however, complexify this opposition between the two models. Both ILGA-Europe and the GPP, as I just demonstrated, came into these transnational relations with larger political projects and understanding of the interdependence of situations regarding LG issues in the EU. Although they may also have had altruistic motives,[31] both of these groups' agendas clearly belonged to the "political solidarity" type. However, such solidarity was still very much of a top-down nature, with Western groups coming up with projects designed beforehand. On the one hand, Polish activists were not necessarily aware of these projects, let alone included in their formulation. If they had been, one can assume that it would have changed the framing of the GPP's "solidarity," for example—recognizing that the European flag with Catholic crosses replacing the yellow stars was counterproductive, given the strategies of the Polish LG movement at that point. On the other hand, the Krakow activists, as the less privileged partners in the relation, seemed to be counting on the support of their Western counterparts in the old-fashioned, altruistic sense. In a difficult local context, they may have treated this strategy instrumentally as a cost-effective way to access resources. This situation, in which the more privileged organizations wish to look at the "bigger picture" with the help of broad, structural analyses while the less privileged ones expect before all to obtain financial and symbolic support, seems paradoxical according to the analytical model presented above. However, it may not be that uncommon and does not equate with a total lack of agency for activists from less privileged contexts. Attempts to use the inequalities between members of transnational movements (that they structurally tend to be more aware of) in order to obtain the resources that they need can typically involve the appropriation of narratives of backwardness (see Neufeld 2018 for the case of Russia) and/or performance of the Eastern/Southern activist waiting to be helped or saved. This tactic, which calls for further exploration and analysis, could also be conceptualized as following a "public transcript" as coined by James Scott (1990).

It should be noted, however, that the initial, structural inequality between positions described here can evolve over time. It was not the case regarding the GPP, with only one activist staying in touch and taking part in the transnational network after the first encounter, but other projects emerged from the initial experiences examined so far. The short collaboration initiated by some of the German activists with the organization *Lambda-Kraków*, built around money and skill transfers from the German groups to the Polish one on HIV/AIDS prevention, although it kept a unilateral West-East approach, put the needs and interests of the Polish organization at the center. Similarly, the human rights monitoring of Pride Marches promoted by ILGA-Europe in CEE intended to respond to the specific needs of local activists with the characteristic tools of the transnational advocacy network—transnational organizing, human rights approach, and lobbying of international organizations. These examples show that, over time, Polish activists established a dialogue with their Western partners and were able to put forward some of their priority issues. But the very structure of these exchanges still resulted in a one-way influence by groups based in Western Europe over the selection of modes of action and frames by Polish activists.[32] However, in the long run, the transformation of ILGA-Europe and of its collaboration with KPH is enlightening in terms of the capacity of these kinds of collaborations to evolve into a more balanced and reciprocal model. After the initial cooperation with the transnational network, KPH's activity as a member organization kept growing. As early as 2006, an activist from KPH was elected on ILGA-Europe's executive board, an event seen as a form of recognition of the Polish organization's role within the transnational one. Following this first election, five consecutive KPH activists served as elected members on the boards of KPH and ILGA-Europe simultaneously, securing a continuous presence of the Polish organization on the transnational organization's board over a period of fourteen years.[33] This makes KPH the most influential member organization from Central Europe within ILGA-Europe, and one of the most influential more generally. Over the same period of time, one could say that the transnational organization transformed from a predominantly Western European network into a truly pan-European organization, with many representatives and staff members from Central Europe, Eastern and South-Eastern Europe, as well as Central Asia.[34]

BRIDGING DIFFERENCE OR (RE)PRODUCING DIFFERENCE? THE PARADOX OF SOLIDARITY

These experiences of transnational solidarity and their deployment through time also point to questions of identity and difference. They invite us to consider how spatialized difference is met, perceived, represented, and dealt with throughout transnational encounters.

On Sameness and Difference: With Whom Do We Mobilize in Solidarity?

In the process of building transnational initiatives, the issue of *identity* is crucial. Whom do we mobilize as and whom do we mobilize for? Tensions around these questions affect the possibility of creating successful transnational identities, necessary for common mobilization. In the cases described here, two distinct types of common identities overlap. The first refers to sexual minorities ("gays and lesbians"): tensions resulting from the globalization of such identities and their translation into local contexts have been abundantly analyzed (for the less researched lesbian identities, see, for example, King 2002; Woodcock 2004; Lewis 2010). The second is a geographical identity, that of European, which is always a political one—when saying "We are on the same land," the GPP activist obviously means more than "we live on the same continent," and refers to the construction of Europe as a political project. These two identities are themselves deeply connected, and their intertwined definition, as Phillip Ayoub and David Paternotte have shown, has been at the heart of LGBTQ transnational activism in Europe for decades (Ayoub and Paternotte 2014). Both of them are political fictions and references to imagined communities, as Christophe Broqua has noted for the idea of an "LGBT people" (Broqua 2018). These transnational fictions—European identity and gay and lesbian transnational "community"—existed for all the actors mentioned in the present study, from ILGA-Europe, to the French GPP, to Polish activists from KPH and the Krakow Festival, who routinely referred to the New York Stonewall riots as a reference point of their activism. However, the definitions of these imagined communities varied from one group to another. Linked to the contrasting political projects described earlier, the understanding of who "we" is clashed in some of the encounters, as between the organizers of the Krakow Festival and the GPP, leading one activist from the latter to reflect, "When we arrived, we thought that we had similar ideas, we are dykes and fags so we have the same goals and fights so it will obviously work. But it did not work. It is not enough."[35] Even more than constructed identities, though, the process of *identification* was often at the core of transnational encounters, with Western groups looking for Polish partners in which they would *recognize* their own political identities and goals. As Wiedlack and Neufeld (2014) have shown, North/Western solidarity mobilizations with Pussy Riot, which wrongly identify them as "punk," suggest that identification and "projection of local desires" (160) are only easy when done from afar. However, while exploring the "market of solidarity" and trying to meet the appropriate partners *in real life*, difference becomes more tangible. In the initial phase, Western groups' possibility or impossibility of identification was thus both crucial and unilateral. Later on, however, Polish groups' identification with their transnational partners, as in the case of KPH with ILGA-Europe, for instance, was indispensable for the relation to last.

Knowledge Production and (Mis)Representation: Epistemic Divides and the Western Gaze

At the heart of the transnational solidarity deployed in these experiences was a process of knowledge production that included pitfalls in terms of representation. In the case of ILGA-Europe and KPH, knowledge was central to the collaboration, as the transnational network needed knowledge about Poland in order to carry on with their lobbying effort at the EU level, and they transferred know-how to Polish activists to produce knowledge ready for international comparison and framed in terms of "discrimination," "human rights violation," and so on. In the case of the Krakow Festival network, the French, Belgian, and German activists spontaneously endorsed the position of conduits of information from Krakow to their own local contexts, where they organized solidarity mobilization in support of the Polish groups.[36] To this end, they produced narratives about the situation of LG people in Poland based on their experience of transnational cooperation with the Krakow group. Two documentary films were produced, one by an activist from Paris and the other one by an activist from Cologne.[37] In contrast with the standardized knowledge produced by ILGA-Europe, these films presented highly personalized narratives. They focused on the encounters of groups from different national contexts, as well as on the shock experienced by activists from France and Germany concerning certain aspects of Polish reality. They especially lingered over the presence of religion in the public sphere and the violent nationalist groups attacking lesbian and gay marches. Despite their obvious differences, the knowledge produced in both cases thus had at least two common traits. First, it conformed to norms defined *by* Western European partners, and *for* the Western European public: they used their own categories, methodologies, or narratives to describe Polish lives and struggles. Second, they concentrated on homophobia, discrimination, and violence rather than everyday life or forms of cultural, identity-based, and/or sexual practices.

Significantly, the documentary films were never screened as part of the festival, despite their directors' wishes. Unspoken tensions between the Polish activists and Western European ones came, at some point, to focus on this issue. Although not in a very direct way, some activists from Krakow expressed their dissatisfaction with the way the festival was, according to them, (mis)represented in those films. They especially criticized the emphasis put on Western European activists' feelings and on public marches and violent counterdemonstrations rather than on the diverse successful events of the festival. Polish organizers of the festival clearly did not identify with these perceptions of their event: they did not *recognize* their action, or at least did not wish to picture it in this way.[38] While attempting, with the best intentions, to produce self-reflective narratives concentrating on their own journey and reactions, Western European activists had still managed, to some extent, to produce "knowledge about" rather than "knowledge with," following the distinction made by Boaventura de Sousa Santos (2018, 156). Confronted with the lack of enthusiasm from their Polish partners, the filmmakers expressed bitter disappointment regarding what they perceived as indifference and closed-mindedness, and this conflict paved the way to the dissolution of the network. This perceived emotional distance, which resonates with Binnie and Klesse's findings (2011) about the orientation of the Krakow group toward their local allies rather than their transnational ones, is also telling about the possibility for contention in such a network. The critical reaction of certain Polish activists happened mostly during interactions within their own group, and was accessible to me only thanks to my participation in informal meetings and my understanding of Polish. Although this issue stemmed from the single contentious episode within the network, it was mostly expressed by Krakow activists through euphemisms and avoidant behavior. Here again, it becomes clear that Polish activists did exert agency in choosing the role they wanted to give to their Western partners, in appropriating or rejecting narratives produced about themselves, or in doing (or refusing to do) the emotional and communication labor necessary to maintain transnational relations. However, their strategies also reflected the high degree of constraint weighing on the communication processes with their transnational partners.

Finally, it should be noted that several features of the films' narratives can be analyzed as characteristic of the "Western gaze." This notion, forged in postcolonial critique and Third World feminism (see especially "Under Western Eyes" in Mohanty 2003), started to be used in the 2000s in the context of the perception of CEE, and more specifically queerness in the region (Baer 2002; Kulpa and Mizielińska 2011; Wiedlack 2015; Mizielińska and Stasińska 2017). The concept of "nesting Orientalisms," coined by Milica Bakić-Hayden in 1995, has been particularly useful in understanding how different processes of Othering carried out by the Western world contrast, compare, and connect to each other. Recently, the conceptualization of the intermediary position of CEE as "semi-peripheral" has spawned analyses of Central Europeans and (South)Eastern Europeans as both "peripherally white" (Safuta 2018) and performing racist hierarchies toward more stigmatized minorities (for instance, Roma) as "strategies to construct intelligible Europeanness" (Tudor 2017, 117–18). Representations of the Polish gay and lesbian/LGBT movement in and by Western Europe, including in these two documentary films, call for systematic analysis that is beyond the scope of this chapter. It is worth noting here, though, that the focus on religiosity and homophobic violence falls under classic Orientalist representations. Religion considered as oppression and backwardness, as opposed to secularism, which is equated to progress, especially in the fields of gender and sexuality, is a classic (post)colonial trope (see, for instance, Mahmood 2011; Dhawan 2013 for its recent deployment). It has been abundantly used regarding the CEE region and, as noted by Wiedlack and Neufeld (2014) about Pussy Riot, is frequently involved in (mis)representations of emancipatory mobilizations in "the East." After all, to most Krakow activists in 2005, Catholics were mainly roommates with whom to ensure peaceful coexistence! Since then, the Polish LGBT movement has been extremely creative in exploring and diversifying the possibilities of connection between religion and queerness—from head-on confrontation to (critical) intersection.[39] Similarly, other categories often described as conservative in their essence by Western progressives and radicals, such as "nation," "family," and "love," have been given different meanings in CEE contexts

(Kulpa, Mizielińska, and Stasińska 2012; for the specific reclaiming of love to the nation, see, for example, Ayoub and Chetaille 2017).

CONCLUSION

Across such different cases of West-East cooperation, several common structural features appeared in the analysis. They all reflect on inequality in positionality between the Western European groups and their Polish partners. The former are used to being the ones who "speak": describing the situation from their points of view, defining the political project according to their agenda. The latter are expected—and expect, themselves—to be the ones to "receive": money, help, knowledge. Yet, over time, more equal and reciprocal relations can develop, both within formal, structured cooperation, as already mentioned about ILGA-Europe and KPH, and within informal, horizontal collaborations.[40] However, the dynamics explored here remain crucial to current politics for at least two reasons.

First, although during the early 2000s, the high level of transnationalization of certain Polish groups was seen as a sign of modernity, legitimacy, and reliability in relation to domestic institutional partners, it was also used as a justification for violent attacks against LGBT groups, when framed as estranged and opposed to Polishness by political opponents and countermovements (Ayoub and Chetaille 2017). Especially after supporters of homophobic heteronationalism gained access to the government in 2005, transnationalization became an ambivalent feature in the domestic sphere. Western European allies of the Polish movement need to be especially careful and knowledgeable about these dynamics.

Second, political context is crucial to the material and cultural dynamics between "West" and "East," even among progressive/radical actors. The return of the same heteronationalist politicians to power in 2015 caused a new wave of politicized homophobia and transphobia in Poland. This context creates, for Polish LGBT organizations, an even higher dependence on their transnational partners for any kind of resources, which is at risk of increasing inequality in these relationships. Additionally, Orientalist representations are easily reactivated in such circumstances. In the summer of 2020, repression reached an unprecedented level with the arrest of a nonbinary activist from the LGBTQ movement and her detention in jail for three weeks. This event fostered a huge wave of transnational protest and expression of outrage from various actors in the (mostly Western) world. The heterogeneous discourses and actions produced in this context, framed in terms of "solidarity with the Polish LGBTQ people/movement" did not, however, always avoid the pitfalls of speaking "in the name of" Polish activists. Many of them used premises or arguments contradicting the local movement's predominant strategies, and reproduced a picture of a backward, obscurantist Poland.[41] There is still a blatant need for self-criticism by Western European progressive and radical groups mobilizing in solidarity with Poland.

NOTES

1. The final steps of research leading to this publication have received funding from the European Union's Horizon 2020 research and innovation program under the Marie Skłodowska-Curie grant agreement MIGREMOV n°797178. I wish to thank Barbara Schuch for trusting me with the rushes shot for the film she made with Sophie Sensier and the many interesting discussions. Many thanks to Dominique Masson, Janet Conway, Pascale Dufour, Roberto Kulpa, and Jakob Zollman for their comments on earlier versions of this text.

2. In the following chapter, I refer to the Polish movement in the mid-2000s as "lesbian and gay" to emphasize that, at that time, its politics were exclusively articulated around homosexuality, and tackled neither bisexuality nor trans* or intersex issues.

3. Within Western European groups mobilized in solidarity, trans* people and trans* issues were only starting to become visible at the same period and were not included as such in any of the exchanges analyzed in this chapter (although the groups sometimes used the acronym LGBT to define themselves).

4. Just as for the North/South opposition, talking about "West" and "East" without reproducing essentialized binary categories is difficult. As for various other authors (Kulpa and Mizielińska 2011, 15; Stella 2015, 147, etc.), what I refer to here is a moving political and symbolic boundary, not a definitive geographic border between two homogenous blocks. Moreover, I refer to "Polish groups" and "Western European/French/German" groups, somewhat obscuring their internal diversity—specifically, on the issue of nationalities, the fact that some Western activists had a (Polish) migration background and that some members of the Polish groups were born and raised in Western Europe. Nuance and attention to intersecting positionality is important. However, I believe that the following analysis shows that, unrelated to individual, often complex, national identities, collective processes of socialization rooted in material, political, and cultural contexts do produce West/East unequal dynamics at the level of group interactions.

5. And a constant observer and ally of the Polish LGBTI movement to this day, which does not imply that I was able to resolve the tensions I identified in the initial period.

6. I thus decided to leave out of the analysis very important aspects which could be explored only with in-depth analysis of a single encounter between two groups. I am especially thinking of how intersecting positionalities in terms of gender, age and generation, class (visible among other things in language proficiency), and race/ethnicity came into play in a complex and subtle way in the relations between transnational partners (for comments on the gender and age/generation aspects, see Binnie and Klesse

2011, 123–24). Processes of both intercultural and "political translation" (Doerr 2018) would also be crucial to add to the analysis at a more micro level.

7. The other large organization at the time, *Lambda-Warszawa*, had a very different trajectory since it was only Warsaw-based and specialized in self-help and community support. Contrary to KPH's transnational strategy, *Lambda* focused on obtaining funding from local and national institutions.

8. The recurring tensions between the Warsaw group and the local branches led the organization to eventually "cut off" the branches in 2011–12, encouraging them to establish new local organizations.

9. ILGA-Europe is a federative association gathering member organizations from all around Europe. Today, ILGA stands for *International Lesbian, Gay, Bisexual, Trans and Intersex Association*, and ILGA-Europe has also developed to include the region of Central Asia.

10. Interview with former ILGA-Europe advocate. London, January 21, 2010. Emphasis added.

11. KPH regularly obtained funding and support from the governmental body from 2003 onwards and gained representation on its advisory board in 2005.

12. Robert Biedroń, founding member and long-time president (2001–2009) of KPH, had, for example, already advocated for the inclusion of an anti-discrimination clause mentioning sexual orientation in the constitution of the political party SLD in 1999.

13. ILGA-Europe was never dedicated to distributing funding and material resources to its member organizations. However, in the EU accession phase, it did fund the realization of surveys on discrimination by CEE-based organizations, and most importantly trained them into accessing funding from international donors.

14. I decided to leave the Western European groups in relative anonymity because I did not collect formal consent from them at the time of the fieldwork. This specific group does not exist anymore, so retroactive collective consent would be impossible to obtain.

15. Interestingly, a few of the French and German activists (especially those with political affinities and somehow transnational lives) maintained contacts on a purely interpersonal basis.

16. Ethnographic notes from meetings with KPH board and Krakow organizers. Krakow, May 6, 2005, and private conversation with 2005 KPH board member. Warsaw, April 5, 2006.

17. See Loudes 2006. The same year, they also published: ILGA-Europe, *Prides against Prejudice. A Toolkit for Pride Organising in a Hostile Environment*, Brussels, September 2006.

18. E-mail on the KdT organization mailing list, April 4, 2005.

19. E-mail on the KdT organization mailing list, April 3, 2005.

20. Transcription of recordings of meeting between GPP activists and organizers of the Krakow festival. April 21, 2005.

21. During the meetings, GPP activists stated many times that their intention was not to tell the Krakow group what to do. However, their preference in favor of breaking free from what they saw as institutionalized, mainstream organizing was so clear

that, at one point, Polish activists heartily laughed when a GPP member told them that he had "no opinion on whether [they] should stay or leave KPH." As previously mentioned, GPP openly expressed criticism of the kind of activism they believed the KPH board was supporting. They also gave concrete advice to the Krakow group to establish financial autonomy and get their own contacts with the media and with transnational organizations.

22. The Krakow groups (KPH branch and later Foundation) were also connected to ILGA-Europe, but never to the same extent as the central KPH. In a symmetric way, KPH has also been part of various horizontal transnational networks, such as the organization of the *Tolerantia Award* ceremony together with *Maneo* (Berlin) and *SOS Homophobie* (Paris). However, I argue that vertical transnationalization represents the most structuring mode of transnationalization for KPH, just as horizontal transnationalization is for the Culture for Tolerance festival.

23. This reasoning was (and probably is) very common in transnational cooperation. A France-based activist who was launching a global transnational campaign for LG rights in the same year (2005) described to me how he saw his work as coordinator in the following terms: "First, there is a sort of casting. For each country I try to identify who would be the person or association best placed to represent the campaign." This process often reveals or intensifies preexisting tensions, resulting in the fact that "it happened to [him] many times to intervene in domestic quarrels," just as in the case of the *Gouines et Pédés Politiques*. Interview with global campaign coordinator, Paris, September 8, 2008.

24. Kultura dla Tolerancji festival, "Letter of Invitation," January 2005 [Personal archives].

25. This idea was widely accepted as obvious by everyone in the situation. It is revealing of a deep and disturbing double standard as to whose safety and life is worth protecting.

26. Or even, one can imagine, establish reversed relations of power with their own "East/South." However, these encounters did not result in continued relations between the Krakow group and the groups from these three countries.

27. The "Polish plumber" became, throughout Western Europe, the symbol of the risks seen in the "Services in the Internal Market Directive" (the so-called Bolkestein Directive), which was to allow any EU worker to work in another EU country under their own labor law.

28. Ambrose Evans-Pritchard, "Atheist Premier Attacks Lack of Christianity in EU Constitution," *The Telegraph*, June 4, 2003. http://www.telegraph.co.uk/news/worldnews/europe/poland/1431975/Atheistpremier-attacks-lack-of-Christianity-in-EU-constitution.html.

29. Transcription of recordings of meeting between GPP activists and Krakow KdT organizers. April 21, 2005.

30. This notion bears similarities with the ones developed by Mohanty (2003) and Scholz (2007). Binnie and Klesse (2011) suggest that transnational LGBT activism would be better conceptualized as "network solidarities" (following Gould 2007). However, the plurality of positioning implied by the term risks to obscure, I believe, the somehow binary hierarchies at play in East/West relations.

31. As emphasized by several authors throughout the book *Political Altruism?*, altruistic motives can coexist with various forms of interest—including, among others, individual psychological interest achieved through moral satisfaction, and gain of political legitimacy by a group involved in this kind of solidarity work (Giugni and Passy 2001).

32. As I demonstrated elsewhere, Polish activists were in no way passive in this process of selection, translation, and appropriation/rejection of frames and action modes (Chetaille 2013). The transfers, however, were structurally flowing in one direction.

33. 2006–2020. Only in 2009 was the KPH representative who ran for the election appointed *reserve member* (and not full member) of ILGA-Europe's board for one year.

34. Almost in a mirroring process, KPH started mimicking the structure of its transnational partner: throughout the 2010s, it implemented many changes in its organization and staff management, most of them inspired by the model of ILGA-Europe.

35. Quote from B. Schuch and S. Sensier, "Des Panthères roses à Cracovie," Documentary film, France, 2005, 30:00.

36. A year after their initial trip to Poland, the *Gouines et Pédés Politiques* issued a statement of solidarity with the next "March for Tolerance" and organized a protest in front of the Polish embassy in solidarity with the Warsaw Equality Parade. They initiated both actions and invited many other French organizations to join. All groups also organized fundraising for Poland at least once in their local contexts.

37. B. Schuch and S. Sensier, 2005, *Des Panthères roses à Cracovie* and N. Volpert and J. Marjanski, 2006, *14 stopni na wschód/14 Grad ostwärtz.* Documentary film, Germany, 62:00. In both cases, the film was made by an activist with a Polish migration background, together with a filmmaker from their country of residence.

38. A film about the festival was produced earlier by a Swedish director (D. Voxerbrant, "Tolerancja! Who would have thought tolerance could be so controversial," Documentary film, Blackraw production, Sweden, 2005, 29:00) and presented similar characteristics (especially the focus on homophobic attacks and violence). Interestingly, probably because it was the only representation of the first edition of the festival, including the founding moment of the first March being attacked, this one was appropriated and used by Krakow activists, mostly as a means for raising international support for the festival during its early years of existence.

39. The most recent development, and probably the most unexpected from a Western perspective, has been the Christ-like discourse of queer-anarchist nonbinary activist Margot Szutowicz, arrested in summer 2020 in Warsaw and detained for several weeks for confronting homo/transphobic demonstrators and hanging rainbow flags and anarchist symbols on statues (including one of the Christ). Upon her release from detention, Margot stated that she was a Christian and was developing queer, anti-traditional family interpretations of the Gospel. See for example "Margot Szutowicz: Chrystus jest nasz" (Margot Szutowicz: The Christ is ours). *Replika* 87. Warsaw. September/October 2020.

40. Another French group, visiting the Krakow festival a few years after *Gouines et Pédés Politiques*, report on more equal and reciprocal relations. See Collectif *Les Flamands roses*, presentation at the seminar "Pratiques et pensées de l'émancipation." Caen, 2016.

41. For a critical reaction and contribution to this transnational debate, cosigned with other social scientists, see A. Chetaille, M. Chmurski, A. Safuta, and J. Struzik, "Violences d'État contre les LGBT en Pologne: quelles solidarités internationales pour quels effets?" (State Violence against LGBT people in Poland: what kind of international solidarities for what kind of consequences?), *Le blog des invités de Médiapart*, August 18, 2020. https://blogs.mediapart.fr/les-invites-de-mediapart/blog/180820/violences-d-etat-contre-les-lgbt-en-pologne-quelles-solidarites-internationales-pour-q.

Part II

SOLIDARITY-BUILDING

3

Solidarity-Building as Praxis

Anti-Extractivism and the World March of Women in the Macro-Norte Region of Peru

Dominique Masson and Anabel Paulos

Solidarity is a key term in social movement organizing, and an important component of both the rhetoric and activity of contemporary social movement organizations, especially in the feminist and social justice movement sectors (see Conway 2012; Routledge and Cumbers 2009). Establishing and maintaining solidarities at various scales is how social movements "draw strength from collectivity" (Massey 2008, 324). Engaging in solidarity-building is viewed as a strategic necessity. Yet, it can be a particularly problematic endeavor. Calls for solidarity are indicative of a recurrent political problem for movements: how to bring together, at least provisionally, individual and collective actors from a variety of contexts around agreed-on goals, demands, or projects of social transformation, in spite of differing geopolitical and social locations, asymmetries in power, and potentially divergent, if not conflicting, interests.

Despite the centrality of solidarity to collective action, the concept has remained largely under-theorized and, consequently, underused in empirical research (Gill 2009, 667; Featherstone 2012, 5; Brown and Yaffe 2014, 37–38; Gaztambide-Fernandez 2012, 45–46). When evoked in mainstream and feminist scholarly work, "solidarity" is more often than not undefined, as if its meaning were ubiquitous. Paradoxically, the multiplicity of its uses reveals variegated understandings of its nature. Solidarity is both about individuals and groups coalescing around a common cause (commonality) and about supporting the struggle of Others (extending across difference). In classical social movement and Marxist-influenced case studies centering solidarity, scholarly understandings of solidarity are often "blurred"

(Scholz 2008, 3) by that of more established concepts—mobilization and collective identities, for instance, or shared experiences, interests, and consciousness, or even transnationalization. In addition, solidarity is also viewed as a political ideal to strive toward in the present—that is, as a pre-figurative political relation that is part of the imagining of the world that is struggled for, as structure of affect—something that individual activists feel, and much more rarely as a collective praxis—something that movement organizations actually do. Finally, in mainstream political theory and political philosophy, solidarity appears as a highly normative concept, one that seeks to prescribe moral, ethical, and/or political responsibilities and obligations to political communities of belonging or affinity (Bayertz 1999, 3; Gaztambide-Fernandez 2012, 46–47), as exposed in the introduction to this book. "Solidarity" is thus a particularly unwieldy concept, yet in our view a necessary one for studying transnational feminist organizations that claim to engage in solidarity-building across different kinds of borders.

In this chapter, we propose to analyze three different contexts in which activists from a transnational feminist network (TFN), the World March of Women (WMW), have been engaged in the building of solidarities with anti-extractivist struggles in the Macro-Norte region of Peru: the struggle against the Conga project in Cajamarca, the struggle of the Indigenous community of Cañaris against the Cañarico project, and the WMW Meeting of the Americas, held in Cajamarca in 2015. Our contribution here is twofold. First, we make a conceptual intervention in the field of feminist theorizing about solidarity. We contend that although "transnational feminism" as a normative analytics offers a number of important insights, its very normativity places important limits on the analysis of practices of solidarity-building in sites where feminist organizing does not conform to its prescriptions. While retaining some of its insights, we combine them with developments in critical geography to conceive of solidarity as a strategic, organizational praxis in the service of movement goals. To access this praxis, we offer an analytical framework that foregrounds the discursive, material, and spatial dimensions of solidarity-building practices, which we further propose to view as embedded in movement goals and broader political projects. It is the usefulness of this intermediate-level theoretical framework that the three contexts studied want to illustrate. Second, we make an empirical contribution to knowledge by highlighting the practices and micro-politics of solidarity enacted at the local scale of a TFN—the WMW—a scale of solidaristic activity that is usually left out of studies of solidarity-building in transnational networks. We also contribute to current understandings of the limits of solidarity-building in the WMW regarding the recognition of Indigenous difference.

CONCEPTUALIZING SOLIDARITY

Starting in the mid-1980s, feminist theory has been the site of a major debate about the grounds for, and the very possibility of solidarities across borders among women who are differently positioned—by class, race, nation, colonialism, sexuality, and the like—in crisscrossing webs of relation of power and difference. In the field of transnational feminist scholarship, such concerns have been articulated within two distinct intellectual strands, one exemplified in the canonical work of Chandra Talpade Mohanty (1984, 1987, 1991a, 2003), the other associated with the work of Inderpal Grewal and Caren Kaplan (Grewal and Kaplan 1994; Kaplan 1994). Taken together, these works are credited with inaugurating "transnational feminism" as a tradition of feminist thought (see Conway 2017a).

Earlier visions of "global sisterhood," which assumed the universality of women's lived experiences under patriarchy as grounds for solidarity among women of the world, were taken to task by Mohanty (1987). Criticizing the essentialism of ahistorical and decontextualized understandings of women's existences, she pointed to the erasure of differences and relations of power and oppression shaped by race, class, and past and present imperialism and coloniality produced by such views of solidarity (Mohanty 1987; see also Mendoza 2002). The politics of solidarity promoted by "global feminism," which saw differences among women of the world to be reconciled if not superseded in the development of a global feminist agenda, were similarly castigated. Global feminism, it was argued, not only minimized issues of power and difference under the cover of liberal pluralism, but it also tended to reproduce the cultural hegemony of Western universalisms and its uncritical celebration of modernity (Grewal and Kaplan 1994; Kaplan 1994; see also Ong 1996).[1]

Both critical strands propose overlapping, if at times distinct, grounds for the building of solidarities across borders of various kinds. Against views of solidarity rooted in the similarity of women's oppressions or the pursuit of Western universalisms, they argue for solidarities anchored in the recognition of the diversity of women's experiences and for making space for the variety of differently located women's and feminist struggles. To enable solidarities that respect differences and specificities, while not remaining mired in particularism, both offer their own variants of a non-essentialist "politics of location" that rejects the fixity and homogeneity of the categories of identity politics.

For Mohanty, the building of solidarities should be based on "the political links we choose to make among and between struggles" (2003, 47). Making these links calls for intersectional analytics of social location attentive to the ways the lives and struggles of various groups of women are shaped differently by the histories and geographies of gender, race, class, nation, and coloniality. It also calls for finding commonality across differences, which depends on the identification of a "common context of struggle." That is, on a "historical, material analysis" (2003, 47) of exploitative, oppressive, or disenfranchising contexts[2] that offers the potential for solidarities among "women with divergent histories and social locations, woven together by the political threads of opposition to forms of domination that are not only pervasive, but systemic" (2003, 46–47). Solidarity-building is thus to be based in a political-analytical praxis, whose outcome is conditional to its success in establishing the interconnectedness of differing locations and their co-implication in common contexts of struggles (2003, 238–43).

In a kindred fashion, Grewal and Kaplan's "politics of location" argues for the founding of solidarities in historicized, contextualized, and detailed understandings of the ways similar structural-institutional arrangements of power—or scattered economic and cultural hegemonies "such as global economic structures, patriarchal nationalisms, 'authentic' forms of tradition, local structures of domination, neo-juridical oppression," religious fundamentalism and colonialism—affect women differently in different groups and different locations (1994, 17). The analyst's task is to map these scattered hegemonies and their impacts on various groups of women, and "to compare multiple, overlapping and discrete oppressions," aiming at unearthing congruencies between them. Such careful articulation of "how people in different locations and circumstances are linked by the spread of, and resistance to" these scattered hegemonies enables the construction of a "terrain of coalition and cooperation" (Grewal and Kaplan 1994, 5). On this basis, political solidarity in the form of a politics of affiliation can bring together "women from different communities who are interested in examining and working against the links that support and connect very diverse . . . practices" (1994, 27).

A normative dimension is intricately woven in the work of these theorists. More specifically, the theorizing of solidarities it proposes is one that aims at the realization of specific feminist projects: explicitly decolonial, anti-imperialist, anti-capitalist in the case of Mohanty, and critical of the material and cultural expressions of modernity—its "scattered hegemonies"—in the work of Grewal and Kaplan (1994, 17). Thus, transnational feminism prescribes analytical, political, and ethical conditions that must be fulfilled for constructing the type(s) of solidarities that correspond to the feminist political projects its theoreticians are advocating. Such normativity needs to be acknowledged. On the one hand, normativity is a constitutive feature of feminist theory as the latter is invested in guiding action as much as in analyzing social phenomena. On the other hand, these two objectives cannot be conflated, and the ways transnational feminist theorists define and approach solidarity and solidarity-building need to be situated with regard to their normative underpinnings.

Feminist moral-ethical frameworks that define solidarity as, and ground it in, the enactment of specific types of political relationships—for instance, in "mutuality, accountability" (Mohanty 2003, 7); reflexivity (Dean 1996); or transversal dialogues (Yuval-Davis 1997; Fultner 2017) should be understood in this spirit.

Conway argues that there is a profound conceptual disconnection between transnational feminism as a normative analytic and the scholarly feminist literature about transnational feminist organizing. In the latter, which is "more realist in its underpinnings, transnational feminism is conceptualized as an empirical phenomenon and the object of study with minimal relation to the central problematics" of the former (2017a, 210). This is also true of empirical analyses of transnational solidarities and solidarity-building, with a few exceptions (see, for instance, chapter 5; Conway 2012, 2017a). Most importantly, Conway further contends that there is also a "misfit" between transnational feminism as a normative analytic and contemporary practices of solidarity-building in movement organizing, as the former seldom engages with the latter.

Transnational feminism as normative analytics offers important analytical insights about solidarity as a political construction and on solidarity-building as a praxis of link-making between discrepant social locations. As well, both strands stress the asymmetries in power and privilege among women and the complicities of some feminisms with coloniality, modernity, and Western universalisms that affect attempts at solidarity-building. Yet, because they largely focus on prescribing "what should be," the normative analytics of transnational feminism are less useful, we contend, for the analysis of "what is"—that is, of actual processes of solidarity-building in feminist organizing and, in particular, of processes that do not partake from the same feminist genealogies and trajectories and, consequently, do not, in part or in whole, conform to their normative prescriptions. We agree with Conway that the practices of solidarity-building in which contemporary TFNs are currently engaged need to be understood first in their own terms (2017a, 221). To further an inquiry into how TFNs "do solidarity," there is a need for an intermediate-level theoretical framework for accessing and analyzing actually occurring praxis. We thus propose to combine selected elements of transnational feminist analytics to key contributions from critical geography.

Drawing on Massey (2008), Routledge and Cumbers (2009), and Featherstone (2012), we thus propose to understand solidarity-building in transnational organizing as an organizational praxis. Studying solidarities and processes of solidarity-building in TFNs means studying this organizational praxis and what it is made of in different movement contexts. Combining transnational feminist theorizing and critical geographical insights, we conceptualize this praxis as involving the active linking together of hitherto geographically and/or socially distant and disparate place-based struggles through the construction of connections between actors, places, and mobilizations. Such conceptualization not only points to the problem of social differences evoked in transnational feminist theorizing of solidarity-building, but also to that posed by the heterogeneous character of the places, organizations, and even of the struggles that are the object of connections. Analyzing how such active linking is made and specifying the (various) nature of the connections that are established, as well as their substantive content, is at the heart of the analysis, which proposes to view solidarity as a praxis made of three interrelated types of practices—discursive, material, and spatial.

The making of solidarities involves the elaboration, in movement discourse, of political imaginaries and forms of political identification that connect movement actors and their struggles (Massey 2008; Featherstone 2012). Indeed, for Routledge and Cumbers, an essential component of solidarity-building is "constructing the grievances and aspirations of geographically, culturally, economically and, at times, politically different and distant peoples as interlinked" (2009, 71). Analyzing discursive practices of solidarity, Featherstone suggests, means paying attention to such imaginaries and identifications, that is, to "the terms on which solidarities are made" (2012, 31), especially to the way causes are defined as being in common. It also involves identifying the discursive constructions of equivalence or articulation through which actors attempt to link together distinct, if not discrepant struggles, as well as the political dynamics that accompany and shape this process (2012, 213).

Solidarity-building is not made solely through discourse. Indeed, enacting solidarity often involves providing very concrete expressions of support and material forms of labor that contribute to the bringing together of actors and of struggles (Routledge and Cumbers 2009; Featherstone 2012). Analyzing such material practices of solidarity-building, or what Routledge and Cumbers call "a practical relational politics of solidarity" (2009, 93) directs scholarly attention toward a variety of practices of organizing, mobilizing, and action. For instance, and without attempting in any way to be exhaustive,[3] coming together in demonstrations, pursuing a given agenda together, coordinating action with others, enabling communication, testimony, and information-sharing, enacting relations of financial, technological, or political support (for instance, political training, sharing knowhow), and so forth.

Finally, critical geographers assert that solidarity is also the object of spatial practices. Translocal and transnational solidarities "are worked through and constructed in and between different sites" (Featherstone 2012, 31; see also Massey 2008), as well as at and between different scales of movement organizing and action (Routledge and Cumbers 2009). The inquiry is thus directed toward the ways specific place-based struggles are linked to struggles happening elsewhere and, in particular, to "attempts to connect up territorially-specific struggles to broader global networks of support, action and debate" (Routledge and Cumbers 2009, 16).

These practices should be approached with a dynamic view—solidarity-building is a process that unfolds over time, through the historical constitution of the discursive, material, and spatial connections established among collective actors. Solidarity-building also possesses a generative character: not only can it shape new connections between actors, causes, and sites of struggles (Featherstone 2012, 19), but it may reciprocally transform agendas, discourses, and practices of the actors involved, as well as foster the emergence of new political subjects. Yet, solidarity-building is not to be romanticized. As transnational feminist theorists have been keen to point out, it is shot through with relations of power that may very well challenge, but also entrench asymmetries and privilege, as well as complicities with various forms of hegemony.

Recent work on solidarity as praxis (Brown and Yaffe 2014; Chazan 2016; Tabar 2017), itself inspired to a variable extent by the critical geographers cited above, suggests that there is a relationship between how goals pursued by an organization are framed (Brown and Yaffe 2014; Chazan 2016) and practices of solidarity it enacts. We understand this insight as an invitation to inquire more closely into the rationale(s) at the core of solidarity-building in different movement contexts. In this view, we claim that solidarity-building should also be analyzed as a political strategy shaped by specific organizational goals and political projects, as well as by the more broadly defined categories of political projects in which these are embedded, from socialist feminism to intersectional or decolonial projects (Chazan 2016), or from Third World and other "old" and "new" Left internationalisms (Waterman 2001; Brown and Yaffe 2014) to contemporary forms of liberal internationalism (Tabar 2017).

In what follows, we use the analytical framework presented above to inquire into the involvement of the WMW in the building of solidarities with anti-extractivist struggles in the Macro-Norte region of Peru, and to demonstrate the interest of analyzing solidarity-building as a praxis in TFNs. We draw on data collected in 2015 by Anabel Paulos as part of her doctoral project on convergence spaces in the WMW in Peru and Dominique Masson's five-year study on solidarity-building around food sovereignty in the WMW.[4] An ethnographic approach guided a two-month fieldwork in the summer of 2015, first in the capital, Lima, and then in the Macro-Norte (MN) region of Peru, the latter proving to be most relevant to the present inquiry. Fifteen formal interviews were conducted in Spanish in various sites of the MN with women who were identified by us and our informants as key activists of the March in the region. Additional informal interviews were also

Dominique Masson and Anabel Paulos

realized with a number of these activists, and observations were made at the events to which we were invited. Anabel Paulos traveled back to observe and collect documents at the fourth WMW Meeting of the Americas, held in the city of Cajamarca in October 2015. The three different contexts examined below were chosen for their relevance with regard to illustrating the different dimensions and potential of our analytical framework. Our analysis does not only draw on the specific interviews and documents quoted in this chapter, but also on the overall picture that emerges from our fieldwork in the MN and our broader knowledge of the WMW. Our data collection is limited by its focus on the WMW, meaning that it did not include the views of local non-March women activists on the March's efforts at building solidarity with their struggles.

SOLIDARITY-BUILDING AROUND ANTI-EXTRACTIVISM IN THE WMW MACRO-NORTE, PERU

The WMW was formally created in October 2001, as the outcome of a five-year process leading to "the world march of women of the year 2000," a three-day, planetary event that mobilized five thousand women's and feminist organizations in 159 countries and territories to denounce women's poverty and violence against women and to demand action from institutions. Lack of response from the UN, IMF, and World Bank, which, with national governments, were the events' main targets, quickly led the March to replace its initial objective of influencing international institutions with a commitment to attain the goal of creating a "worldwide women's movement," that is, of creating a commonality of struggles among the world's women in opposition to patriarchy and neoliberal capitalism. Building solidarities and sustaining the self-organization of women around the world were seen as the primary means to attain this goal (Dufour and Giraud 2007, 315–17). Since then, the WMW has transformed into a multi-issue network embracing a wide range of questions and claims. It is loosely coordinated by an International Secretariat and an International Committee that operate on a shoestring budget and organize "global actions" every five years. The network currently comprises approximately sixty national coordinating bodies (NCBs), themselves composed of national, regional, and local organizations that mobilize "as WMW" at will between global actions (for more detail on the WMW, its history, and political platform, see Dufour and Giraud 2007; Conway 2012).

In Peru, the WMW started forming at the end of the 1990s, when a group of activists from Quebec (Canada) asked Peruvian women's organizations to take part in organizing the 2000 global action. This process morphed into the creation of a national coordination of the WMW in Lima and into efforts at building the WMW in other regions of Peru. By 2005, the March Macro-Norte (March MN) counted on local member groups and self-identified March activists in the departments of Piura, Cajamarca, and Lambayeque, and on a regional coordination located in the city of Chiclayo. Participation in the international meeting of the WMW in Rwanda, in 2004, was a turning point for Regional Coordinator Rosa Rivero, who was particularly inspired by the self-definition of the March as a mass, popular movement of women from "the base" (interview[5] with Rosa Rivero).[6] In 2015, the main political priorities of the March MN were described to us as being struggles against extractivism and more specifically mining, water, and environmental protection, LGBT issues, violence against women, climate change, and the promotion of food sovereignty.

BUILDING SOLIDARITY WITH STRUGGLES AGAINST EXTRACTIVISM IN CAJAMARCA

In the city of Cajamarca (Macro-Norte), the organization of the March initially rested on a small number of activists, who met sporadically to discuss issues such as violence against women and gender equality, as well as feminist ideas. However, at the time of the interviews, the main struggle of the March Cajamarca was said to be resistance against mining and extractivism. In fact, since 2011–2012, the March Cajamarca has been heavily invested in the protest movement against the "Conga project" proposed by the Yanacocha Mining Company, which has been operating one of the world's largest gold mines in the department of Cajamarca since 1993. Earlier protests denounced this mine as a threat to the lagoons, lakes, and freshwater springs on which the subsistence production of local communities depended. The Conga project was similarly condemned as a vector of environmental destruction (Viitala 2016, 11–19; Hallman and Olivera 2015) and of land grabbing (Bebbington et al. 2008, 2895), whose most publicized case was the resistance put up in the area by peasant woman Máxima Acuña.[7]

The involvement of the March in the *Conga no va* (Conga won't happen) protests begs the questions of why and how a struggle against extractivism, an issue far removed from classical feminist ones, became defined as a priority for the feminists of the March in Cajamarca. According to the then-coordinator of the March Cajamarca, Mirta Villanueva, with the 2011–2012 mobilization against Conga, "thousands of women came out of their houses" where they had so far "remained passive . . . in their reproductive role" and poured into the streets to be part of the protest. For Villanueva, seeing women come out shouting in the streets was not only "a miracle" wrought by the Conga protest at the time, but it also opened an opportunity for the March to attempt to expand local women's mobilization to issues of violence against women and the defense of women's rights. Her reasoning was: if these women were already in the streets, shouting against the Conga project, they could be brought to shout about women's issues as well.

Villanueva's understanding of the March's own interest in engaging in practices of solidarity was thus highly strategic and calculated, and the discursive practices of solidarity in which the March Cajamarca engaged in the process of mobilizing against Conga should be understood in this light. In Cajamarca, the March went on to produce a political imaginary that connected feminism with anti-mining struggles. Interviews show that it did so by breaking the apparent gender-neutrality of the protest through elaborating a feminist discourse centered on local women's relationship to water and to the land. Women, the March's activists argued, need water from dawn to dusk for most of their everyday activities (interview with Mirta Villanueva).[8] "The women are in direct contact with water for the care of their animals, for their small gardens, for the food they prepare, the clothes they wash" (interview with Aurora Portal).[9] They were the ones, it thus followed, who were the most affected by water contamination and the drying out of the springs, lakes, and lagoons wrought by mining. Women were further understood as bearers of a relation to the land marked by a greater preoccupation for having a place to stay for their families and greater concerns for the future of their children (interview with Mirta Villanueva). Consequently, women's opposition to the Conga project was viewed as a result of their acute consciousness that water and the land were crucial components of their lives (interview with Aurora Portal).[10]

The decision to join the protests against Conga—that is, to act in solidarity—had transformative effects on the political imaginary of the March in Cajamarca. In this particular case, it prompted activists from Cajamarca to produce a locally novel, vernacular feminist discourse in which the participation of women in the *Conga no va* protest was rearticulated as an instance where women were mobilizing "as women." Identified as a "women's issue," the Conga project thus became a shared terrain of struggle for local women and the March's feminists in Cajamarca, and anti-extractivism was redefined as a political activity falling within the purview of the WMW. Such discourse was shared by activists in the cities of Tambogrande and Chiclayo where the March was also involved in protests against extractivism.

SOLIDARITY-BUILDING AGAINST EXTRACTIVISM WITH THE INDIGENOUS COMMUNITY OF CAÑARIS

The district of Cañaris covers 285 square kilometers and has a population of thirteen thousand inhabitants. Together with the districts of Incahuasi and

Salas, it represents the biggest Quechua-speaking area of Northern Peru. However, the status of the community of Cañaris as "Indigenous people," which would mean entitlement to the right to prior, free, and informed consultation in cases of projects impacting Indigenous communities, was denied by the government who proceeded to grant mining concessions in the district. In 2010, the community discovered geologists and technicians of the Candente Copper Corporation carrying out the exploration phase for a multi-metal mine, the Cañarico project. According to Cañaris activists and environmental experts, this extractive project would greatly impact the eco-system, water sources, and, in turn, the agricultural activities on which the community's way of life and survival depended. The people from Cañaris started organizing. In 2012, they held a consultation in which 95 percent of the voters opposed the project. An indefinite strike was declared in January 2013, followed by a road blockade that was repressed by the police (twenty-eight people were injured). Action was undertaken to bring the Peruvian state before the Inter-American Commission of Human Rights for not respect-ing the community's Indigenous rights (Mendez 2013; *Comité Solidarité Cajamarca* 2015).

It is in these circumstances that activists from the coordination of the March Macro-Norte first encountered women activists from Cañaris. The lat-ter were participating in a protest in the city of Chiclayo against the Conga project, carrying banners saying *"Conga no va. Cañariaco tampoco"* (Conga won't happen. Neither will Cañarico) and *"Cañariaco no va"* (Cañarico won't happen) that, using juxtaposition in the first case and mirroring the lin-guistic construction of the anti-Conga banners in the second, created in politi-cal discourse a relation of equivalence between the two struggles. Activists of the March MN report that, upon seeing the banner-carriers from Cañaris, they moved through the crowd to join them, bringing to them their *batucada* (the March's drums) and shouting with them *"Conga no va. Cañariaco tam-poco"* and *"Cañariaco no va"* (interview with Yuli Peralta).[11] Solidarity was thus enacted in concrete, material form by the activists of the March as they physically bridged the distance between the two struggles by moving through the crowd and joining in the shouts denouncing Candente Copper's Cañariaco project. It is on this occasion that the activists of the March MN met and talked with Indigenous leader Rosa Sara Huaman Rinze, who was to become their main point of contact with the women and the community of Cañaris.

The March MN decided to start supporting the Cañaris struggle from its base in Chiclayo (interview with Yuli Peralta). In terms of the discursive construction of solidarity, this decision was presented to us by a local activist from the March MN as resulting from an identification of the similarity of struggles in Cajamarca (against Conga/Yanacocha) and in Cañaris (against Cañariaco/Candente Copper).

The *compañeras*[12] were fighting. We became more involved when we identified that there was solidarity: the struggle for water, for life was similar to the
one in Cajamarca, but in another kind of context, that of a Quechua speaking
Indigenous community . . . (interview with Lourdes Contreras).[13]

Building solidarity across differences was a challenge for the non-Indigenous and mostly young, urban, and highly educated feminists of the March
Chiclayo, as members of the community of Cañaris initially expressed their
distrust, "At the beginning, they did not want us there, they kicked us out"
(interview with Lourdes Contreras). Even when the relationship had become
more amiable, another activist from the March reflected that often "it was
like climbing a hill of sand with them" (interview with Rosa Rivero). Such
reticence was variously interpreted by the March's activists as rooted in the
history of the community (interview with Rosa Rivero), in geographical
isolation and social exclusion (interview with Yuli Peralta), and in a distrust
from a people who "had resisted the conquest by the Incas, had resisted the
Spanish conquest, and now resisted the capitalist conquest" (interview with
Lourdes Contreras). These explanations allude to, but at the same time elude,
at least in our interviews, a more explicit understanding by the March's
activists that they may have been perceived by the Cañaris community as
belonging to the world of colonial and neocolonial relations of power that had
negatively shaped their experience as Indigenous people.

Confronted with such challenges to their efforts at solidarity-building,
activists from the March decided to tread carefully and, for some time,
limited themselves to offering logistical support. Food and clothing were
collected by the March in Chiclayo for Cañaris strikers and blockaders, community members who had been wounded in the confrontations with the police
and were in the hospital were helped, money was found so that those who
had been arrested and were in jail could eat, and lawyers who would work
pro-bono were sought to help them navigate the judicial system (interviews
with Yuli Peralta and Lourdes Contreras).

Enacting concrete, material practices of solidarity eventually contributed
to building a level of trust. In the opinion of local activists of the March,
the relationship with the community also changed when Cañaris leaders
understood that WMW members really believed that the Cañaris struggle
for water and for the protection of the territory was also their own struggle.
". . . because the struggle for water is the struggle of all, as is the struggle
for the territory, so we were fighting against something bigger, which is this
capitalist system that wants to steal everything from us and wants to destroy
everything" (interview with Lourdes Contreras).

In this imagining of solidarity, the cause of the Other (the Cañaris
Indigenous community) was made into the cause of the March MN, not only

through the discursive construction of a (purported) similarity of issues but also through the projection of a common adversary: capitalism.

From that point on, material practices of solidarity of the March expanded from purely logistical to more directly political forms of support. Activists from the March MN explained to leaders in Cañaris what the political interests were among the NGOs and politicians who were involved (interview with Yuli Peralta). They arranged a meeting with environmental organizations that could assist the struggle (interview with Lourdes Contreras). They also brought knowhow to Cañaris activists, helping them to plan actions and mount the documentation necessary to claim their rights, a point which was underscored by Rosa Sara Huaman Rinze, one of the leaders of the community. Turning to the March, she further stated, was a way for the community to gain from "the strength and solidarity" of the March's activists:

> We have always called on the March when we wanted to take action . . . in defense of our territory, say a peaceful strike or a claim to institutions about our rights, that's when they support us, as well as in the preparation of documents that we want to send to the ministries, be it the Ministry of Environment, of Energy, or Mines, to see if they can help us with that, or by looking for legal advisors. . . . In these moments, we let the March know what we need in order to draw on their strength and solidarity. (Interview with Rosa Sara Huaman Rinze)[14]

Finally, core activists from the March MN in Chiclayo repeatedly visited the community of Cañaris. Rosa Sara Huaman Rinze stated in her interview that it was through these visits that they, the peasant, Indigenous women of Cañaris, came to know about their rights: "our right to the land, our right to the territory, our right to water," as well as about "the rights of women: the right not to be discriminated against, the right to gender equality." On these occasions, activists from the March MN contributed to the politicization of social relations by speaking to women's assemblies and by engaging in political training on Indigenous and women's rights. Such practical political support is part of the practices of solidarity-building deployed by the March in its relationship with the community of Cañaris; it is also a practice of solidarity-building with its women, attempting to build Indigenous women's mobilizations "as women's" and, eventually, as feminist mobilizations. The years that followed saw the creation of the Indigenous Women's Association of Cañaris "Juana Callaypoma," which became a member of the March MN. The solidarity-building process in which the March was engaged with the women of Cañaris proved generative in that it contributed significantly to a transformative process already underway among the women of the community, fostering the emergence of a new, organized political subject: the Indigenous women of Cañaris.

SPATIAL PRACTICES OF SOLIDARITY AT THE 2015 WMW MEETING OF THE AMERICAS IN CAJAMARCA

The 2015 Meeting of the Americas of the WMW took place in Cajamarca from October 23 to 25. Nearly 100 delegates of the March from Mexico, Guatemala, Panama, Cuba, Venezuela, Chile, Brazil, Quebec, and Peru participated. The presence of the March Macro-Norte was strong, with activists from Cajamarca, Chiclayo, and Cañaris, as well as from other localities. This event provides us with the opportunity to further our inquiry into solidarity as an organizational praxis by analyzing the spatial dimensions of solidarity-building around anti-extractivism in the March. Because the March exists not only in different sites, or locales, but is also instantiated at different scales—with NCBs, national and local member organizations, an International Committee and an International Secretariat, as well as regular continental and international meetings—its spatial practices of solidarity involve relations between sites (translocal) and between scales (interscalar).

Cajamarca was sixteen hours by bus from the capital, Lima, where the international delegates first arrived, and six hours by bus from Chiclayo, where the coordination of the WMW Macro-Norte is located. Such impractical logistics speak to the significance for the International Committee of the March of choosing this site. Holding the meeting in the remote setting of Cajamarca was a practical and symbolic act of solidarity: "We are in Cajamarca in recognition of the struggles in defense of water and territories against predatory extractivism. We want to show our solidarity with women's and peoples' day-to-day resistance against mega-mining in the region" (World March of Women 2015, 27). Meeting there was also a means to reinforce the engagement in, and solidarity with similar struggles in other sites of the March in the Americas, and in the March itself as a TFN.

Practices of solidarity at the meeting included devoting a full day and a half to struggles against extractivism in the Macro-Norte. In the opening panel, after welcoming her audience in Quechua, Rosa Sara Huaman Rinze from Cañaris told the story of her community's resistance to the Candente Copper mining company. Dina Mendoza, an activist from the March, spoke of women's involvement in the struggle against the Conga project in Cajamarca (World March of Women 2015, 3), while Maria Tempora Pintado[15] recalled her experience of founding a women's association (ADIMTA, member of the March MN) in Tambogrande to resist a mining project by Manhattan Minerals. On another panel, internationally known local emblem of resistance

Máxima Acuña was invited with her daughter to share the experience of Máxima's personal struggle against the Yanacocha Mine. The meeting also featured a protest against the Conga project in which international delegates from the WMW and activists from the Macro-Norte and Lima marched together in the streets of Cajamarca, shouting *"Agua si, oro no"* (Water yes, gold no) to the sound of the *batucada* and under strong police surveillance (4). Scarves worn for the occasion read: *"Conga no va—MMM"* (Conga won't happen—WMW) and banners affirmed: *"Por nuestros cuerpos y territorios libres"* (Freedom for our bodies and territories) and *"¡Todas somos Máxima!"* (We are all Máxima!) (5).

Bringing in speakers to give testimony of their struggles to the participants in the meeting was a practice of solidarity that braided these four place-based mobilizations (Cañaris, Cajamarca, Tambogrande, and Máxima's) together at the scale of the Macro-Norte. Being the focus of panels and of the protest also projected these struggles onto a spatially wider arena, that of the March in the Americas. International Coordinator of the March Graça Samos further extended solidarity-building across distance by establishing, in her public speech, connections between the testimonies of the morning and anti-extractivist struggles occurring in the March in Africa and around the world (World March of Women 2015). These examples of how links between local struggles and other sites and scales of the March were established during the meeting illustrate the translocal and interscalar dynamics of solidarity-building at work.

On the second day of the meeting, the delegates were invited to construct collectively a map of the resistances and alternatives of the March in the Americas. Mapping enabled all the participants to further connect resistances to extractivism in the March Brazil, Guatemala, Mexico, Quebec, and Peru to the wide variety of feminist struggles comprising the March's agenda in its various sites (for instance: resistances to gender-based violence, to the effects of neoliberal policies on women, as well as to gender discrimination, heteronormativity, and the sexualization of women's bodies). As an exercise in solidarity-building, such mapping worked to expand activists' understanding of the actual or potential connections between anti-extractivism and other kinds of struggles in their own locales as well as in more distant sites. Establishing such translocal "geographies of connections" across differences is intrinsic to the internal solidarity-building processes in which the March is consciously engaged.

The one-page final statement of the meeting devoted two full paragraphs to affirming the solidarity of the delegates of the March from the Americas with the struggles, in Cajamarca and elsewhere, in the defense of water and territories against mega-mining industries and "predatory extractivism." To those involved in those conflicts and resistances, the document reaffirmed the

March's opposition to "the commodification of our bodies, land and territories" and stated, in a final declaration of translocal and interscalar solidarity: "*¡No están solas!*" (You are not alone!) (World March of Women 2015, 27).

SOLIDARITY-BUILDING AS MOVEMENT-BUILDING

Practices of solidarity-building as well as their limits are shaped, we contend, by organizational goals and by the political projects in which they are embedded. The WMW's goal of creating a commonality of struggles among "women of the world" should be understood in light of the socialist feminist character of its politics. Informed by a Latin American-born popular feminism that seeks to articulate the concerns and struggles of poor and economically marginalized women (working-class, rural, peasant, Indigenous), the March is animated by a dual project of movement-building—that is, of building the March as a mass movement of women and as a feminist movement, and of building a broad-based, "counter-hegemonic, anti-capitalist and popular politics" in alliance with other progressive social movements (Conway 2016, 16). Our research on the March Macro-Norte (Peru) demonstrates how the strategic enactment of practices of solidarity-building at the local scale is intrinsically tied to this political project.

Constructing solidarity with nonfeminist activists and collective actors involved in the anti-mining struggles in Cajamarca, Cañaris, and elsewhere in the region was crucial to the March's goal of movement-building. Engaging in solidarity against extractivism was the entry point for activists from the March MN to further encourage women's organizing through offering political training aimed at transforming political subjectivities, helping to constitute women's mobilizations as "women's" (and eventually as feminist), and supporting the creation of local organizations that became members of the March (in Cañaris, Tambogrande). Making women's existing involvement in anti-mining struggles part of the March thus contributed to building the March in the Macro-Norte by expanding the assemblage of actors that self-identified as members of the March MN, as well as by extending its political platform to include anti-extractivism and the protection of water as newly re-signified women's and feminist struggles. The involvement of the March in the protests against Conga in Cajamarca, its support of the struggle of the Indigenous community of Cañaris, and its taking up of anti-extractivism as one of its priority issues should also be understood in the context of major anti-mining protests in the region, in which a broad alliance of movements was participating (Bebbington et al. 2008). In that, the solidaristic activity of the March in the MN is in line with the broader organizational project pursued internationally by the WMW.

There were, nevertheless, limits to solidarity-building as it was enacted by the March in the Macro-Norte. Solidarities are not only constructed as interventions in a field of power that they seek to unsettle, but they are also shaped by structural relations of power around difference, which their actors may not always recognize or attempt to alter. In this regard, and drawing on the normative analytics of decolonial perspectives, we contend that activists of the March MN have largely failed to appreciate fully and engage with "the difference that difference makes" (Gaztambide-Fernandez 2012, 42), in particular in the construction of solidarity with the Indigenous women of Cañaris. Although "difference" was named by the March MN's activists—Cañaris was clearly identified as an Indigenous community marked by a history of 500 years of Indigenous resistance—there was no recognition, at least in our interviews, of the impact that occupying differing positions in colonial and neocolonial relations of power may have on the building of solidarity. Yet, it is these differing positions that, at least initially, fostered distance and distrust on the part of the community. Eliding the examination of the March's own relation to neo-colonialism eventually produced contradictory constructions of political solidarity. The March MN claimed to respect the processes, ideas, and decisions of the community; yet, it trained the women of Cañaris in its own version of feminism and of the defense of Indigenous rights.[16] The WMW Meeting of the Americas started with a welcoming ceremony celebrating the Pachamama, the earth goddess of the Andes, yet during the meeting no translation was provided for the Indigenous women who were attending, which limited participation to those among them who could understand and speak Spanish.[17]

More fundamentally, the indigeneity of the community of Cañaris was "a difference that ma[de] little difference" (Conway and Paulos 2017, 21). According to Alvarez et al.'s (2003) study, "mis-encounters" between Indigenous women and white/mestiza feminism have been a regular feature in the history of the Latin American women's movement. Tensions around the lack of recognition of Indigenous women's issues, they suggest, stem from the rooting of dominant, white/mestiza feminisms—including the popular feminism of the March—in the discourse of the political left, which has tended to subsume Indigenous (and other) differences under the categories of capitalism and class (2003, 565). As argued by de la Cadena (2010), such mis-encounters are, more broadly, the consequence of non-Indigenous and Indigenous people inhabiting worlds of radically different ontological natures, and in which Indigenous worldviews are only partly intelligible within the hegemonic, modernist discourses of the Left and other non-Indigenous actors. Thus, when the women of Cañaris speak of defending their territory, nature, "sacred mountain," and "water as a life force" (Chambeu 2015), which de la Cadena analyzes as the irruption of sentient "earth beings" in social protest (2010, 336), the March MN ignores the excess meaning carried by their voices and reinterprets their claims under a rationale for solidarity against extractivism that makes capitalism into the "common" enemy. These limits to solidarity-building hark back to feminist theory's debates on solidarity across differences, which are marked both by the necessity of building feminist solidarities that truly respect differences and avoid reproducing power relations and modernist hegemonies, and by skepticism over this very possibility (Mendoza 2002; Grewal and Kaplan 1994; Conway 2017a).[18]

CONCLUSION

This chapter has provided an ethnographically rich contribution to empirical knowledge about the practices and micro-politics of solidarity-building around extractivism in the WMW in the Macro-Norte region of Peru. Our case shows how solidarity-building as the process of linking distant and sometimes initially discrepant struggles is constructed on the ground, very practically, through interrelated discursive, material, and spatial practices of solidarity. Further, our study brings to light local processes through which the struggles of "Others" have come to be part of the struggles of the March, and how such processes contribute to the expansion and transformation of the WMW as a TFN at various scales. Attempts to build solidarities with the Indigenous struggle of Cañaris also reveal contradictions and limits that stem from the broader political project in which these efforts at building solidarities across differences are embedded. Yet, as solidarity-building is generative and in-progress, its story may very well be open to further transformation in the March.

Conway has written extensively about the (mis)fit between transnational feminism as normative analytics and the practices of the WMW. The main differences that the WMW is attending to in its processes of solidarity-building are those linked to the realities and political organizing of poor and economically marginalized women (working-class, rural, peasant). The March also recognizes the diversity of women's struggles, especially those stemming from place-based differences (local and national). Its political project is anti-patriarchal, anti-capitalist, and anti-imperialist. Where the WMW distances itself considerably from the perspectives developed in the scholarly work examined in the first part of this chapter is by its silence on coloniality, as well as on race and sexuality (Conway 2017a, 212–23), and by its alignment with the Left's assimilationist and modernist desire for a unified struggle that eschews radical difference.

In keeping with the (mis)fit, what our case study also demonstrates is that the process of solidarity-building in the WMW does not rest on the kind of careful and detailed comparative analysis (the "politics of location") proposed in Mohanty (2003) and in Grewal and Kaplan (1994) which ultimately calls on the deployment of academic feminism's expert knowledge. Rather, establishing the interconnectedness of distant/discrepant socio-spatial struggles involved much less complex intellectual operations on the part of activists. Creating vernacular articulations in feminist discourse defining water and land as "women's" and as feminist issues, asserting the similarity of issues, struggles, and enemy, and using juxtapositions—in slogans, in storytelling and testimonials, in pedagogical mapping exercises—that enabled analogies to be drawn all contributed to constructing relations of equivalence between struggles (Laclau and Mouffe 1985). The making of connections between differently located struggles and actors was also enacted through the very concrete, material practices of bringing bodies together in demonstrations, of chanting together and repeating each other's slogans, and of providing logistical and political support. Finally, a variety of translocal and interscalar practices of solidarity-building, from the composition of panels to public speeches to mapping exercises, linked place-based struggles across socio-spatial differences and established a geography of connections at the wider scale of the Americas and of the planetary WMW.

To conclude, transnational feminism and other normative analytics are certainly helpful for identifying the shortcomings of activist attempts at forging solidarities. Yet, as we hope to have shown, from the point of view of knowledge production, such critique cannot replace or occur in abstraction from the fine-grained analysis of why, when, and, most importantly, how solidarities—the strategic forging of connections between actors, places, and struggles—are sought and built by feminist collective actors in the first place. We have argued that feminist analysis of solidarity-building in TFNs needs more tools for identifying, documenting, and analyzing the variety of practical incarnations that solidarities and efforts at building them can take on the ground. To further this inquiry, we have proposed to consider solidarity as a strategy to realize visions of change and, as such, as a praxis that collective and individual movement actors undertake to change the world. In this perspective, we have offered to conceptualize solidarity-building in TFNs as an organizational praxis, made up of sets of discursive, material, and spatial practices whose nature and content are the object of investigation. In line with feminist theory's insights, these practices are to be seen as generative and transformative; they are also fraught, maybe inevitably, with asymmetries, relations of power, and complicities with various forms of domination. Finally, we have offered an understanding of organizational praxes of solidarity as shaped by the character of the specific feminist projects of solidarity-building in which they are embedded. This potentially opens up the analysis to the existence and enactment of a variety of feminist projects of solidarity at various scales, as the following case studies exemplify—socialist feminist (the WMW in this chapter; Conway 2017a); intersectional (Feminist Dialogues at the WSF in Conway 2012); anarcha-feminist (ProNet in Mott 2018); decolonial (Canadian Raging Grannies in Chazan 2016). Actually occurring practices of solidarity-building in feminist organizing, we contend, all beg for more sustained attention from feminist scholars.

NOTES

1. For a detailed and more generous analysis of global feminism as a project of solidarity, see chapter 1.

2. In the second part of "Cartographies of Struggle," Mohanty (2003, 57–83) suggests "multiple contexts for the emergence of contemporary Third World feminist struggles" and, thus, for the building of political solidarities: the "socioeconomic, political, and discursive configurations [of] (1) colonialism, class, and gender, (2) the state, citizenship, and racial formation, (3) multinational production and social agency, (4) anthropology and the Third World woman as 'native,' and (5) consciousness, identity, and writing" (57).

3. For more examples, see Johnston and Laxer (2003, 64–67); Brown and Yaffe (2013, 2014); Chazan (2016); Tabar (2017).

4. This five-year research project was funded by the Social Sciences and Humanities Research Council of Canada (SSHRC). We would like to thank SSHRC for its support, the activists of the WMW for their participation in the project, and the members of the research team, Janet Conway, Pascale Dufour, Elsa Beaulieu-Bastien, and Carmen Diaz for their comments on earlier versions of this chapter.

5. Participants whose interview material is cited here all chose to be identified by their name in the publications resulting from our research.

6. Rosa Rivero, regional Coordinator of the March MN. Interview conducted August 20, 2015.

7. See the webpage of The Goldman Environmental Prize—"Máxima Acuña, 2016 Goldman Prize Recipient South and Central America," http://www.goldmanprize.org/recipient/maxima-acuna/.

8. Mirta Villanueva, activist and former Coordinator of the March Cajamarca. Interview conducted August 8, 2015, in Cajamarca.

9. Aurora Portal, Coordinator of the March Cajamarca. Interview conducted August 7, 2015, in Cajamarca.

10. Women are affected by mining projects in a variety of other ways. See Jenkins (2014) for a comprehensive review.

11. Yuli Peralta, activist of the March MN. Interview conducted August 5, 2015, in Chiclayo.

12. *Compañeras* is the feminine form of *compañeros*, which means comrades or "companions in struggle."

13. Lourdes Contreras, activist of the March MN and Coordinator of CAFEM (*Circulos de Acción Feminista*). Interview conducted August 10, 2015, in Chiclayo.

14. Rosa Sara Huaman Rinze, female leader of the *rondas campesinas* (rural self-defense groups) of the community of Cañaris and self-identifying as member of the March MN. Interview conducted October 24, 2015, in Cajamarca.

15. Maria Tempora Pintado, activist of the March Tambogrande. Interview conducted October 24, 2015, in Cajamarca.

16. These power relations were not challenged in our interview with the Indigenous female leader of the community of Cañaris. That they were identified or not by the women of Cañaris remains an open question, knowing that voicing such critique may not have been considered desirable in a context where maintaining a good relationship with the March MN was considered important politically.

17. Thanks to Carmen Diaz for signaling this point to us.

18. De la Cadena (2010) and Gaztambide-Fernandez (2012), among others, offer normative proposals that could be helpful for the construction of new, decolonizing relationships of solidarity. At the same time, they are acutely aware of the difficulties involved.

4

Allowing Rural Difference to Make a Difference

The Brazilian Marcha das Margaridas

Renata Motta and Marco Antonio Teixeira

A number of different concepts have been used in social studies to denote processes of alliance building: coalitions, alliances, networks, cross-movements, solidarity. Although solidarity has been a key concern and praxis for social movements, the concept is not theorized and does not even take a central role within social movement studies. Rather, the terms coalition and alliance are often used interchangeably to describe strategies of solidarity-building among social movements (Van Dyke and McCammon 2010; Van Dyke and Amos 2017). Other common concepts, coming from political science, are advocacy networks and advocacy coalitions, while social movement coalitions are conceptualized as networks (Diani and Bison 2004). When emphasis is placed on bridging social movement sectors, in particular, between workers' movements and other social movements, the term "cross-movements" has been coined (Zajak et al. 2018). Finally, the category of solidarity is used generically to refer to alliance building among activists and organizations, but it has not yet been theorized further. We believe that this is because the field of social movement studies, in particular in its Anglo-Saxon dominant strand, has increasingly become concerned with analytical differentiation for quantitative purposes that often yield very descriptive results.[1] However, as pointed out in the introduction to this book, the under-theorization of the concept of solidarity hides the Euro-modernist political-normative projects and assumptions at play in this literature. Particularly problematic are universalist accounts of the political subject and the political community that are complicit with relations of domination and exclusion along racial lines. What inscribes a colonial legacy in conceptualizations of solidarity is the idea that difference can only be contemplated through assimilation, that is, its denial, and the attendant difficulty of dealing with issues of power, inequalities, difference, and alterity.

In contrast, within critical social theory and feminist scholarship, a normative theorization and analysis of solidarity prevails. Black feminists in the United States have coined the term intersectionality in order to highlight difference and inequalities within what had been perceived as a unified feminist movement. Building on that, postcolonial feminisms have challenged European-modernist universalist assumptions behind transnational categories of feminist solidarities, such as global sisterhood, while also criticizing attempts to reduce the colonial difference into simplified categories such as "Third World women." Intersectional and transnational feminisms build solidarities of difference, as described in the introduction to this book, by sharing a clear anti-racist and anti-colonial stance and centering the problem of difference. Concerned with the political problem of inequalities among women in different contexts, and how to build alliances across inequalities of class, race, citizenship, coloniality, sexuality, and/or other axes of difference and inequality, postcolonial feminism brings to the fore the broader normative and political question of solidarity-building in emancipatory struggles. However, as argued by Masson and Paulos (chapter 3) and Conway (2017a, 2018), the normative analytics of transnational feminism can also limit the analysis of practices of solidarity-building taking place in struggles not informed by the same histories and legacies.

We believe that this is not just a matter of the correct "fit" between normative theory and empirical research, an always-evolving praxis, or finding a middle ground for analysis. Such normativity within feminist theory approaches to solidarity must also be considered within the geopolitics of knowledge. In the English-language dominated field of feminist theories, as well as Black and postcolonial studies, a specific understanding of feminist intersectional analysis and of race is expected from anyone wanting to publish in English about women's movements and feminism. In our contribution, we develop the argument about the implications of both the geopolitics of knowledge and the coloniality of knowledge (Giraldo 2016; Mendoza 2015) in the analysis of solidarity. We argue for the need to theorize and analyze the specific categories of difference that emerge endogenously from processes of solidarity-building in actual struggles, rather than those established in the canonic intersectionality analysis.

U.S.-based Black and postcolonial feminists have discussed categories such as "women of color" and "Third World women" as political coalitional identities organized across axes of race, class, and citizenship in postcolonial settings of the British empire. In Latin American postcolonial societies, another difference gains salience in the struggles for rights and against discrimination: the rural/urban difference. The persistent condition of the coloniality of power in rural settings cannot be overstated in Latin America, where land concentration indexes surpass already high levels of social inequality, and are accompanied by violent conflicts over land and resources such as water. The reprimarization of the economy in the subcontinent in the past two decades was also marked by the disposability of racialized, ethnicized bodies, and of environmental and rural activists (Wade 2018). Rural contexts have witnessed the emergence of decolonial feminisms that do not conform to the prescriptions of mainstream feminist movements and pose challenges to analysis by feminist scholars.

The *Marcha das Margaridas* (Daisies' March, from now on, *Marcha*)[2] is one of the most impressive instances of women's organizing and praxis of feminist solidarity in rural contexts in twenty-first-century Latin America. First, it is impressive due to its size and mobilizing capacity, bringing between twenty thousand to one hundred thousand women from all of the twenty-seven Brazilian provinces—and very remote areas—to the national capital, Brasília. Second, and, related to that, the *Marcha*'s diversity is noticeable, as women situated in various specific rural contexts (with varying land property relations, types of food production, histories of struggles and specific conflict lines, dynamics of racialization, relations to the natural resources) come together. Women situated in different urban contexts also join the mobilization. Third, although rural working women make up the majority of the grassroots base, due to the organizational and political leadership of the rural trade union movement, the *Marcha* emerged through a politics of alliances with women's movements, feminist movements, urban trade unions, agrarian movements, and NGOs (Teixeira and Motta 2020). Finally, the *Marcha* is an interesting case to investigate processes of solidarity-building, thanks to its durability. With its first edition taking place in the year 2000, they have managed to establish a timetable of periodic mass actions, with six editions so far (2000, 2003, 2007, 2011, 2015, and 2019). The *Marcha das Margaridas* brought visibility to rural working women as political subjects. Over time, negotiations over the coalitional identity *Margaridas* (Motta, forthcoming) have resulted in the diversification of rurality and the political subject has progressively changed to include "women from the field, the forest, and the waters."

We examine the process of emergence and solidarity-building in the *Marcha das Margaridas* since 2000 by drawing on different types of data that are part of a broader research project. We combine documentary analysis of archival material produced by the *Marcha*, ethnographic fieldwork, and semi-structured interviews with activists that represent different social movements and NGOs in the coalition. Regarding archival sources, a myriad of documents are typically produced during their process of mobilization, which can be classified into two phases. A document for discussion is written by the national organizing committee and distributed among all organizations through a number of activities in preparation for the march, which is itself understood as a permanent process of mobilization and political training (*formação*). This process involves around one million rural women according to the organizers. After discussions at the local, regional, and national levels, the rapporteurs develop a text with demands. A two-month period of fieldwork was carried out during the fifth edition (Marco Antonio Teixeira) and sixth edition (both of us). Additionally, we conducted twenty-one formal interviews in Brasília, São Paulo, Rio de Janeiro, and Belo Horizonte with leaders of organizations and movements that are part of the coalition. We have attended other events of the *Marcha das Margaridas* and the National Confederation of Agricultural Workers (Contag), to which we have been invited over the past four years and where we noted down observations in a field diary. Although this chapter centers on the context of the emergence of the coalition, and we rely mostly on archival data, our analysis draws on the broad body of knowledge that we have been building together that helps us to understand how the coalition works and how it has developed over time.

The chapter proceeds as follows. We first discuss solidarity-building in postcolonial, intersectional feminist theories and build on Masson and Paulos's definition of solidarity (chapter 3), drawing on insights from critical geography to propose our own conceptualization of solidarity. Next, we analyze solidarity-building as a set of praxes bridging place-based struggles. Third, we make our case about rurality as a category of difference and solidarity-building in the *Marcha das Margaridas* as a praxis of recognizing socio-spatial inequalities within the rural difference. Rurality becomes the main intersection, also articulating generational, racial, and ethnic inequalities. Finally, we draw some conclusions about the key role of the rural difference in allowing for multiple rural identifications in order to expand solidarities.

BRINGING IN THE RURAL DIFFERENCE IN A FEMINIST POLITICS OF SOLIDARITY

The debate about the politics of solidarity is one of the main concerns of postcolonial feminist scholar Chandra Talpade Mohanty in her book *Feminism without Borders: Decolonizing Theory, Practicing Solidarity.* Mohanty's starting point is the critique of the assumption in much of Western feminist scholarship that women act together based on sisterhood, which assumes that a commonality of oppression makes women work together. Opposed to this view, she asserts: "I believe the unity of women is best understood not as given, on the basis of a natural/psychological commonality; it is something that has to be worked for, struggled toward—in history" (Mohanty 2003, 116). For that, she outlines a notion of feminist solidarity, which is not defined, but includes the following meanings: (1) ". . . mutuality, accountability, and the recognition of *common interests* as the basis for relationships among diverse communities"; (2) *"the practice of solidarity* foregrounds communities of people *who have chosen to work and fight together"*; (3) *diversity and difference* are central values "to be acknowledged and respected, not erased in the building of alliances"; (4) it is *an achievement, "the result* of active struggle to construct the universal on the basis of particulars/differences" (Mohanty 2003, 7, emphasis added). We can summarize Mohanty's concept of solidarity as a praxis based on common interests, while recognizing internal differences as well as an achievement through political struggle.

Two concepts are central in Mohanty's discussion: common contexts of struggle and common interests. She asks: "How do we conceptualize the question of 'common interests' based in a 'common context of struggle,' so that women are agents who make choices and decisions that lead to the transformation of consciousness and of their daily lives as workers?" (Mohanty 2003, 161). Criticizing Western feminism's understanding of Third World women as an identifiable group on the basis of shared dependencies, Mohanty argues that it is "the common context of political struggle against class, race, gender, and imperialist hierarchies that may constitute Third World women as a strategic group at this historical juncture" (Mohanty 2003, 24–25). In another quote, Mohanty says: "Thus it is the common context of struggles against specific exploitative structures and systems that determines our potential political alliances" (Mohanty 2003, 49). She argues against generalizations, but for historic and context-specific analysis of the effects of racial, class, gender domination. Relations of rule are not binary oppositions, but complex intersections. Feminist struggles are thus positioned at such intersections of relations of ruling (for which she borrowed Dorothy Smith's term). She claims that "it is also by understanding these intersections that we can attempt to explore questions of consciousness and agency without naturalizing either individuals or structures" (Mohanty 2003, 56). Women are thus not victims that unite on the basis of oppression, but agents with common interests who build their solidarity in their practices of struggle.[3]

> I argue for a notion of political solidarity and common interests, defined as a community or collectivity among *women workers* across class, race, and national boundaries that is based on *shared material interests* and *identity* and *common ways of reading the world.* This idea of political solidarity in the context of the incorporation of Third World women into a global economy offers a basis for cross-cultural comparison and analysis that is grounded in history

and social location rather than in an ahistorical notion of culture or experience. (Mohanty 2003, 144–45, emphasis added)

Here further analytical elements enter her definition of solidarity: a political subject of "women workers" with shared material interests, identity, and common interpretations. However, she does not deepen this analysis. Throughout the book, though, Mohanty chooses to use the category "Third World women" more than women workers, but she does not assume any a priori political subject: it is a potential for collaborations across boundaries.[4] She explains that there is no biological or cultural bases for alliances, no inherent characteristics, no homogeneous formation, and also no clear-cut oppositional identity (such as the sexual difference, the third-world difference), but this political subject results from political action, that is, the construction of links between political struggles. The social category is a result of an engagement with feminisms. The focus is less on the actors but more on the common context for their political engagements: "What seems to constitute 'women of color' or 'Third World women' as a viable oppositional alliance is a common context of struggle, rather than color or racial identifications" (Mohanty 2003, 49).

Mohanty's postcolonial feminist theory of alliances thus offers a critique of a focus on questions of identity that are treated without considering the everyday experiences of socioeconomic and political exclusion.[5] Analytically, this means first and foremost looking for the intersections of relations of rulings in which the political process of actively constructing interrelationships and alliances between political struggles takes place. The joint definition of a coalitional identity expresses discursively the social praxis of building solidarity among differently situated feminists. However, a conceptualization of solidarity as a potential, as a political project that must be constructed by linking struggles, has clear analytical shortcomings.[6] It offers the analyst a strong normative lens, in the search for potential contexts of struggles, but does not help describe how, or explain why and when such potentiality actually unfolds into solidarity. Social movement theory has long argued that structural deprivation provides no explanatory shorthand for actual mobilization; that instead depends on organizational basis, social ties, and networks, common interpretations that identify causes, ascribe responsibilities, and suggest solutions, and leaderships and brokers, as much as opportunities. In other words, there is a long way between common deprivation and solidarity resulting from political work.

We thus find it useful also to incorporate, as suggested by Masson and Paulos (chapter 3), the distinction between solidarity, as a political construction, and the praxis and process that generates it, solidarity-building. Drawing on insights from critical geography, they conceptualize it as an organizational praxis of "the active linking together of hitherto geographically and/or socially distant and disparate place-based struggles through the construction of connections between actors, places, and mobilizations" (chapter 3, 61–62). This means that solidarity does not involve only bridging social differences, but also places, organizations, and struggles. Masson and Paulos specify how three interrelated types of praxis create solidarity: discursive, material, and spatial practices. They further conceptualize the dynamic nature of solidarity, both as a process that evolves over time and as generative of transformations, new connections, and new political subjects. Finally, they caution against not romanticizing solidarity-building, as it is embedded in organizational strategies and goals, and permeated by relations of power.

However, we believe that the problematic is more than a "fit" (Conway 2017a) between normative analytics of transnational feminism and its praxis, and that the solution lies in an appropriate theorizing at the intermediate level (chapter 3). We would like to contribute to this debate by following Giraldo's (2016) provocation about the geopolitics of knowledge and coloniality of knowledge and the need to theorize and generate concepts from practices of solidarity-building taking place in struggles not informed by the histories and legacies that became dominant in English academia and postcolonial feminist thinking. Even though categories such as women of color do not travel so well (Alvarez et al. 2014) to contexts in which racialization has other histories and dynamics than in contemporary United States and former colonies of the British empire, they have provided important impulse for feminist struggles and theorizing elsewhere. Similarly, intersectionality features a strong normative call to retain its initial concern for the specific situation of Black (poor) women in the United States, but inspires many struggles in which the intersections of race, gender, and class have different trajectories. The problem arises when these situated understandings of transnational and intersectional feminisms are expected to guide any analysis of feminist solidarity. With that in mind, we want to suggest rurality as a category of difference that has emerged in solidarity-building in Latin American decolonial struggles.

> [The] . . . relentless wars waged against peasant and indigenous communities by current nation-states, imply that needs and issues differ considerably between rural and urban populations. While a neoliberal gender equality rationale has permeated urban areas, strands of feminism in a decolonial vein have proliferated in rural ones. (Giraldo 2016, 162)

Since the 1980s, there has been a rise of women's organizing within rural and Indigenous movements fighting for land (Deere and León 2001; Aguiar 2015, 2016). Rural and Indigenous women increasingly understand themselves as feminists and challenge the Western, white, middle-class conceptualization of feminism, proposing instead their own framings of feminism. For many activists not identified with historically dominant concepts of feminism, a consequence of such a distance has been a skepticism of theory, in favor of activism (Giraldo 2016). At the same time, feminist theories have had troubles in making sense of Latin American feminisms' drawing on figures such as mother Earth and what appear as essentialized relations between women and nature and motherhood (Rocheleau and Nirmal 2015). We would like to propose a way of learning from concrete struggles in Latin America to contribute to an open-ended, feminist theorizing of solidarity, suggesting rurality as a category of colonial difference.

Ruralities as a locus of enunciation challenges the urban bias of social theory (McMichael 2008) in which the rural poor were deemed to disappear, according to modernist theories of both liberal and Marxist tendencies. The rural difference is characterized by a coloniality of power, which stands in opposition to traditional accounts of modernity and citizenship. Citizenship rights are associated with urbanization and industrializations (Sauer 2010). But rurality is just as well a part of modernity, in the ambivalence of modern forms of plantation as the dominant model of food production that was installed in the colonies, with the domination of nature by monocropping, and the exploitation of work, based on enslaved work and the racialization of others (Tsing 2012). However, critical agrarian studies, which have concentrated analysis on struggles surrounding agrarian change, often reproduce the blindness of class analysis. The contribution of a decolonial feminist critique would then include the intersection between the coloniality of nature in commodity extraction, the coloniality of power in the racialization of Others, and the coloniality of gender. It would further combine the feminist critique of the binary logics of modernity and development, the narrative of linear progress contraposing tradition-modernity, rural-urban, agrarian-industrial, and the belief that interventions would improve the lives of rural subjects, whether through modernizing agriculture or expelling them to the urban factories (Chowdhury 2015). The binary logic thus is socially and spatially inscribed; rurality becomes a social-spatial inequality, a category of difference. This categorization contributes to making sense of the war on racialized and ethnicized bodies of environmental and rural activists and movements (Wade 2018).

Taking such considerations into account, we understand that solidarities do not automatically result from a common context of struggle nor from a structural analytical perspective, but from the political work of actively constructing common diagnostics of such contexts, and from the joint definition of a coalitional identity. Thus, we welcome Masson and Paulos's definition of solidarity-building as a dynamic organizational praxis that includes material, discursive, and spatial practices (chapter 3). We want to contribute by including social-spatial differences related to the coloniality of power in Latin

America—and other possible regions of commodity extraction, not reduced solely to the Global South—as further complicating the intersectionality in categories of difference. In what follows, we take a closer look at how solidarity-building can link different contexts, that is, place-based struggles, related to geographies and biomes. Then, we analyze how rurality is diversi-fied in the political subject and intersects with other categories of difference like generation, race, and ethnicity in *Marcha das Margaridas*. We do these two analyses to distinguish analytically between solidarity-building as con-nections across socio-spatialities and rurality as a category of difference, which the politics of solidarity must recognize.

PLACE-BASED STRUGGLES

Recognizing specific sites in which rural working women struggle is an important dimension of the solidarity-building process within the *Marcha*, which enables the bringing together of women from all over the country. In the documents of the *Marcha*, they state that one of the mobilization's aims is to improve their agenda by taking into account the diversity of their contexts: "Update and qualify our agenda of demands, taking into account the regional, political, economic, social, cultural, environmental and organizational diversities where we are based" (Contag 2003, 4). This process involves both material and spatial practices. Material practices are those involved in organizing and mobilizing for action, ". . . providing very concrete expressions of support and material forms of labor that contribute to the bringing together of actors and of struggles" (chapter 3, 62). Women leaders of Contag draw on many types of resources related to the organiza-tional structures of the rural unions, which gives them the capacity to act as brokers in the mobilization for the *Marcha* (Teixeira and Motta 2020). Their practice of solidarity-building is facilitated by (1) the political experience of unionized women in making alliances within the union movement itself, (2) the extensive experience of the rural trade union movement in articulating their positions alongside other social movements, a skill developed through-out the organization's history since the 1960s, (3) the political reach of the trade union movement across the country, and (4) the human and material resources of the movement itself.

The *Marcha* involves a continuous, less-visible, political work that does not begin or end during the two days of street mobilization. Officially, the *Marcha* is publicized more than a year in advance, in conjunction with actions related to International Women's Day. The organization process involves several internal meetings with Contag's board and women's representatives from state federations of rural workers. Then, they invite the partners for a number of organizational meetings. Another important step is the mobilization of women throughout the country. The organizing committee has the goal to discuss the *Marcha's* agenda with rural women to broaden and facilitate debate among a wider audience beyond those who manage to go to the street mobilization in Brasília. This is also a strategy of political training. Finally, during the march itself, the *Marcha* is a place for socializing, interaction, exchange of experiences and knowledge, creating bonds, and political articulation involving women from all states in the country—which means that it brings together women from different social, political, and economic backgrounds. Being part of the *Marcha* as it occurs has an important meaning for the participants. It is the materialization of a long process of work, when they create solidarity-building in a face-to-face setting.

Spatial practices relate to the construction of solidarity between different sites and scales, including alliances between place-based struggles and their connection to networks at other scales (chapter 3). While the literature focuses on translocal and transnational scales, the *Marcha* is the strongest at a national scale, when its strength is shown in the numbers of women from all over Brazil marching together. The *Marcha* brings many place-based struggles under a national umbrella, different regional realities, and specific conflicts that take place at distant locations, far from the view of the urban sites and locus of political power. It is difficult to separate some material practices from spatial practices, such as activities of political training taking place in various regions, in which women are invited to elaborate and discuss a diagnosis of their context of struggles, and their list of demands to be incorporated in the political agenda of the *Marcha*. They also discuss the documents of the *Marcha*, assessing them according to their contexts of struggle.

Brazil is a continental country and it can be divided in many different ways. The most common social-spatial classifications found in the practices of the *Marcha das Margaridas* are political administrative regions, biomes, and specific subregions. The documents of 2003 refer to regions, biomes, and subregions: The South and Southeast, the Semi-arid, Cerrados, Pantanal, Amazon, Carajás. These socio-spatial contexts inform the specific meanings and struggles of rural working women, as shown in the following quotes: "In the northeastern semi-arid region, women's living and working conditions are even worse. Faced with precarious and difficult conditions, women workers play an essential role in the mechanism of living with and addressing drought" (Contag 2000, 12–13). Because of the sexual division of labor according to which women are responsible for fetching water, the list of demands includes: "Guarantee the construction of . . . artesian posts in the rural communities of the semi-arid Northeast as one of the mechanisms to address and live with drought" (Contag 2000, 22).

Mentions of the socio-spatial context appear mostly linked to the environmental theme within the *Marcha*, mainly during the 2003 march. The

socio-spatial dimension stands out in the 2003 documents as a way of referring to specific environmental conflicts and problems, which is a way to
express solidarity and to position place-based struggles under the overarching collective struggle of the *Marcha das Margaridas* and the mobilization
of rural working women. The debate on water is central, as this is important
for domestic consumption as well as for agricultural activities. Concern for
water is generally a task socially assigned to women. Moreover, access to
water varies among regions and biomes. In 2003, references to place-based
struggles appear in themes such as soil, water degradation, and pollution,
conflicts arising from the energy model and hydropower plants in Pará, Mato
Grosso, and in the south region of Brazil, and conflicts around the agroextrac-
tive activities in the Amazon.

In 2007, access to water remained central to a specific region, the semi-
arid, while also reflecting a wider concern of all regions: "The women rural
workers have been actively participating in the strategies of coexistence with
the semi-arid region and of actions that protect and defend the quality of
water for all in the diverse regions of the country" (Contag 2007a, 12). The
issue of water remains in 2011: "The concentration of water mainly affects
rural areas. Most of the time, women are responsible for the water supply in
the family units of production, mainly in the Northeast region, where they
need to travel long distances to have access to water" (Contag 2011a, 21).
Accordingly, water is on the agenda of demands: "Ensure that the assistance
to families in the northeast region, during periods of drought, through the
Programa de Operação Pipa, is carried out after prior analysis of the water
quality and monitoring of the beneficiaries" (Contag 2011b, 11). In 2015,
water appears in the title of the second axis of demands: "Land, Water and
Agroecology."

> We know that each biome has its own challenges and demands. For example,
> in the Amazon, there is enough available water to wash clothes, but there is no
> drinking water, because many municipalities do not have sanitation, leaving the
> rivers that surround them completely contaminated. The Southeast is impacted
> by mining, leaving entire communities homeless because, overnight, they dis-
> cover that they no longer have the land they owned, and the subsoil does not
> belong to them. The families who resist are harmed by the contamination left
> by mining, both in the soil and in the water. We need to raise awareness of this
> debate in each region, based on the local experience, considering the issue of
> quality, consumption and excessive use of water. (Contag 2015, 30)

Most interesting is the goal to further elaborate their political demands
according to the diversity of situations experienced by rural working women.
Different environments and biomes create specific working possibilities and

restraints, entail specific types of resources for production, and thus concrete demands. These are place-based struggles. Therefore, starting from common-alities in the intersection between class, gender, and rural space, the *Marcha* understands that it is politically desirable to further specify the contexts of struggles and what it means to be a rural working woman in different places. In this way, the *Marcha* is not to be understood as a static alliance, but as a process of solidarity-building to build collective power in making demands of the state and of organized civil society.

Socio-spatial differences are not only expressed at the discursive level of documents. Respect for the specificities that play an important role in the construction of solidarity is also expressed in the way in which the *Marcha*'s street action takes place. Participants march in separate regional delegations, each carrying banners with the central points of the political platform of the Margaridas as they are related to their socio-spatial context. In 2019, the women of the North, for example, marched with banners: (1) for the protection and conservation of sociobiodiversity and access to common goods and (2) for the self-determination of peoples, regarding food and energy sovereignty.

THE RURAL DIFFERENCE IN THE POLITICAL SUBJECT: FROM RURAL WORKING WOMEN TO WOMEN FROM THE FIELD, THE FOREST, AND WATERS

Drawing on Chantal Mouffe, Aguiar (2015) argues that it is through political praxis that various social movements and civil society organizations that support the *Marcha das Margaridas* are able to articulate, in common collective actions and in a joint discursive platform, a provisional and contingent "we."

> The links established between the various organizations and movements, how-ever, do not make the Marcha a unified or homogeneous entity, but imply a certain form of unity and common action, established from precarious forms of identification around the category "woman from the land, the forest and the waters," from which a discourse is created that is capable of articulating several demands of the different organizations and movements that compose it, constituting what Mouffe (1999) would say was the nodal point that allows the construction of a symbolic unification, of a relation of equivalence, of a "we," capable of giving a unity to the movement, although in a partial and contingent way. Such discourse is not a mere sum of words, but it is the result of concrete articulations that unite words and actions, and produce meanings. (Aguiar 2016, 285)

In line with the arguments of Aguiar (2015), we identified in our documentary analysis three main axes of difference intersecting in the formation of the political subject of the *Marcha*: gender, class, and rurality. While there are strong class differentials between the women from the *Marcha*, as within the rural trade union system, ranging from wage workers and small to medium family farmers, this is not central to their identification process as part of the coalition. Rurality becomes a social position of difference that does matter, which must be acknowledged to strengthen solidarities and political engagements. In a long political process, in which the political identity of "rural working women" becomes permeable to negotiation, a contextual analysis of what being a (working, rural) woman means is necessary. The way that women from the *Marcha* express their identification with the rural space has changed over time.

The text from 2000 presents the *Marcha* as a mobilization of rural working women, in alliance with the World March of Women and many partner entities. Throughout the text, "women" (*mulheres*) or "rural working women" (*trabalhadoras rurais*) are the main words used to refer to the political subject marching and demanding rights. The politics of language is important: the document always refers to the male and female forms of workers and farmers. The "women" identity is articulated with the class identity of the worker and the spatial difference of rurality: "The MARCHA DAS MARGARIDAS is a mobilization of twenty thousand rural working women . . ." (Contag 2000, 1). In their list of demands: "We, Rural Working Women from all Brazil, understand that the lack of access to land, to natural and productive resources for promoting agrarian and non-agrarian activities, to labour and pension rights, and to social services is a limitation to rural development" (Contag 2000, 18). Rural working women are specified as encompassing women farmers, fisherwomen, women in extractive activities (*extrativistas*), as well as rubber tapper women, and palm and women *babacu* coconut breakers. The *Marcha* highlights different worker identities that arise as socio-nature companions, according to material practices relating to their environment: farming, fishing, extracting (products from the forest, such as nuts and rubber), breaking specific types of nuts. Thus, already in the year 2000, it was clear that the identification with rurality means different working relationships between women and their environments that are spoken out in the political discourse of the *Marcha*. Such working identities are often understood as "subsistence" activities in the framework of economic development, and thus not recognized as an "economy" (Shiva and Mies 1993). These women thus fight to be recognized as working women who have labor rights.

In the 2003 documents, the main reference to the political subject remains "rural working women." In 2007, it coexists with a new identification, "women from the field and the forest": "The MARCHA DAS

MARGARIDAS is a strategic action of rural working women to guarantee and broaden the achievements of the women from the field and the forest" (Contag 2007b, 1). This new expression appears more often in debates on health (Contag 2007b, 15–16), environment (Contag 2007b, 6), food security and sovereignty (Contag 2007b, 9), and education (Contag 2007b, 16). In 2011, the key role of rural working women in the *Marcha* is reaffirmed, and their diversity as "women from the field and the forest," while other political identities are called upon to join in solidarity. Urban working women are situated in an unambiguous class solidarity, while feminists are clearly defined as partners, not as the political subject of the struggle.

> It is with great satisfaction that I present this document to you, comrades, working women from the field and the forest, working women from the cities that share with us the ideals of justice, autonomy, equality and freedom, and to you, partners, feminist activists who have been building with us this trajectory of learning, struggles and achievements. (Contag 2011a, 5)

In 2015, the category has expanded to "women from the field, the forest and the waters." Water here refers to communities living near riversides, coasts, and mangroves, who often depend on fishing and gathering of animals, such as crawfish. These include many Indigenous communities and others identified as "ribeirinhas" fisher villages. "We look at the slogan of the *Marcha das Margaridas* from the rural environment, which is where the women from the field, the forest and the waters live and work" (Contag 2015, 9). It is also in the agenda of 2015 that a feminist politics of difference takes form in a most innovative way: not only divided in themes/axes (i.e., health, education, violence) but also by regions and by categories/identities. The section "Margaridas voices from all regions" lists demands from women from the Amazon, Pantanal, Northeast, Southeast, and South. "Margaridas voices of all ages" lists youth and elderly women. Next come the categories of employed rural women, women from the forest, from the waters, quilombolas, and Indigenous. Up until 2015, the *Marcha* documents often referred to racial, ethnic, and generational inequalities that affected women differently in the rural space, but did so in a broad and generic way that did not translate into a systematic treatment of differences and their politicization, as shown in the following example: "Inequalities based on sex, age, race and ethnicity confirm that the countryside hides a form of deep inequality through the relationship between women and men, and a rather oppressive patriarchal structure" (Contag 2003, 8).

The generational difference has been more debated than ethnic and racial inequalities. Initially addressed in 2000, 2003, and 2007, it progressively gained prominence (in 2011 and 2015). The youth received more attention than the elderly, as they continued to see less of a future as rural working women.[7] Indigenous women only appeared as generic references up until 2015. In regard to race, instead of the "Black woman" identity, the *Marcha* documents refer to the ethno-racial category "quilombolas," who are residents of rural Black communities formed by descendants of enslaved Africans. In 2015, a list of proposals of quilombola women addressed themes such as the following: land regularization, education, health, culture, work, access to public policies to support production, and agroecology. Drawing on Aguiar (2015), we consider that the strengthening of the quilombolas' agenda since 2015 seems to reflect an increased articulation with quilombola movements at the local level, which is reflected in the final documents. But there is also a clear politics of solidarity-building at work here, which becomes clear in the words of the Coordinator of the 2015 *Marcha*.

> . . . We have made a twist in the structure of the agenda to list it by segments, . . . to show that rural women are several perspectives and that it is not enough to say, "ah, rural women, politics is the same for everyone." No, the demand of the forest is one, the demand of women in the Northeast is another, the demand of women wage earners is another, and demand of quilombolas is another. So to do this classification by social groups too. They are all women, but there are different demands. So giving that voice, even by the organizations, was very well received. . . . Because so the women take it up, the women from the waters came, they never came with such a strength as they came this time and what did we do? We went there to build, the women of the waters and the tides (*marés*) through Confrem[8]—"this is our agenda," it is in its entirety, right, in the agenda of the *Marcha*. The one from indigenous women we had never been able to add and we brought it just as they presented.[9]

The quote makes clear how the feminist politics of difference at play in the *Marcha* takes the highest priority, especially when considering intersecting ruralities. The attention to the rural difference between various ruralities is key in their solidarity-building. The reason they have been changing how they name themselves is to have a more inclusive term that allows more women, with different identities, to recognize themselves in the coalition. It means that if there are commonalities in how they perceive their context of struggles shaped mostly by gender, class, and rurality, which somehow allows women to join in a coalition, their political work of solidarity-building also needs to recognize difference within rural working women, so that all different segments see themselves represented in the political agenda. More than different places, the rural difference relates to a worker identity and specific human-environmental relations involved. A politics of location, which is not place-based, but socio-material, takes into account the diversity of rural situations in which women work and live, and informs a feminist politics of difference in the *Marcha* subject's formation. The rural difference becomes a central axis that intersects with class and gender. The diversity within rurality informs, in its analysis of their context of struggle and their demands for rights, what work means precisely in each context. Recognizing this diversity means inquiring into what natural resources are important for production, how these are distributed, how work is divided and recognized. Allowing the rural difference to make a difference means posing the question of what it means to be a rural working woman in different relations to environments, such as farming the land, fishing from the rivers and coastal areas, extracting nuts from which type of tree and which forests, where different types of threats and problems in access exist.

In 2019, a section in the *Caderno de Textos* is entitled: "Who Are the Margaridas?" The answer given is: "They are the working women from the field, the forest and waters, who, marching, weave their common experiences of life and struggle" (Contag 2019, 5). It is clear that the political protagonist role belongs to these categories of women, although not as given social groups, but rather as those that engage in the coalition's work. The text also explains that the political subject of the march has been evolving over time, starting with women from the field, expanding to include women from the forest in 2007, and women from the waters in 2015.

[T]o affirm the diversity of rural women, as family women farmers, peasant women, landless women, camped women, "settled" women [(acampadas) inhabitants of land reform settlements], women wage laborers, artisan women, women in extractive activities, women coconut breakers, rubber tapper women, fisherwomen, river women (ribeirinhas), quilombolas, indigenous and many other identities built in the country. (Contag 2019, 5, emphasis added)

In defining the political subject, diversity relates, above all, to the human-environmental relations in their working experience, involving both material relations and symbolic identification in subject formation. Racial and ethnic differences are incorporated. However, they do not decenter each of these other categories. Instead, they are expressed in specific relations to their lands: Indigenous women and quilombola women. The diversity of rurality challenges the identification of rurality with agrarian activities, showing how rural working women also work in the fields, but do more than that. They gather and extract food and materials from the forests and waters, they fish, they do handcrafts, they engage in wage work, they fight for land. Many rural working women also identify themselves ethnically as quilombolas and Indigenous.

CONCLUSION

Solidarity-building in the *Marcha das Margaridas*, as analyzed here, has been an ongoing, dynamic process over the past two decades. Informed by feminist theorizing on both normative and practical dimensions of solidarity, we searched for how the *Marcha* recognized differences within the political subject as well as for their practices of solidarity, as they sought to create links between different contexts of struggle. Drawing on our fieldwork, our interviews, and on a documentary analysis of the archives from the *Marcha*, we looked for how differences within the political subject, namely, rural working women, were acknowledged and reflected in its political agenda during the two decades since its emergence in the year 2000. Through the process of women's organizing within trade unions that culminated in the *Marcha*, the affirmation of "women" as an identity was at first necessary in a context in which discrimination occurred on the basis of sexism. But such gendered identity had already been articulated through class identity, and the struggle was recognized as that of women workers, more precisely, as rural working women. More than just affirming essential identities, the building of a political subject has been informed by a contextual analysis of what being a (working, rural) woman meant.

As we have showed, rurality was the main intersection in which the discourse of the *Marcha* identified similar relationships of exploitation and struggles that boosted the solidarity within the *Marcha*. To consider how these different social-spatial contexts are differently felt by women in diverse Brazilian ruralities has had a core importance in bringing women together for the biggest march of rural women in Latin America. The diversity within the rural condition involved not only the specificities of place-based struggles but also the broader political identifications which women working in nonurban settings feel. The rural difference is thus both a diversity within rural contexts and a relational category of Otherness to the dominant urban identifications of political subjects of struggles and rights. In this sense, the rural difference is an expression of decolonial difference that decenters the whiteness and urban predicaments of European-modernist conceptions of solidarity. It can be better situated within pluriversal solidarities, as conceptualized in the introduction to this book. Therefore, the political subject "women from the field, the forest and the waters" is not seen as a description of concrete places and struggles, that is, not geographical locations. Rather, we understand it as the political subject of a coalitional identity, that of Margaridas, resulting from solidarity-building. The diversity informs the coexistence of many worlds within the rural difference. While work (class), gender, and ruralities are the main intersections that build their common context of struggle, ethnicity, race, and generation are other axes that appear in the narrative, but have not structured their discourse until recently. However, and particularly since 2015, racial, ethnic, and generational categories were reflected in the agenda of demands. Still, the articulations of gender, class, racial, ethnic, and generational differences are played out in specific ways when intersected with rural differences. Thus, we argue that the Margaridas are actively constructing their political subject in an ongoing political work of building solidarity. This is a precondition of the success of their politics of alliance as well as its achievement.

In short, we identified rurality in our research as a central category of intersectionality, which has played an important role in solidarity-building in the *Marcha*. It was only possible because our analysis was open to let categories emerge from the texts, and account for their relative salience. It means that we combined deductive and inductive approaches to the categories of difference. Considering that the genealogy of intersectionality is related to the struggles of Black women in the United States, and acknowledging that racism is a persistent condition in Brazil, our analysis searched for the consideration of the racial difference in the discourse of the *Marcha*. Also, taking stock of postcolonial feminist theorizing and the Latin American contributions on the coloniality of power and the Indigenous struggles for land in Brazil, we were concerned about the presence or absence of the category of indigeneity. We also encountered generation as an important axis of difference, as women in the countryside of Brazil are confronted in their youth with fewer future prospects and, in old age, with more vulnerability to poverty.

The strength of transnational agrarian movements (Borras, Edelman, and Kay 2008) has challenged observers and scholars to rethink the urban epistemology of social theory and consider movements of the rural poor as political subjects that, more than just being a return from the past, are strong political actors capable of shaping democratic futures (McMichael 1997, 2008). The resistance of the *Marcha das Margaridas* combines a historical resistance with a new, forward-looking struggle to redefine rurality as a context for citizenship and rights. The mass mobilization of variously situated rural working women in Brazil challenges critical agrarian studies to incorporate a feminist perspective. In addition to questioning the urban-rural bias of social theory and politics, it contributes with a feminist epistemological stance that argues knowledge is better constructed by establishing networks of solidarity between differently situated positions. We have tried to learn with and from the rural feminists of the *Marcha das Margaridas* to understand the rural difference as an intersection of gender, racial, ethnic, class, and socio-spatial inequalities. This rural difference intersects many axes of Otherness in relation to the abstract subject of modernity. It is characterized by a coloniality of power, a coloniality of knowledge, and a coloniality of gender, as nonurban subjects are deemed to disappear, are disposable bodies, and are suffering a war on bodies in zones of agrarian and commodity frontiers.

Coming from such a marginal position, the struggles of these rural feminists are envisioning new connections across the urban-rural difference. Far from an established category in feminist analytics and politics of difference, rurality might be more than an endogenous category from our case study. It could inform other struggles in the subcontinent and elsewhere, in particular in a global context of increasing violence and conflicts in areas of commodities extraction, such as in mining regions and agrarian frontiers. Rurality is a social location that articulates diversity within Otherness to the urban subject that underlies social theory, public policies, and also often feminist struggles. The rural difference is a different standpoint, a different social positioning, which does not appear in canonic intersectional analysis. Just as racial inequalities and north-south inequalities are central for the construction of the coalitional identities "women of color" and "Third World women," the urban-rural difference is the central axis of inequalities for "women from the field, the forest and the waters." Those coalitional identities that became taken for granted in intersectional and transnational feminist theorizing do not always travel so well. Feminist theorizing thus must be always open to see its own exclusions and learn from the margins. A feminist analytics and politics of difference, thus, will be more open for inclusion when it ideally combines a normative and analytical understanding of solidarity, for which questions concerning exclusions and inequalities must be always stated, in addition to a praxis of connecting different contexts of struggles and recognizing differences within a feminist political subject.

Our chapter contributes to the conceptual debates of this book by identifying the tensions in the normative horizon and praxis of the *Marcha* between the three modalities of solidarity as identified by Conway, Masson, Habrih, and Dufour (introduction): counter-hegemonic, intersectional, and pluriversal. Following documented praxis of twenty years of solidarity-building, we describe the process in which emancipatory solidarities that are quintessential to union movements are under continuous redefinition through the engagement with cross-borders and intersectional feminist praxis. The *Marcha* is, in a similar vein as the WMW, a contemporary expression of popular feminism situated within the global left and thus of counter-hegemonic solidarities. It engages in a critique of global agrarian capitalism from particular rural contexts and localized struggles. The *Marcha* embraces difference in an open-ended construction of a decolonial political subject that accounts for differential consciousness, allowing many worlds to coexist within the identity Margaridas: women from the field, the forest, and the waters. In this sense, solidarity-building is translocal and crosses not only geographical borders of localized struggles but also across difference. This pluriversal solidarity emerges from an engagement with intersectional feminist solidarities, in which the rural difference becomes a key category of inequality that articulates racial and ethnic differences within rural working women. The *Marcha*'s intersectional feminism, while not centered on race as a main category of inequality, nevertheless articulates racialized rural women through their political struggles for land and resistance in quilombola communities.

NOTES

1. A telling example is the work from Diani and Bison (2004), which differentiated coalitions from social movement networks in that the latter also include collective identity and a conflictual element. The main distinction is between movement, coalitional, and organizational processes, as in "coalitional processes, where alliances to achieve specific goals are not backed by significant identity links, and organizational processes, where collective action takes place mostly in reference to specific organizations rather than broader, looser networks" (281). They "measure" collective identity of a coalition when there is sharing of members and participation in joint events. If organizations participated in three events together, one could deduce a social movement identity. But such a quantitative study has clear limitations in measuring what it purports to measure, namely, solidarity ties and identity.

2. The translation does not refer to the flower daisy, but the given name Daisy. The *Marcha das Margaridas* was named as a tribute to Margarida Maria Alves, a union leader from Paraíba, a state in the northeast of Brazil. Margarida was murdered in 1983 because of her fight for rural labor rights.

3. Mohanty sometimes uses the term "common differences" as the basis for deeper solidarity across differences and unequal power relations, but the term is not further conceptualized.

4. It is important to mention that in the third part of the book "'Under Western Eyes' Revisited: Feminist Solidarity through Anticapitalist Struggles," written in 2002, Mohanty prefers to adopt the term One-Third/Two-Thirds instead of Third World women. "Rather than Western/Third World, or North/South, or local/global seen as oppositional and incommensurate categories, the One-Third/Two-Thirds differentiation allows for teaching and learning about points of connection and distance among and between communities of women marginalized and privileged along numerous local and global dimensions" (Mohanty 2003, 243).

5. "Above all, gender and race are relational terms: they foreground a relationship (and often a hierarchy) between races and genders. To define feminism purely in gendered terms assumes that our consciousness of being 'women' has nothing to do with race, class, nation, or sexuality, just with gender. But no one 'becomes a woman' (in Simone de Beauvoir's sense) purely because she is female. Ideologies of womanhood have as much to do with class and race as they have to do with sex" (Mohanty 2003, 55).

6. We agree with Masson and Paulos's critique on the need to acknowledge the normative underpinnings of the political projects advocated by Mohanty as well as with their decision not to throw the baby out with the bathwater (chapter 3). In other words, it is important to retain the normative dimension of solidarity as the need to always take into account inequalities of power among the political subjects of feminism, correcting the blindness of Western middle-class white feminism to the relations of domination associated with coloniality, modernity.

7. "With no expectation of a better future, and being forced to help in the family income, many young women leave their homes to work in neighboring cities as maids, waitresses, and mining, etc. Most of these girls start living in areas of prostitution and misdemeanor" (Contag 2000, 16).

8. National Commission to Strengthen Extractive Reserves and Coastal and Maritime Traditional Peoples (Comissão Nacional de Fortalecimento das Reservas Extrativistas e Povos Tradicionais Extrativistas Costeiros e Marinhos).

9. Interview with Coordination of the *Marcha das Margaridas* 2015, given to Marco Antonio dos Santos Teixeira on October 25, 2015.

5

The Cosmopolitical Challenge of Building Border-Crossing Feminist Solidarities

Johanna Leinius

THE POLITICS OF FEMINIST SOLIDARITY IN BORDER-CROSSING ACTIVISM

Research on transnational feminist activism has discussed how activists negotiate the complex relationship between difference and commonality in order to build and sustain coalitions across borders (Grewal and Kaplan 1994; Mohanty 2003; Conway 2012). Solidarity as a "praxis of making linkages and sustaining relations" (Masson and Paulos 2018, 3) between "communities of people who have chosen to work and fight together" (Mohanty 2003, 7) has been identified as an integral part of emancipatory coalitional efforts. In these debates, solidarity has been understood to function "in terms of mutuality, accountability, and the recognition of common interests as the basis for relationships among diverse communities" (Mohanty 2003, 7). The crossing of borders—not just national and state borders but also the numerous other ways that activists negotiate difference in their daily practices, normative outlooks, and strategic orientations—continues to shape solidarity practices. Tracing the role of difference in linking diverse struggles can help to assess not only the potential but also the hierarchies, contradictions, and ambivalences of border-crossing organizing and solidarity practices between women. From Audre Lorde, who sees difference as a "fund of necessary polarities between which our creativity can spark like a dialectic" (Lorde 1984, 113), to Chandra Talpede Mohanty's "common differences" (2002, 503), or Chela Sandoval's method of "oppositional consciousness" (2000), feminists theorizing cross-border engagements from a postcolonial and transnational perspective generally see difference as a resource and not an obstacle to be overcome. But what kind of difference can be engaged? How do different kinds of difference emerge and interact in border-crossing activism? And how do they shape practices of solidarity?

As Pascale Dufour and her colleagues have argued, in transnational activism, the shape and scope of solidarity practices depend on the "decisions made, strategies formulated, and specific mechanisms established within [the] respective organizations, movements, or networks" (Dufour, Masson, and Caouette 2010, 4). Following their insight, I approach border-crossing solidarity as a transformative and relational mode of linking different struggles and not only as an affective outlook or political value. Solidarity efforts strive to create "shared understandings of situations, problems, and, sometimes, solutions" (Dufour, Masson, and Caouette 2010, 4). To do so, they employ different modalities whose logics are counter-hegemonic, intersectional-feminist, or pluriversal, to follow the helpful systematization presented by the editors of this book (Conway et al., introduction, xxiv; see Conway 2019). In this contribution to the debate, I analyze empirically how these modalities are interwoven and create ambivalent positions for those cast as different, but also how the hegemonic position of unmarked difference sustains solidarity practices by examining two encounters between social movements that took place in Peru. They were explicitly counter-hegemonic in the sense that they shared the conviction that the differences between the activists encountering each other should not be overcome, but instead be engaged with as a valuable resource for building coalitions against the dominant system characterized by neoliberalism, patriarchy, and coloniality. The encounters consequently strove to facilitate dialogue across difference. But even though both encounters used a similar vocabulary and many of the same actors were involved in their organization, different kinds of difference were articulated, which shaped the border-crossing solidarities enabled. While the XIII EFLAC was primarily guided by an intersectional-feminist perspective, the V Diálogos strove to put into practice pluriversal modes of connecting different worlds. My analysis traces the effects of this divergence. I put forward cosmopolitics—"the politics among heterogeneous worlds" (Blaser and de la Cadena 2018, 12)—as an analytical perspective able to grasp the politics involved in bringing together those united by the common concern for emancipation that, however, do not necessarily share the same understanding of emancipation, the same interests, or, in fact, inhabit the same worlds (see Stengers 2011, 60). The cosmopolitical challenge in this context, I argue, lies in fostering border-crossing solidarities able to bridge differences that can and should potentially neither completely be understood nor recognized by those encountering each other. Striving for intelligibility, in fact, can actually complicate solidarity efforts by reproducing asymmetrical and colonizing modes of encounter. Resisting the desire to understand the Other completely is, I argue, a crucial aspect of pluriversalizing border-crossing solidarities.

First, I examine the Thirteenth Latin American and Caribbean Feminist Encounter (XIII *Encuentro Feminista Latinoamericano y del Caribe*, XIII EFLAC). The Feminist Encounters are regional feminist meetings organized since the 1980s that have served as a central space for Latin American feminist organizing (see Alvarez et al. 2003). Intended as an invitation to dialogue, the organizers of the XIII EFLAC positioned difference as a common denominator able to transcend the conflicts within Latin American feminisms. Second, I analyze the Fifth Dialogues of Knowledges and Movements (*V Diálogos de Saberes y Movimientos*, V Diálogos). The V Diálogos were part of a workshop series organized by the *Programa Democracia y Transformación Global* (PDTG), a Peruvian urban collective of popular educators, eco-feminists, and activist researchers that accompanies social movement struggles in Peru, since 2010. The V Diálogos[1] intended to gather heterogeneous emancipatory actors—in particular Peruvian and Latin American social movement representatives, activist researchers, and artists—to create transversal alliances against extractivism, neoliberalism, and patriarchy. Both meetings took place in 2014 in Lima, the capital of Peru.

I have closely accompanied the organization, implementation, and evaluation of both encounters. My involvement with the V Diálogos was deeper than with the XIII EFLAC, as I was part of the team that facilitated the V Diálogos. Concerning the XIII EFLAC, I was welcome to support the event but not involved in the internal processes of the organizing committee. Apart from committed ethnographic research undertaken in four fieldwork stays in the period from 2013 to 2017 that included the participation in both encounters, I conducted thirty-one in-depth interviews with the organizers and participants of the two events. Moreover, I collected documents that helped me to both embed the encounters in the history of Peruvian emancipatory struggles and to trace their genealogy within and beyond Peru. I analyzed the discourses and practices at the two encounters by using discourse and situational analysis.[2]

In the following, I first examine how, in the two encounters, difference has been constituted and with what effects. I then introduce the concept of the cosmopolitics of solidarity and explain how translation and intersectionality serve as analytical tools to scrutinize whether and how cosmopolitics of solidarity were practiced at the two encounters. I conclude by discussing how the latter can serve as both analytics and an ethical call to decolonize solidarity-building in border-crossing encounters across difference.

ENGAGING WITH DIFFERENCE AT TWO INTER-MOVEMENT ENCOUNTERS IN PERU

Articulating Difference as Inequality: The XIII EFLAC

The XIII EFLAC, attended by approximately 1,400 women,[3] took place from November 22 to 25, 2014, in the center of Lima. As part of a series of regional encounters that have taken place in Latin America since the 1980s, its development and character were heavily shaped by the EFLACs preceding it[4]: Since the VII EFLAC 1996 in Colombia, the conflict between the so-called institutionalized feminists working for NGOs and the state and "autonomous" feminists had been central in structuring Latin American feminist movements (Vargas 2008, 151–58; Alvarez 2000). Indigenous, poor, Black, and other marginalized women had challenged Latin American feminist movements for representing mainly the interests and experiences of mestiza, educated, and urban middle-class women (Curiel 2014, 328).

Both conflicts shaped the outlook of the XIII EFLAC. The organizers of the encounter—of whom many might be counted as "institutionalized" feminists though only few would self-identify as such[5]—intended to open a dialogue between the different factions to strengthen Latin American feminist movements. Following mainly an intersectional-feminist modality of solidarity, they emphasized the value of difference not only for sidestepping the ongoing polarizations or for explicitly recognizing the criticisms voiced but specifically also for facing "discrimination in all its forms" (XIII EFLAC 2014b, 2).[6] As they write in their Political Manifesto—published before the XIII EFLAC as an invitation for dialogue—"[t]he diversities that characterize our societies are tinged with inequality and violence and reflect severe imbalances of power" (XIII EFLAC 2014b, 2). Taking inequality and difference as starting points was seen as a powerful, but inevitably conflictive process that would, however, lead to improved understanding not only of each other but also of the multiple, but yet connected systems of oppression.

The methodological challenge of the face-to-face encounter was, then, how to articulate the inequality constitutive of diversity so that the conflicts arising could be turned into dispute that would foster deliberation and, in the end, understanding. On an organizational level, this challenge was met by organizing thematic panels on topics seen as sufficiently broad to interpellate a variety of women and sufficiently specific to allow for the particularity of different experiences to be articulated. Up to seven participants for each panel were chosen "taking into account the diversity of perspectives, identities, and Latin America political proposals" (XIII EFLAC 2014c, 43).[7] The topics of the panels were "Interculturality and Intersectionality" (day one), "Sustainability of Life" (day two), and "Body and Territory" (day three).

After the panels, it was intended that the audience would be divided into sub-plenaries in which the experience-based knowledge of the audience members would complement the discussions that had taken place at the panels and lead to reflection on what was heard on the panels. These sub-plenaries were organized on only two of the three days due to time constraints (XIII EFLAC 2014c, 43).

On a discursive level, the XIII EFLAC strove to foster dispute by positing the body as focal point. As the body is "produced and transformed by the social relations in which we are immersed" (XIII EFLAC 2014b, 1), it evidences the specific oppressions experienced. The body can consequently serve as the entry point for understanding how oppression works, if the different experiences of violence against one's body and other bodies are reflected on.

This discourse on the body as transversal axis prefigured how the participants of the encounter were categorized: those who had recognized that difference, though valuable for tracing how violence works to constitute different bodies, serves mainly as resource for reflection, and those that were (still) drawing their identity primarily from their difference.

> These movements—ethnic-racial, territorial, generational, transgender, lesbian, of persons with disability—enrich the feminisms in their diverse currents with their new perspectives and causes of struggle, but they also place us in front of important challenges. (XIII EFLAC 2014b, 1–2)

While feminists attended the encounter as individuals, those cast as different were assumed to participate as representatives of a particular movement. The panelists were assumed to be clearly identifiable by their difference and chosen accordingly, while, in a logic mirroring the logics of "whiteness" (Ahmed 2004, §1), feminists positioned themselves against the particularity of these movements. Addressed both as different and as "new" to feminism, the difference of these "other" movements was seen as both positive—making available the resources needed to foster dispute—and potentially threatening. There should not be "too many" Indigenous women speaking as panelists, for example, as one of the organizers commented during the preparation of the encounter.

Especially when the feminism of those identified as different stood to question, their participation became conditional on them being part of a movement. When, during the organization of the encounter, the question was posed whether trans men would be allowed to participate in the XIII EFLAC,[8] it was made clear that if trans organizations would come forward and ask to participate, the question might be considered by the plenary of the XIII EFLAC. When one of the organizers remarked that, in Peru, no trans organizations existed that could put forward such a request, it was made clear that trans activists without links to a "proper" movement would not be granted entry.

The standard according to which difference was to be assessed was set by the organizers, who assumed that those cast as different would be identifiable by one primary difference. During the encounter, however, participants resisted the ascription of exclusive difference. The declaration of the "Lesbians, Bisexuals, Transgender, Sexuality and Gender Dissidents That Participate in the XIII EFLAC," formulated and presented during the encounter, states that "transgender, bisexual, lesbian, feminist persons are also black, disabled, Indigenous, young, sex workers, and mestizas" (XIII EFLAC 2014a, §8).

Building Affective Ties across Difference: The V Diálogos

The V Diálogos were a three-day workshop that took place from September 21 to 23, 2014, in Lima. The largest groups of the sixty participants were activists involved in eco-territorial struggles (38%) and scholar activists (35%). Representatives of Peruvian political parties, NGOs, LGBTQ collectives, the urban and afro-Colombian movement as well as artists participated in smaller numbers. Thirty-three people identified as women, twenty-five as men, and two as queer. The encounter was facilitated by eleven people, nine identifying as women and two as men, all working for or with links to the PDTG.[9]

Difference, for the organizers from the PDTG, is constructed continuously by people being embedded in different webs of social relations, which are tied to specific territories. As each person is always part of multiple webs of social relations and lived experience overflows the boundaries of rigid identities, difference is necessarily multiple, fluid, and relational. Difference is conducive for learning as "one learns from difference and complementarity" (Daza et al. 2016, 99), as stated in a publication in which they reflect on the workshop series. But, according to the organizers, the fragmentation that is characteristic of modernity "creates borders of identity and dichotomous positions [and also] hierarchizes us" (Daza et al. 2016, 99). Therefore, difference becomes hierarchized and fixed to exclusive identities. Learning is inhibited. In this context, "The power to build bonds and commonalities is highly revolutionary" (Daza et al. 2016, 99). The methodology of the Diálogos was consequently aimed at:

> [R]ecovering the important histories, moments, or situations lived, finding paths that allow to express them in their complexity and richness, problematizing them and creating spaces of dialogue for the more plural inter-learning between the subjects. (Daza et al. 2016, 93)

Foregrounding emotion and experience, it was hoped, would allow participants to recognize the fluidity and multiplicity of identities each person articulates in the course of their lives and enable pluriversal solidarities to be built.

On a discursive level, participants were interpellated as learners (Daza et al. 2016, 92): The "subject that learns" how to incite emancipatory change (Daza et al. 2016, 92) was encouraged to be "thinking, reflecting, feeling, doing, creating, remembering, desiring, dreaming . . . and all simultaneously in the being" (Daza et al. 2016, 92). Seeing the hegemony of speech and debate in social movement spaces as part of the system of oppression that needs to be overcome, the V Diálogos strove to mobilize the senses in other ways: painting, moving, singing, and touching were employed to allow for other modes of sharing experiences and linking struggles (PDTG 2014, 145). These moments were accompanied by spaces of personal and collective reflection on how these moments had been experienced. The importance of the affective side of encounters across difference for recognition is underlined by an Indigenous activist, who told me in an interview:

> Well, look, many times it seems silly, but when a compañera grabs you and tells you; "Continue, continue, compañera," that she takes your arm and lets you rest and you realize—That meant very much to me, very much. It was necessary. (Interview, November 21, 2014, § 24)

Being touched means letting somebody else come close, which, as Sara Ahmed argues, might move the subject "from her place" (Ahmed 2000, 40). But allowing intimacy, especially across difference, is, as Gloria Anzaldúa has commented, a risky endeavor: "To bridge is to attempt community, and for that we must risk being open to personal, political, and spiritual intimacy, to risk being wounded" (Anzaldúa 2009, 246).

While for the Indigenous activist quoted above being touched conveyed support and recognition, it can also be perceived or intended as threatening and violent, especially in a context in which power is asymmetrically distributed. The facilitators consequently strove to create an atmosphere that was empowering and appreciative of each contribution. This, to a certain amount, made the articulation of uneasiness, frustration, or anger difficult. When tensions arose within the group of participants that organized the místicas[10] taking place each day of the encounter, the difficulty of articulating conflict within the context of the V Diálogos became apparent. While the first mística was a collective offering organized by Indigenous women, the subsequent místicas were focused on singing afro-Colombian spirituals. Rather than a consensual decision within the group, the Indigenous women felt that the decision was unilaterally taken by the afro-Colombian activist.

When they brought the issue to the facilitator responsible for the místicas, asking for an intervention, she did not intervene. When the situation was brought up during the facilitators' collective evaluation of the V Diálogos, she justified her decision by pointing to the marginalization of afro-Latin spirituality. Latin American emancipatory activism, she argued, tends to invisibilize afro-descendant perspectives, mobilizing Indigenous perspectives and practices when trying to include the Other. It urgently needed to become "open to other places," she argued.

Organizationally, group work was preferred to plenary discussion because it was seen as more conducive for exchanging experiential knowledge. The groups changed depending on the task to be completed, and participants were encouraged to reflect on how the groups that were formed reproduced or transcended hegemonic constructions of difference. Methodologies from popular education that engaged creativity and the body were used, in particular to visualize knowledge through exercises of collective mapping. On the first day, after the inaugural mística and after the central questions that the participants wanted to work on during the encounter were formulated, the participants were asked to constitute groups based on their main struggle. In these groups, they were encouraged to share their personal stories of how and why they became activists and, by compiling the different life stories, a timeline of the movement's history was then collectively created. On the morning of the second day, after a mística, a plenary took place in which the timelines were linked and the context in which the movements (inter-) acted was reflected on. During the plenary, a pre-organized panel consisting of three participants, who were asked in advance to prepare short ten-minute statements, discussed how extractivism, patriarchy, and coloniality interacted to form the contemporary system of oppression. Then, groups composed of representatives of the different struggles present were tasked with mapping the alternatives that the movements put into practice. The actual mapping of the struggles, it was hoped, would make the participants realize the partiality and situatedness of knowledge and underline the necessity of building alliances. On the third day, after the morning mística, these maps were presented and another pre-organized panel of three participants shared their views on the alternatives to the current system and the challenges of implementing them. The V Diálogos ended with group discussions on the questions compiled on the first day of the encounter and the presentation of the results of these discussions in a short plenary. Due to time constraints, the participants were asked to write down on cards what they liked the most and what they liked least about the encounter, with these cards not being discussed with the participants but taken as basis for the facilitators' evaluation of the V Diálogos.

The Difference That Difference Makes

In the two encounters, different kinds of difference were constituted both by the discourse on the encounters and the organizational and intersubjective practices of those gathering at the encounter. This had effects for the modalities of solidarity that emerged.

To grasp the dynamics that bring difference into being and shape solidarity, I use the analytics of cosmopolitics. The concept is inspired by the debates in political ontology[11] and especially the work of anthropologist Marisol de la Cadena. In her work (2010, 2015), she examines how communities in Peru articulate the presence of what she calls "earth-beings." Seeing the interpellation of these entities only from hegemonic logics, she argues, means limiting their articulation as expression of either religious beliefs or a political strategy that strategically mobilizes culture. Both explanations strive to fit into preconceived categories what is unintelligible in political logics that grant subject status only to humans—the presence of "earth-beings." In doing so, they miss this presence as a political moment in which other worlds are enacted that potentially practice other kinds of political subjectivity and agency. Mario Blaser (2013, 553) cautions against associating such ontological conflicts with the involvement of Indigenous peoples. As "partially connected heterogeneous social worlds" (Costa 2013, 84) can be enacted in all kinds of contexts, political ontology primarily involves a shift in perspective in which modernity and its constitutive logics are not automatically assumed to be the only and exhaustive reality-producing machines out there (see de la Cadena and Blaser 2018). Juan Ricardo Aparicio and Blaser (2008, 85) argue that such an analytical stance is especially relevant when empirically examining encounters between different social movements. In such encounters, it should not be assumed a priori that there is only one way of performing reality that structures the interactions at the encounter. The complex negotiations that take place should be empirically traced instead. To analyze these negotiations at the two encounters, I use the concepts of intersectionality and translation. I take as starting point the central conundrum for border-crossing solidarities in the pluriverse: unfamiliar and possibly unintelligible experiences and demands need to be articulated in terms that are relatable, but not colonizing or universalizing, allowing for a cosmopolitics to take place (see Spivak 1988; May 2014, 99).

Translation, then, denotes "not just [the translation] of languages, of course, but of incommensurable local differences, trajectories, practices, experiences and cultures" (Nunes 2005, 315). Within the debate on the role of translation in border-crossing activism, there are those that hold that solidarity across difference is not possible without mutual intelligibility (see Santos 2005, 19). The task of translation would be, then, "to turn incommensurability into difference, a difference enabling mutual intelligibility among the different projects of social emancipation" (Santos, Nunes, and Meneses 2007, xi). Another approach to translation is offered by María Lugones, who argues that translation needs to address the material and epistemic underpinnings that subordinate some worlds to others (Lugones 2003, 3). Instead of striving to achieve intelligibility, translation represents "a much larger act, a much more faithful act, a more loving act, a more disruptive act, a more deeply insurgent act" when it "interprets what is happening and gives voice to it in the subaltern language" (Lugones 2003, 3–4). Translation, as Lugones understands it, hinges on the creativity and imagination of the translator. Echoing her argument, imagination is seen, in the broader debate on solidarity across difference within transnational and postcolonial feminisms, as indispensable ethical impetus: "Radical alterity—the wholly other—must be thought and must be thought through imaging" (Spivak 2000, 99) because there is "a limit, an unknowable alterity, an excess, which elides comparison and exchange but to which equality must extend" (Birla 2010, 97). For Gloria Anzaldúa:

> Imagination, a function of the soul, has the capacity to extend us beyond the confines of our skin, situation, and condition so we can choose our responses. It enables us to re-imagine our lives, rewrite the self, and create guiding myths for our time. (Anzaldúa 2009, 248)

Solidarity then is a "problem of relation rather than a problem of knowledge" (Spivak 2000, 105), though lack of knowledge of course might provide a challenge for border-crossing solidarity as well. According to Gayatri Spivak, the transformation of subjectivities into subjects capable of ethically relating to each other across difference, of perceiving themselves as subjects and of imagining a different future, is slow work (Spivak 2009, 35). The encounter across difference in face-to-face meetings can contribute to this but should not be expected to resolve the asymmetrical relation between different worlds characteristic of modernity.

A productive way of making sense of the effects this asymmetrical relation has for conditioning the relation between identities and difference is intersectionality. The concept has been applied to make sense of how racism, classism, sexism, and other forms of hierarchizing difference interlock to create different experiences of oppression (Crenshaw 1989). It sees systems of oppression as mutually constitutive, shaping lived realities in complex ways that always overflow fixed categories of identities. And yet, in modernity, demanding redress and recognition often means articulating experiences of oppression in ways that make them intelligible to hegemonic discourse. Intersectionality thus challenges single-issue politics, but, as feminists critical of how the concept has entered academic debate have argued, can also stabilize identity categories (see Puar 2007, 212–15). Paula-Irene Villa (2012, 177) argues that the "quest for categories" that some intersectional approaches pursue makes it difficult to grasp the "complex 'doing' of people." AnaLouise Keating similarly notes that intersectionality can stabilize rather than challenge "status quo thinking" and make differences "function like walls, not thresholds" (Keating 2013, 36–37).

When taking seriously these critiques and reflecting on how categories are constituted, intersectionality can provide fruitful analytics for engaging with the effects that hierarchizing difference has on solidarity practices. As Vivian M. May argues, intersectionality centers emphasis on the "both/ and" thinking of Black feminism (May 2014, 97). Solidarity, then, is not a practice of building community based on *one* common cause, but a practice that recognizes the intersectionality of different struggles *as* common cause (Davis 2016, 187–88). Anzaldúa similarly imagines border-crossing activists as threshold crossers, *nepantleras*, involved in various struggles at the same time, sometimes having experienced the oppression that is challenged, sometimes struggling in solidarity. Lorde has posited the "very house of difference rather than the security of any one particular difference" (Lorde 1982, 226) as common ground for coalitional work. It can therefore provide both an analytical lens and political outlook conducive for understanding and practicing solidarity as cosmopolitics, as I show in the following.

The (Cosmo-)Politics of Intersectionality and Translation at the Two Encounters

The political and analytical challenge of emancipatory solidarity can be seen when considering the dynamics that positioned Indigenous women ambivalently in both encounters. Notions of class, "race," language, culture, education, religion, and geography interwove to create a situation in which they took on a central position discursively by representing both womanhood and indigeneity/rurality as ultimate markers of difference within the Peruvian context.

In the XIII EFLAC, Indigenous women were given a prominent place. The three thematic axes "Interculturality and Intersectionality," "Sustainability of Life," and "Body and Territory," for example, drew on concepts and demands raised by Latin American women's rural and Indigenous movements, specifically. Their presence was, however, also perceived as a risk— remember the comment of one of the organizers that there should not be "too many" Indigenous women invited as panelists. During the encounter, the participation of rural and Indigenous women dwindled during the morning panels. This was observable both in their attendance and the number of their contributions to the discussions. According to the conversations I had with rural and Indigenous women during the XIII EFLAC as well as to different instances of collective reflection in the wake of the encounter, they felt that the conflicts that dominated debate did not interpellate them. Conflicts cited were the question of whether trans men should be allowed to participate in the EFLACs and the debate concerning the place of the next EFLAC, which mainly articulated the conflict between "institutionalized" and "autonomous" feminists. Nonetheless, the report on the XIII EFLAC holds that Indigenous women "proposed to open a debate about realities and demands from different visions" (XIII EFLAC 2014c, 74). They seem to have achieved this by their mere presence—there was no joint declaration of rural and Indigenous women and the contributions of the panelists and the members of the audience that commented on the panels were rather heterogeneous.

In the V Diálogos, rural and Indigenous women were positioned as the protagonists of counter-hegemonic struggles. The methodology applied strove to construct the persons making possibly unintelligible demands as embedded in a web of relations that made these demands necessary and urgent for them. As rural and Indigenous women were seen as more familiar with such a relational ontology, their experiences were centered as valuable moments of learning for all participants. Group work was seen as primary space for the exchange of experiences, the creation of affect, and of learning. It was conditioned, however, on the need to produce results to be presented in the plenaries. This need to translate created barriers for participation, intimidated especially rural and Indigenous women, and privileged those familiar with abstraction and systematization, fluent in Spanish, and familiar with speaking in front of large audiences. This issue was made explicit in a previous Diálogo when an Indigenous woman acknowledged that:

> [M]any times, we think many things, but we do not say them, we do not express them for fear or because they could make fun of us or could say [things]. And another situation is that I want to say something and I do not know how to say it; therefore I rather stay silent and accept the things that I see. (PDTG 2010, 42)

During a conversation with a rural woman during the V Diálogos, she echoed this assessment: "Sometimes I am lacking the words. I would have liked to ask the compañeros, but I lacked the words and so I kept quiet. I would love to know more" (interview, August 25, 2014).

While not necessarily the intent of the organizers, both encounters also privileged formal education and familiarity with academic concepts. The methodology of the XIII EFLAC, with "expert" panels and discussions, mirrored the format of an academic conference at least during the morning panels. Its Political Manifesto, in tone and style, was an academic treatise that, though it was intended as an invitation to dialogue for all Latin American women, spoke to only a specific group of feminists familiar with abstract academic concepts. Those not interpellated by the dense academic jargon were implicitly cast as lacking the capacity to engage in the dispute striven for. They were welcome to bring their difference as resource but were not included (yet) in the community of feminists able to strengthen the Latin American feminist movement by engaging in dispute.

The V Diálogos did not presume that the struggles present would already be intelligible to each other. Discursively, the participating scholar activists were cast as those needing to listen and learn from the Other. Yet, discussions were oriented toward concepts stemming from academic worlds—neoliberalism, extractivism, and patriarchy—and the participants were asked to articulate their experiences in a way that made them intelligible by connecting them to these concepts. The frame in which this was supposed to happen was put forward by the "experts," who were given the privileged position of being able to present prepared statements to which the other participants were then expected to respond.

The binary ordering of difference in Peru structured by the geographically framed distinction between the "urban" coast and the "rural" highlands (see Greene 2006) invisibilized the Amazon and its peoples in both encounters. In the XIII EFLAC, the Amazon was mentioned neither in the Political Manifesto nor the report on the encounter, no Amazonian representative had been invited as a panelist and there was only one workshop organized by the "Amazons for the Amazon," a group composed of Amazonian and Spanish young feminist artists. In the program of the XIII EFLAC, the workshop was listed as being organized by activists from "Spain." The Amazon remained invisible also during the V Diálogos. The organizers had tried to rectify this, but as a former member of the PDTG sustains, "we did not have a link to the Amazonian movement" (interview, November 5, 2014), also because the Amazonian federations had no interest in initiatives they perceived as steered by activists from Lima.

THE COSMOPOLITICAL CHALLENGE OF BORDER-CROSSING FEMINIST SOLIDARITIES

What follows from these brief glimpses into the practices of and at social movement encounters? Understanding feminist solidarity as border-crossing solidarity that allows for cosmopolitics would mean perceiving it as a practice striving to bridge different worlds to encounter the Other without assuming eventual intelligibility. As my analysis has shown, the engagement with difference through a pluriversal modality of solidarity—behaving as if a "world in which many worlds fit" (EZLN 1996) is already reality—is tied to the conditions under which subjects encounter each other. It is an endeavor hinging on the active confrontation with colonizing logics that form and structure encounters across difference even in spaces based on the recognition of and the wish to build and sustain understanding across difference. Mere co-presence does not suffice.

The orientation of the V Diálogos toward mutual learning and the multiplicity of identities was able to contest exclusive identity categories and allowed for the building of connections across difference based on letting the Other get closer by touch, affect, and imagination. By highlighting positive emotions, however, conflictive issues were blinded out, which led to the silencing of conflicts that might have allowed for the power imbalances that continued to exist to be articulated. The emphasis on dispute as crucible for transformation of the XIII EFLAC, in turn, allowed for the articulation of conflict. But the prior categorization of difference and its enclosure in specific bodies made it difficult to question the inequalities that contributed to the construction of these very differences. Anticipating the common ground shared by the participants as the experience of violence against women's bodies limited the possibilities for encountering difference on different terms and reinforced identity categories instead of questioning them.

If there are no moments of critical reflection, the certainties of those organizing and facilitating border-crossing encounters tend to be reinforced. Allowing cosmopolitics as irritation and "fright that scares self-assurance, however justified" (Stengers 2005, 996) is therefore an indispensable first step for opening up spaces for other kinds of difference to emerge and, in turn, for solidarity between different worlds to become possible. Moments of irritation should be taken as a starting point to unravel the constellations of power that distribute the possibilities of bringing into being different worlds unequally, asking about power and privilege by posing the question: "Up to what point does [the encounter] not turn into another space of specialization for some who know very well how to conduct themselves there, and not a place of more collective creation?" (interview, June 22, 2016), as a facilitator of the V Diálogos remarks self-critically.

Opening spaces for solidarity as cosmopolitics means abandoning the desire to maintain control of the encounter at all times. It means fighting the urge to produce results and the tendency to center on those issues that are felt to be of primary importance for those in a position to steer the encounter. Seeing difference as eventually intelligible tends to result in those in a dominant position fitting difference and those perceived as different into pre-constituted categories—as happened during the XIII EFLAC. While conscious of the unequal power relations that constitute categories of difference, the mode of encounter reproduced the very relations fought against in identifying the participants according to preconceived categories of difference. But when difference is contained in preordained boxes and seen as the property of certain groups instead of a relationally constructed marker of differentiation in a terrain shaped by inequalities of power and knowledge, the terrain for solidarity shrinks. Marguerite Waller and Sylvia Marcos (2005, xxv) have argued that it is not the lack of desire for engaging with those perceived as different on horizontal terms, but the inability to destabilize one's certainties that makes difference that does not respond to hegemonic logics potentially invisible to feminists. Only when difference is seen not as evident, not as outside ascription, but as a collective and relational process of identification, will different kinds of difference have the potential to emerge. Then, cosmopolitics both as analytics and politics can foster solidarity as pluriversal practice.

NOTES

1. For more information, see http://www.democraciaglobal.org/index.php, last accessed November 20, 2019.

2. For more information on my research design and its ethical, political, and normative implications, see Leinius (2020a).

3. There were 1,391 women who participated in the encounter, of which 43 percent were from Peru. Strongly represented were also other Latin American countries, especially Mexico (8% of participants), Nicaragua, Colombia, and Bolivia (6% of participants each). There were also some women from Europe and North America, me included (XIII EFLAC 2014c, 40–41).

4. As Sara Ahmed (2000, 7) holds, face-to-face encounters are mediated events in that they presuppose "other faces, other encounters of facing, other bodies, other spaces, and other times."

5. The organization of the XIII EFLAC was an open process that started in July 2012 with a meeting attended by forty women (XIII EFLAC 2014c, 12). In 2013, in the face of organizational difficulties, the Centro de la Mujer Flora Tristán, the Manuela Ramos Movement, and the feminist human rights organization DEMUS, all important Peruvian feminist NGOs, took charge of the process (XIII EFLAC 2014c, 34).

6. All quotations that follow in the analysis of the V Diálogos and the XIII EFLAC are originally in Spanish and have been translated by the author.

7. Each panelist had seven minutes for presenting, from their experiences, their reflections on what the topic of the panel meant to them, followed by a round of comments and questions from the audience, a brief round of responses from the panelists, and another round for the audience.

8. During the X EFLAC 2005 in Brazil, its plenary as main decision-making body allowed trans women to participate. Since then, the question of whether trans men would be granted entry to the EFLACs has been the topic of heated debates. For more on the issue, see Heumann et al. (2017, 165).

9. Thirty-four participants were from Peru and twenty-six from abroad, of whom the majority were from elsewhere in Latin America. The facilitation team consisted of four Peruvians, three Europeans (me included), one Colombian, one Bolivian, and one Argentinian.

10. Místicas are a pedagogical and cultural practice first used by the Brazilian Landless Rural Workers' Movement to foster other modes of creating a sense of commonality among social movement activists (see Issa 2007; Leinius 2020b). Mística can be performed as theater performance, spiritual ritual, a sharing of stories or a combination of these practices, the common denominator being the intent to create a "subjective experience in collectivity" (Issa 2007, 126).

11. The turn to political ontology can be seen as "an attempt to take others and their real difference seriously" (Carrithers et al. 2010, 175). As a field of study, it focuses on "the conflicts that ensue as different worlds or ontologies strive to sustain their own existence as they interact and mingle with each other" (Blaser 2009, 11).

Part III

TRANSLATION

6

Power, Translation, and Localized Transnational Feminism

Geneviève Pagé

In the contemporary scenario of fragmented identities, contact zones, and border epistemologies, it is incumbent on feminist critics to scrutinize the processes of cultural translation of feminist theories/ concepts so as to develop what has been dubbed as "a geopolitical or transnational ability to read and write" (Friedman 1998; Spivak 1992) toward "the articulation of transnational feminisms" (Grewal and Kaplan 1994).

Costa (2014c, 24)

Traditionally, transnationalization has been studied either as a movement emerging from different locales coming together in an imaginary or material global space (World Social Forum, anti-globalization movements, etc.) or as a global movement shaping and influencing local organizations (Friedman 1999; Alvarez 2000). However, as Aili Mari Tripp argues, when looking at transnational feminist movements, it is important to recognize that "the influences have always been multidirectional, and that the current [transnational] consensus is a product of parallel feminist movements globally that have learned from one another but have often had quite independent trajectories and sources of movement" (2006, 52). Thus, this contribution will focus on one of the ways in which local feminist movements have learned from and interacted with one another transnationally, contributing to the development of a transnational feminist movement: the exchange and translation of ideas and concepts across linguistic and cultural barriers. In this chapter, I argue that, as social scientists as well as activists, we need to pay attention to the multiple and conflicting power dynamics ubiquitous in the processes of conceptual translation if we aspire to build a feminist movement critical of its own power imbalances.

This chapter addresses the issue of conceptual border crossing, mainly from a theoretical perspective. Yet, to illustrate this theoretical reflection, I rely on the example of the travel of and resistance to the concept of "intersectionality" in the Montreal francophone feminist movement. I have chosen to focus on this one case study to facilitate the cohesion of the text. However, the ideas presented here were developed while doing research on multiple conceptual voyages. In fact, my research over the last fifteen years has been concerned with the travels, appropriation, and development of conceptual tools by Montreal feminists, touching on different ideas and concepts, from "gender" to "queer," from "reproductive justice" to "transformational justice," among others. In addition, I personally grew up in Montreal and have been active in both its francophone and anglophone feminist community for over twenty years. Thus, for this chapter, I draw on personal experience, rigorous funded and unfunded research, as well as existing literature.

This case study is particularly interesting to highlight multiple lines of power negotiation. First, the travel of intersectionality is embedded in French/English power relations. Coming from the United States, its integration in francophone feminist groups has been denounced as participating in U.S. hegemony. Yet, because it emerged in Black feminist circles, it is also imbued with resistance to mainstream and dominant U.S. feminist conceptual hegemony, namely through its anti-racist critique. Furthermore, its integration into mainstream U.S. feminist vocabulary is also contested because of the perceived appropriation and depoliticization of the word by white feminists (Bilge 2015). Thus, as we follow its integration into mainstream francophone feminist circles in Montreal, it is subjected to criss-crossing power dynamics tied to language (anglophone/francophone), tied to anti-racist critiques of white feminism, and tied to resistance to appropriation of Black-produced theories to serve white feminists. By paying attention to the (micro)politics of conceptual translation, this analysis is rooted in the careful study of the making of solidarities, which, according to Masson and Paulos (chapter 3, 62), "involves the elaboration, in movement discourse, of political imaginaries and forms of political identification that connect movement actors and their struggles." In this sense, this chapter contributes to the documentation of one of the types of practices (see chapter 3) involved in solidarity-building as a praxis: discursive practices, highlighting that, like any other practice (material or spatial), it is imbued and disfigured by power dynamics. Words and concepts become a battleground for legitimizing or condemning actors, groups, or even whole movements.

After a short review of translation studies (Bassnett and Trivedi 1999; Venuti 1992, 2004; Simon 1996, 1999; Rodriguez 2003; Spivak 2004), including recent work on cultural translation (Alvarez et al. 2014; Costa 2014c; Thayer 2000, 2014), I start by conceptualizing Montreal as a contact zone and as a transnational space. I then briefly describe the Montreal feminist francophone community and its complex relation to both anglophone and racialized feminists. Finally, I argue that four main types of power dynamics are at play to facilitate or impede the translation of concepts within a localized transnational space: (1) the strength and state of local theoretical tradition and movement, (2) the presence of "bridge actors" with enough social capital to command a change in conceptual framings, (3) the capacity/desire of the movement to reconfigure its borders, and (4) asymmetries of power between languages.

TRANSLATION STUDIES

Translation, both in its literal and metaphorical senses, provides tools for analyzing the traveling of ideas. As Simon has written, the concept of translation allows one to identify "the intellectual and linguistic points of contact between cultures, and make visible the political pressure that activates them" (1996, 136). I rely on the words of queer theorist Juana Maria Rodriguez to explain how translation is understood not only as finding equivalence for words between languages, but also as a process that involves an exchange between symbolic and semiotic structures of both the original and the new communities. She writes, "The process of translation involves more than merely translating languages, it involves translating cultures, values, and institutions of power" (2003, 19). Translation, even in its literal sense as one of the processes that allow concepts to travel, needs to be understood as both informal and formal. When two linguistic communities live among each other, different official and informal spaces allow for the coining and borrowing of words, ideas, and sounds in ways that may defy formal processes. Thus, translation refers not only to the meaning of words but also to a range of social and political meanings and associations.

Translation allows one to identify "ways to link the issues and analysis generated from one campaign or social movement to another in order to strengthen praxis" (Naples 2008, 9). Conceptual translation refers to how one community makes sense of concepts or practices taken from another community in a way that does not always retain all of the original meanings and intentions. It also explores how communities and discourses are heard differently depending on their audience (Mani 1990). Translation studies provide us with a framework to analyze how concepts cross borders and how communities interact with each other to make sense of the other, not only through language but also by different modes of exchange and at different scales. This framework assists in understanding the possibility of a common transnational political ground. Finally, translation studies address the "messiness" of these exchanges, the faults and the successes of transference and modification of ideas (Simon 1996; Foucault 1977).

Some have used the concept of cultural translation to describe how "any process of description, interpretation, and dissemination of ideas and worldviews is already caught up in relations of power and asymmetries between languages, regions and peoples" (Costa 2014c, 20). This is particularly true when discussing the translation of concepts that are central to political organizing. Thayer further suggests that "translations—or refusals to translate—play a strategic role for social movements and represent a significant form of political agency" (2014, 402). With this in mind, this chapter engages with the complexity of exchanges between actors and ideas by acknowledging the multiplicity of sources of influences and their instability across time and location. Furthermore, it centers the notion of power—empowerment as well as power imbalances—to revisit the movement of ideas and concepts across feminist locales in the context of transnationalization. The goal is to foster literature that pays attention to how transformation in the conceptual apparatus of feminist communities is also connected and interdependent with transformation in power dynamics among and between actors and groups in these communities.

Contact Zones, Borders, and Transnational Space

In order for conceptual translation to happen, there needs to be a point of encounter between two (sub)cultures. Linguist and literary expert Mary Louise Pratt has used the term "contact zones"—the space where two or more communities of practices come together and interact—to attend to the different and conflicting power relations that structure and regulate the erection, the crossing, and the policing of borders, in all their diversity. She defines "contact zones" as "social spaces where cultures meet, clash, and grapple with each other, often in contexts of highly asymmetrical relations of power, such as colonialism, slavery, or their aftermaths as they are lived out in many parts of the world today" (Pratt 1991, 34).

Contact zones allow our lens to zoom in to specific locations where the exchange happens and to localize the point of contact. Contact zones can be ephemeral (an international gathering) or long-lasting (World March of Women), structured or spontaneous, local or transnational. Sherry Simon has described Montreal as a more or less permanent contact zone: francophone and anglophone communities live next to each other, interacting only in certain spaces and in certain contexts. Furthermore, as a diverse city, it is also the site of convergence between an array of different cultures, traditions, and ways of thinking. This is also true of the Montreal feminist movement: the ongoing in flux of anglophone feminists (from the rest of Canada as well as from the United States), namely because of the two English universities, in addition to the influx of feminists from a diversity of cultures and traditions, ensures a constant yet timid interaction between different feminist traditions.[1]

As Janet Conway (2004) has aptly described, social movements are all situated in "time space." Yet, "places can no longer be conceived as pre-given or bounded locals. Places are being constituted in significant ways by forces and conditions arising beyond the place, including the globalization of production, trade, finance, international migration, environmental crises and transnational social movements" (Conway 2004, 36). Social movements both contribute to the constitution of spaces and are constituted by it.

Research on urban movement has stressed that place should be understood as "constructed out of a particular constellation of social relations, meeting and weaving together at a particular locus" (Massey 1994, 154). For instance, transnational migration flows "touch ground" in different ways in different places; the way racialized and immigrant feminists have contributed to shape feminist politics in Montreal is part of the past and present history of immigration in the city, as compared to that of the rest of the province or other metropolises. Thus, Massey urges us to consider the different scales of these social relations, ranging from the global to the local. Yet, we are reminded that the local also participates in the production of these different scalar social relations. "The local and the global are mutually constituted; they *and* other spatial scales are constantly being produced and are constituting social relations as well" (Conway 2004, 44).

Particularly when thinking through transnational translation, contact zones help us think through the notion of different "scales" when, moving away from a narrow understanding of national border crossings, we pay attention to navigations between the local, regional, national, and transnational exchanges that permeate any community. This is particularly true when one looks at the converging scales of conceptual referencing. As this chapter demonstrates, the theoretical influences are both global and local, provincial and city-based. Hence, Montreal is also a place where different political discourses, which are also scaled in terms of the territory they explicitly refer to (the Canadian state's discourse on multiculturalism, the globalist/planetary discourses of the World March of Women and other transnational movements), are taken up (or opposed) at the "local" level of Montreal by activists.

Furthermore, Masson suggests that "what defines the transnational in movement activity is the cross-border nature of the forms of connectivity established among movement actors, practices, and discourses" (2010, 40). With the rise of "border studies" numerous conceptualizations of borders have emerged. Linda Bosniak defined the border as:

[A] site that divides insiders and outsiders, and where decisions about who may or may not become insiders are made. It is, moreover, a sphere with its own normative logic, one that itself is structured neither entirely by insider nor outsider but which lies at the interface between them. (2006, 126)

This understanding of the border helps us locate the border as repository or defining of power relations. Gloria Anzaldúa (1987, 3) also identified the fluctuating and sometimes immaterial nature of borders as important elements. Feminist theorist Chandra Mohanty in her book *Feminism without Borders* analyzes borders critically when she writes:

Feminism without borders is not the same as "borderless" feminism. It acknowledges the fault lines, conflicts, differences, fears, and containment that borders represent. It acknowledges that there is no one sense of a border, that the lines between and through nations, races, classes, sexualities, religions, and disabilities, are real—and that feminism without borders must envision change and social justice work across these lines of demarcation and division. (2003, 2)

Feminist theorist Nancy Naples emphasizes the importance of recognizing "the myriad of ways borders are constructed, how they function to divide us, and what purposes they serve for different constituencies" (2008, 8) in order to foreground asymmetrical power relations and their impact on the development of the feminist movement.

Because Montreal is a site where so many of those borders are negotiated and remade, I follow Conway's idea that a specific space can be understood as a transnational space. Thus, in this chapter, I consider Montreal to be, at times, a transnational space where global social relations converge and meet localized relations, influenced by regional, provincial, and national social relations, and institutional levels of decisions. Montreal's francophone feminist community is thus localized in the transnational space that is Montreal, with "its own specific and multiple history(s), geography(s), political culture(s), national articulation(s), identity(s) and so on, which are distinct from [other cities]" (Conway 2004, 43).

FRANCOPHONE FEMINISM IN MONTREAL: CONTEXT AND ALLIANCES

In Montreal, francophones and anglophones usually circulate in different social and political circles. Although 54 percent of the population in Montreal report being bilingual (English-French) (Statistics Canada 2011), the two communities operate in relatively separate spaces. The concept of two solitudes—two linguistic communities living side by side, cohabiting, yet separated by a virtual border that prevents cross-border exchanges—also applies to feminist communities in Montreal; very few groups or organizations navigate both languages on a daily basis.

This border is also fueled by political traditions and specific language power dynamics. The revival of the feminist movement in the 1960s and 1970s was concomitant with the rise of the Quebec nationalist movement, a movement very invested in language politics. As a result, apart from a few historical moments of alliance between French-speaking and English-speaking feminists, both communities developed fairly separately. At times, this border is policed by francophone feminists' refusal to participate in mobilizations organized by anglophone feminists (collaborating with their oppressors) or targeting the federal government (refusal to recognize it as a legitimate government) (Pagé 2012). Furthermore, the theoretical grounding of the francophone movement became increasingly fueled by texts produced in France, while their anglophone counterparts were more influenced by their southern neighbors (Pagé 2012). As a result, the conceptual apparatus of francophone Montreal feminists is quite different than that of their anglophone counterparts.

Another particularity of Montreal's francophone feminist community, again linked to the influence of nationalism, is its historical inattention to racialized and Indigenous feminists. Until a few years ago, the historical positioning of francophones as oppressed by "conquering anglophones" had prevented real discussions of the domination of whites (English or French) over native communities[2] and over marginalized racialized women. For francophones in the 1960s, racialized women were either associated with the anglophones (they won't learn French; hence, they participate in the oppression of francophones) (Pagé 2015), left out, particularly as political actors and feminists (Williams 1997; A. Ricci 2015), or, in the case of Indigenous women, venerated as models from the past, nonexistent in the present, especially as political actors and feminists (A. Ricci 2015; Pagé 2015).

Montreal's feminism has, in the past twenty years, increasingly revived its "contact zone" quality, especially among younger feminists who are more and more exposed to English-based theoretical traditions. Furthermore, starting in the early 1990s, the concerns and voices of racialized feminists started emerging in documents by and for the white majority. Yet, the space and strength of these voices was irregular and easily dismissed.[3] The 2000s began a new set of relationships, namely with the signing of a solidarity agreement between Quebec Native Women and the Fédération des femmes du Québec (FFQ). But this integration of the demands of racialized and Indigenous feminists did not happen without resistance.

The *États généraux du féminisme* between 2011 and 2013 was in part designed to address these tensions and became the battlefield for what

Marie-Ève Campbell-Fiset (2017) describes as the "intersectional turn." Over this period, the FFQ pushed to adopt an intersectional framework and was faced with resistance from "universalist feminists" (Campbell-Fiset 2017) who advocated for minimizing differences among women in order to foreground women's common oppression. As a case in point, in 2013 a new feminist group, *Pour le droit des femmes du Québec* (PDFQ), claimed in the media to be a counterweight to the FFQ. PDFQ not only criticized FFQ's support of women's right to wear the headscarf, but they also denounced the use of an intersectional framework as a form of cultural relativism and of sectarian or ethnic separatism (*communautarisme*) (PDFQ n.d.; Caron 2014).

It is in this contact zone, situated in time and place, but also imbued with transnational, translocal, and multiscale influences, that the struggle to integrate the concept of intersectionality in the francophone feminist movement takes place. Next, I delineate contextual elements that influence the interplay of power and foster—or prevent—the translation of concepts from one community to the next.

TRANSLATION AND POWER

Strength and State of Local Tradition—Fulfilling a Need

Studying the voyaging of concepts and ideas reveals that one of the most important elements influencing the importation of concepts is whether there is a need for theoretical tools. A fertile ground for translation is defined by a context where a foreign concept explains a reality that is felt by a group of people or a movement, but is not sufficiently addressed by their existing theoretical tools. Furthermore, dominant theoretical traditions need to be compatible with the incoming ideas.

First, the need for a new conceptual tool must be felt by significantly organized groups, groups that wield some power over the definition of (pertinent) theory. In the case of intersectionality, the increasing pressure exercised by racialized feminist individuals and groups, denouncing mainstream francophone feminist conceptions as unable to account for their reality and thus furthering their marginalization within the feminist movement, led to a questioning of the local theoretical tradition.

It is telling that resistance to the integration of intersectionality often suggests that it is not suited for Quebec's reality. For example, a board member of PDFQ argues that:

> Although there are similarities, the social reality at the source of the development of the intersectional analysis is not present in Quebec. This approach, grounded in Afro-American feminists, is born out of a culture historically based

on "race," and this reality is not transposable here, contrary to what certain Quebec feminist groups argue. (Caron 2014; my translation)

As this example demonstrates, the legitimization of the need is as much a field of struggle as the value of the concept itself.

Second, the dominant local theoretical tradition needs to be compatible with the conceptual innovation. The strong influence of French materialists on Quebec feminism has shaped a specific resistance to intersectionality. Just as in France, or maybe because of the way the debate was happening in France, Quebec feminists first associated intersectionality with an individualist, neoliberal, postmodern understanding of feminism. This ran contrary to the structural anchor of the dominant materialist feminist understanding of oppression.[4]

In fact, the local tradition of materialist feminism also offered an alternative concept to fulfill the need for conceptualizing the interaction between multiple structures of oppression. Mirroring the French debate, some Quebec feminists sought to use the concept of "consubstantiality of oppressions" (Kergoat and Galerand 2014) instead of intersectionality, arguing that it was more compatible with materialist feminism.[5] Yet, Quebec feminists of color favored a concept that highlights Black feminists' contributions to feminist theory.

Third, timing needs to be right. For example, Quebec "revolutionary" feminists in the late 1960s and early 1970s were actively looking for conceptual tools to help them make sense of a tripartite struggle: one against patriarchy, capitalism, and colonialism.[6] They searched whatever literature they could find, from the United States and Europe, for theoretical help. Here is how one activist details the thought process that happened in her 1969 group:

It is extremely important to develop our own analysis. Thus, we are always searching for texts in French that stimulate our thinking and are in agreement with our line of thought. Because for us, *Québécoises*, it is not easy to try to combine three kinds of struggle! Another difficulty is to justify theoretically why the feminist struggle comes "first," that it is prioritized over the struggle for independence and socialism. Impossible to find texts that talk about that, and even harder, in French! (Péloquin 2007, 31; my translation)

Unfortunately, the conceptual tools developed by Black feminists in the United States came too late to satisfy their quest. By the time the Combahee River Collective publish their germinal text in 1977, or by the time the "matrix of oppression" (Collins [1990] 2000) or the idea of intersectionality (Crenshaw 1989) comes along, radical feminists in Quebec are so disillusioned by the nationalist project and so alienated by the local left that they revert to defining patriarchy as the main/only structure of oppression regulating women's lives (Pagé 2012). In short, by the time the conceptual tool becomes available, the need no longer exists for mainstream and "radical" feminist groups in Quebec. One will have to wait until women of color and their allies reactivate the need for a conceptual tool articulating multiple sources of oppression with enough voice to be heard in the 2010s.

It is ironic that the same local theoretical tradition that sent the 1970s "revolutionary" feminists in search for an intersectionality-like tool served as an excuse not to adopt it fifty years later. As documented by many, the strong influence of the Quebec nationalist movement on some feminists has veiled their capacity to see themselves as participating in racist and colonial structures, and recently increased their resistance to the integration of an anti-racist agenda and the concept of intersectionality (Bilge 2010; Pagé and Pires 2015; Pagé 2015; Campbell-Fiset 2017).

This analysis needs to be further nuanced by an analysis of power in any given feminist movement. Who defines "dominant theoretical tradition"? Who is able to voice a conceptual need? Whose reality is centered in any given conceptual tool? Racialized feminists who kept demanding a better integration of their experiences and an ensuing positioning against racism among Montreal feminists (A. Ricci 2015; Williams 1997), to no avail, would rightly disagree that the "need" for intersectionality disappeared in the mid-1970s. At that historical moment, however, they lacked the means and voice to command a conceptual transformation. Thus, we need to nuance the idea of conceptual need, of existing dominant theoretical tradition, and the notion of timing in light of the power differential between the different subcultures within the feminist movement.

The Presence of Bridge Actors

Zooming in even more, to understand conceptual translation, one needs to pay attention to how emotions—personal conflicts, hatred, and divisions, along with love and friendship—and social bonds—kinship, faith-based network, or geographical proximity—might have as much to do with the development of ideas as the political potential they hold or the need they fulfill (Foucault 1977, 140–42; Tarrow 2005, 103).

The importance of certain individuals and their relations to both the origin and the translating cultures is documented in social movement literature through the process of brokerage (Gould and Fernandez 1989; Tarrow 2005). One way repertoires of actions as well as conceptual framings are disseminated is through mediation by key individuals or institutions. These individuals or institutions that facilitate resource flows and conceptual flows have been designated as "brokers" (Diani 2003; Tarrow 2005). Research has shown that both their social prestige and their relationships with the adopting communities are important factors in facilitating the importation process (McAdam and Rucht 1993; Strang and Soule 1998).

The study of Montreal's feminist community confirms that for translation to take hold, key actors need to act as brokers. Facing strong resistance, it took a very strong commitment on the part of the staff and president of the Fédération des femmes du Québec—the main feminist umbrella organization in Quebec—to meaningfully translate the intersectional framework (Campbell-Fiset 2017) and make it resonate for Quebec feminists.

Yet, it is not only important for key actors to give credence to an external theory or concept; these actors must transform the concept—sometimes skewing its meaning—to make it compatible with a pre-existing framework. In this sense, I regard their work as more than "brokers"; they need to construct a theoretical bridge between the two cultures. While some activists and intellectuals tried to make intersectionality relevant to Quebec's specific feminist history (Pagé 2014), others started to denounce the watering down and the depoliticization of the idea—the "whitening of intersectionality" as Bilge (2015) has termed it. Thus, the work of bridge actors is a delicate balance, between making an idea intelligible by using existing ideas and conserving its original meaning and its political potential.

The Capacity/Desire of the Movement to Reconfigure Its Borders

Especially when thinking of transnational feminism, it is easy to understand translation as border crossing. However, in this section, I want to suggest that translation is not so much about border crossing as it is about border reconfiguration. As we have seen previously, borders are here understood as "a site that divides insiders and outsiders, and where decisions about who may or may not become insiders are made" (Bosniak 2006, 126).

Conceptual translation—the integration of a new meaningful concept imported from "outside" the border—works to reconfigure borders, reshaping the "us" and "them." In the process of this translation, for a time, there are those who know about it and those who don't, as well as those who understand it, those who pretend to, and those who don't. There are those who teach it, those who claim it, and those who listen. There are those who refuse and reject it. There are those whose lives are made more central to the struggle because of it and those whose experience loses salience. There is, inevitably, a power struggle, a new definition of insiders and outsiders. Thus, the work of translation is not only a border crossing, but a reshaping of borders. In this sense, translation necessitates a negotiation of power dynamics embedded in the creation, maintenance, policing, and crossing of borders.

Once again, examples from the Quebec feminist movement support this idea. The integration of intersectionality in Quebec francophone feminist theory required a new definition of "who we are," of the "us" and the "them," thereby stimulating a strong resistance among feminists (Pagé 2012), or a backlash as Campbell-Fiset (2017) has theorized it. At stake are definitions of who we are as Quebec feminists, including debates about our history, our values, and our future.[7] To illustrate, here is an example of how a rigid understanding of "us Quebecers" is being used to oppose the integration of an intersectional analysis among feminist groups:

> In fact, this whole intersectional approach is erected on an ethnic separatist (*communautariste*) and multicultural structure of thought—a vision of society not shared by the majority of Quebecers, who still struggle to build themselves as a nation in a country where they only have a lease. *Thus, intersectional feminism, self-proclaimed as third wave [feminism], is the outcome of a thinking that breaks with the general thought common to francophone Quebecers* (Caron 2014; emphasis in original; my translation)

In this example, there is a reaffirmation of an "us Quebecers" that is set in opposition to proponents of intersectionality, who are repositioned outside of the nation. At the core of the debate is a struggle about who is at the center of the feminist community (Campbell-Fiset 2017).

It is also telling that much of the debate about the integration of intersectionality is reinterpreted around the notions of inclusion and diversity (Anctil Avoine, Veillette, and Pagé 2019), which tends to depoliticize and overlook how domination is perpetuated. It thereby protects the status quo (S. Ricci 2015; Ahmed 2012), falling short of questioning how power dynamics operate to center the experience of some, while marginalizing the experience of others; this strategy avoids the painful reconfiguration of borders.

Asymmetries of Power between Languages

Finally, one cannot think about conceptual translation without paying attention to how different languages are imbued with historical and contemporary power asymmetries. I take for granted, like many authors before me, that any intellectual production needs to be understood as the product of power relations. Thus, as scholars, we need to be aware of the different structures that allow or prevent one from producing recognized and legitimate knowledge, and the structures that facilitate or impede translation.

Translation theory has been criticized for its lack of attention to power imbalances tied to different languages (Jacquemond 1992; Mehrez 1992). Especially in (post)colonial countries, the colonizer's language becomes the mark of the empire, imposed through schooling institutions and representative of potential upward mobility in a highly hierarchized system where the native language is that of the sinner or that of the savage. And in most countries, one can add the class/caste hierarchies revealed through language patterns, dialects, and accents. This power imbalance, however, is not limited to postcolonial countries, although it carries in those sites a substantially different weight.

To illustrate this fact, Quebec feminist theorists Francine Descarries and Laetitia Dechaufour have documented the limited impact of francophone feminist texts on English feminist texts. Using the example of French is especially telling since French is usually considered a "legitimate" language of knowledge production. Yet, it is rather frustrating for French-speaking feminists to see the limited impact of their own theoretical developments on feminist theory globally as a result of this English hegemony.

> Our almost daily frequenting of English literature especially leads us to observe to what extent, with a few exceptions, anglophone feminists—all countries included—know of or use very little, if at all, francophone feminist works. And what to say about the fate reserved for other linguistic communities such as Latino-American or Asian? As an inevitable consequence of this lacuna, *mainstream* feminism ignores and de facto rids their theoretical contributions of notions or concepts as fundamental as *rapports sociaux de sexe*, domestic mode of production, sexual division of labor, or even patriarchy. (Descarries and Dechaufour 2006; my translation)

This limited impact is in addition to the numerous instances of misunderstanding, misinterpretation, and ideological misrepresentation of certain schools of thought or concepts developed in languages other than English.[8]

Consequently, for a theory to penetrate the canons of, in this case, feminism, it needs to be mediated through either published translation or the intellectual capacities and labor of individuals in influential circles. The first type of mediation, translation, is at the mercy of laws of the market, of publishers' choices and preferences and their personal and socially constructed understanding of what is "worth" translating.[9] In the case of feminist communities of practice all over the world, this is especially relevant because the vulnerability of theories to this tyranny is reinforced by the marginality of certain types of knowledge produced.[10] Although such work is at times paradigm-shifting in its content, its audience remains relatively small and has limited resources, as the low rate of survival of feminist periodicals can attest. Hence, feminist theorists have to rely on small autonomous or university presses to publish their work in translation.

Thayer (2000) further argues that economic and discursive barriers prevent feminist theories and concepts from traveling from the South to the North, forcing diasporic intellectuals to take on this task if they want to see it happen. This dependence on publishing institutions is shared across the world as a function of not only the actual audience for each linguistic community but also of the state, and the development and progressive nature of publishing institutions.

Furthermore, the politics of translating forces us to think about whether translation reinforces or challenges power imbalances between different communities. Some translators have praised the inherently democratic nature of translation, suggesting that it makes a text more accessible. French theorist Jacques Derrida says, "I must speak in a language that is not my own because that will be more just" (cited in Spivak). However, Spivak warns against the romantic notion of accessibility: "In the act of wholesale translation into English, there can be a betrayal of the democratic ideal into the law of the strongest" (Spivak 2004, 371). We see here how difficult it is to negotiate the dissemination of knowledge without re-inscribing the hegemonic domination of English.

In addition, because so much of the conversation on feminist theory and praxis happens in English, local non-anglophone communities need to rely on translation to stay afloat of the newest developments in the field. To counteract this problem, feminist theorists will sometimes take it upon themselves to do the tedious work of translating important work into their own language in order to make it accessible to their community. Yet, this very difficult task takes time and labor away from the development of new theory, research, and scholarship. For example, Crenshaw's article was only translated into French in 2005 while the Combahee River Collective's Statement was translated in 2006, along with a few key Black feminist texts in 2008.

Finally, in the case of the travel of intersectionality through the transnational space that is Montreal, the relationship between the French and English languages must be also considered. The constant fear of the disappearance of the "fait français" in Quebec is in the background of some of the resistance. As such, the importation of a terminology from the United States is often read as imperialist and as participating in the maintaining of English hegemony.[11] Yet, this line of reasoning, although with some merits in certain cases, does not account for power inequalities among English-speaking conceptual innovators. To equate the importation of ideas developed by Afro-American feminists with U.S. imperialism is to discount the internal power struggles within the United States.

From this discussion of translation, one can see the importance of language not just in terms of translating concepts from one movement to another, but also in positioning knowledge production and different communities, interacting with each other, onto a wider grid imbued with power.

CONCLUSION

As we strive to strengthen transnational ties among feminist communities, it is important to critically reflect on the conceptual language we use to define issues, how this language has come to be meaningful, what might be lost, and who gains and who loses in the process. As Masson and Paulos (chapter 3) have demonstrated, the building of solidarities across communities and differences requires attention to discursive practices and their role in creating common political imaginaries and identifications. As cultural translation theorists have argued, words are not just symbols of stable meanings. They carry with them political histories inscribed in complex multiscalar power relations. The travel of concepts not only reflects those complex web of power relations but also participates in them, by disrupting them and/or reproducing them.

Using the example of the arrival of intersectionality to the contact zone that is Montreal feminism, I have suggested that conceptual translation is not "good" or "bad" per se, but is fraught with power imbalances. This study of the importation of a politically charged term into a spatially situated transnational movement highlights the messiness of solidarity-building. Understanding the state of local theoretical traditions, the differential needs of groups within a community, the importance of key individuals, the transformation of borders required, and the power asymmetries between languages are all key elements to critically evaluate the importation of concepts across borders. Moreover, they help us map how collective identities are maintained or redefined and force us to pay attention, not just to the concepts used but also to the reconfiguration performed by the translation of concepts.

NOTES

1. For more on these dynamics, see Pagé (2012).

2. One of the narratives present among Quebecers is the idea that French colonizers were much more egalitarian with the First Nations than the British conquerors. This discourse is present even among scholars (see, for example, historian Denis Veaugeois in an interview [Arseneault 2019]) and has been heard among francophone feminists.

3. For example, in 1989, groups representing racialized and immigrant women walked out of the *Forum pour un Québec féminin pluriel* because the organizers refused to change the keynote speaker, Lise Payette. She had just coauthored the documentary *Disparaître* (1989) which denounces immigration as a menace to the Quebec people. In contrast, the demands of the 1996 march *Bread and Roses* included some demands emanating from groups representing immigrant women, such as the

retroactive application of the reduction of the sponsorship time (from ten to three years) for women who were sponsored by their husband or partner for immigration.

4. Early writings on intersectionality in Quebec and in France refused the idea on the basis of its lack of structural analysis (Kergoat 2009; Juteau 2010).

5. It is interesting to note that prior to the pressures for the integration of an intersectional approach into feminist theory in France (circa 2005), very few materialist feminists used—or even knew about—this concept developed by Danielle Kergoat in the 1980s. A preliminary review of the literature suggests that the popularity for this idea grew as a way to refuse the concept of intersectionality.

6. Colonialism, in their understanding, refers to the colonization of French settlers by English-speaking settlers, however problematic that is.

7. For a very detailed and poignant analysis of how representation of religion and "laïcité" (secularism) has been used to reconfigure the collective understanding of who we are as "Quebec feminists," see Jacquet (2017).

8. See, for example, the case of "French Feminism" as criticized by Claire Moses (1998) and Christine Delphy (1996).

9. Even in less marginal fields, the translation of texts is dependent on markets and relationships of value imbued by the notion of "worthy scholarship." Translation theory needs to address the context of production of the text not only in terms of local significance of individual words but also its wider positioning within the matrix of text production. Translator and theorist Richard Jacquemond estimates that translations of texts from the Global South represent "at best 1 or 2 percent of the translated book market of the North, while in the South 98 or 99 percent of this market" is composed of texts produced in the North (1992, 139).

10. Claudia de Lima Costa exposes similar dynamics as they are happening in Brazil (2014c).

11. For a similar debate in France, see among others Bourdieu and Wacquant (1998) and Noiriel (2018), and refuting their argument in regard to intersectionality and "race" respectively, Lépinard and Mazouz (2019).

7

(Mis)translations in Translocal Solidarity-Building and the Need for Controlled Equivocation

Cuerpo-territorio *in the World March of Women*

Nathalie Lebon

Building solidarity is indispensable to creating and maintaining cross-border networks and to their role in sustaining progressive social change, and yet, it presents unique challenges. Building solidarity relies on building connections, and building connections in such highly and complexly diversified terrain as cross-border networks requires deep understanding of one another—or some other form of deep trust. Linguistic and conceptual translation thus become indispensable tools for translocal network participants to successfully make sense of each other's discourses and meanings and to allow discourses to "speak to" one another. Conceptual translation refers here to the "exchange and translation of ideas and concepts across linguistic and cultural barriers" (chapter 6, 119).

Power infuses every step of conceptual translation efforts, as Quebec political scientist Geneviève Pagé argues, and in multiple directions at once, as I explain below. Movement practices which level out power asymmetries to facilitate effective conceptual translation are thus key. Missteps and failures in conceptual translation are bound to occur along the way. In some cases, participants from different (political) cultures may believe homonymic concepts refer to the same reality when in fact they do not, as each context alters the meaning of the concept. In fact, they are dealing with a case of equivocation (Viveiros de Castro 2004). I argue that peeling away the layers of such misunderstandings can reveal deeper differences in positionality among network participants, which imperatively need to be addressed if long-lasting solidarity bonds are to survive.

This paper explores translocal networks' practices and negotiation strategies as they strive to build solidarity toward movement-building in the context of conflicting preexisting localized political cultures and ideologies, with a special attention to discursive practices, language, and translation. In so doing, this paper seeks to answer Masson and Paulos's call for studying what social movements *do* to promote solidarity-building, as they encourage scholars to conceptualize solidarity as "a strategic, organizational praxis in the service of movement goals" (chapter 3, 58). The paper explores situations where network members work across geographically distant contexts which are geopolitically at odds, while also paying attention to hierarchies of difference (race, class, gender and sexuality, indigeneity, citizenship) at the local/national and transnational levels stemming from intersectional power relations.

The empirical points of departure for this paper are the practices, structural features of, as well as challenges encountered by the World March of Women (hereafter WMW or the March). Since we can learn a lot from failures in conceptual translation, I am particularly interested in the challenges the March faced in crafting a common theme/slogan for their 2015 International Action around the concept of defending the autonomy of women's bodies and the territory of their communities, a concept first formulated by Indigenous women's organizations in Central America. The WMW is a translocal popular feminist coalition particularly successful in Latin America, which is broadly dedicated to ending poverty and violence against women within an anticapitalist framework. It has been present in sixty countries around the world for two decades now (Giraud and Dufour 2010). Some have argued that the March is one of only two fully transnational global networks, although interestingly, the English-speaking world, notably the United States, Anglophone Canada, most of Anglophone Africa, and India, participate only minimally. Indeed, languages have played a role in how the network spread around the world, with its being prevalent in countries where Spanish, French, and Portuguese are spoken. Every five years since 2000, the various chapters of the March come together to orchestrate an International Action. These mobilizations are meant to promote consciousness-raising and organizing, and to link together protests around issues of poverty and violence against women within a socialist feminist framework.

This paper is based on ethnographic fieldwork, mostly participant observation and interviews, with participants in the WMW in Brazil and France in 2013–14 as the March was preparing its 2015 International Action. I also observed proceedings at the ninth International Meeting of the WMW in São Paulo in August 2013, where decisions regarding the 2015 International Action were made.

SOLIDARITY-BUILDING AS ORGANIZATIONAL
PRAXIS IN TRANSLOCAL CONTEXTS

Masson and Paulos "understand solidarity-building in transnational organizing as an organizational praxis [that] involves the active linking together of hitherto geographically and/or socially distant and disparate place-based struggles through the construction of connections between actors, places, and mobilizations" (chapter 3, 61–62). Solidarity-building in translocal contexts thus involves weaving struggles together not only across difference resulting from geographical distance (across borders) but also across difference resulting from differential positionality *within* a given society (along axes of race, ethnicity, migration status, class, gender and sexuality, religion, age, ability). This is a notion Sonia Alvarez labels "translocation": "linking geographies of power at various scales (local, national, regional, global) with subject positions (gender/sexual, ethnoracial, class, etc.) that constitute the self" (2014, 2). As such, while building solidarity *among already constituted struggles*, as highlighted by Masson and Paulos, is key, attention to existing intersectional power dynamics along the axes mentioned above even when attending organized struggles have not yet budded is also essential.

Following Alvarez, I will refer to the March and other such movements as translocal rather than transnational. I wish to move beyond the artifice of the "nation/national" to a more fine-grained analysis as it highlights both the heterogeneity present within a nation's borders (intersectionally) as well as the unevenness of movements' presence and rooting on any given "national" territory (geographically) (Alvarez 2014, 1–2).

Translocal solidarity work is complicated by the fact that such intersectional power dynamics are structured differently across geographically distant sites, producing misalignments in political cultures. Each context reveals differentiated racial formations, class stratification, and gender and sexuality systems, and so on. Maylei Blackwell refers to these misalignments as "unaligned geographies of difference" (2014, 300). She underscores the role of our current neoliberal globalized political economy which both sharpens inequalities in any given locale and simultaneously obscures these differences "through the illusion of inclusion in market multiculturalism" (300) as adding to the challenges translocal movements face to translate social meaning of differences across social scales. This paper will explore challenges to solidarity-building resulting from misalignments in terms of coloniality and indigeneity in the WMW, a movement whose focus, like most self-identified popular feminist movements, was originally built around gender and class issues (Lebon 2014; Giraud 2015).

This paper attends to translocal movements' discursive, material, and spatial practices, since "solidarity as a praxis [is] made of three interrelated types of practices—discursive, material, and spatial" (chapter 3, 62). However, a focus on discursive practices is unescapable since an essential component of solidarity-building is "*constructing* the grievances and aspirations of geographically, culturally, economically and, at times, politically different and distant peoples *as interlinked*" (Routledge and Cumbers 2009, 71; chapter 3, 62). As such, discursive practices will have a place of choice in these pages.

TRANSLATION AND POWER IN SOLIDARITY-BUILDING

Constructing linkages and highlighting commonalities require translation, both linguistic and conceptual, but such translation also needs to attend to unaligned geographies of difference. This is far from easy as "transnational social and political actors negotiate vectors of power organized around axes of gender, sexuality, race, indigeneity, class, citizenship, and geopolitics through a form of translation that involves representational struggles over meaning, identity, strategy, ideology, and power" (Blackwell 2014, 301). One important goal of this translation is to "transform identities and movement meanings across translocalities without erasing differences" (Blackwell 2014, 301).

Avoiding the erasure of differences in conceptual translation requires a deep understanding of the source and destination contexts/cultures, along with a keen awareness of power imbalances. Some of us are particularly well suited to identifying the power dynamics involved as a result of their multi-sited locations. In fact, they often find themselves to be "necessarily translators" (Alvarez 2014, 5). Alvarez emphasizes in her introduction to the volume *Translocalities/Translocalidades* the key role played by diasporic subjects, such as Afro-Latinas in North America, and especially those who are also "world travelers" and experience their "multiple locations or subject positions shift[ing]" in traveling along misaligned geographies of difference. Alvarez provides as example her own shifting ethnoracial identity from Cuban American (an ethnicized label) in South Florida to Latina (an oppressed racialized position) in New England and to white (a privileged racialized position) in São Paulo, Brazil (Alvarez 2014, 3). Because their "subjectivities are at once place-based and mis- or dis-placed," and they "are simultaneously and intermittently self and other" (2014, 3–4), such diasporic world travelers are in a privileged position to translate movement meanings.

The importance of power and of who does the translating is also highly relevant in Nicole Doerr's (2018) work on political translation, which she defines as a broad set of [disruptive and communicative] practices designed to address marginalization based on gender, class, race, and other differences—even within groups whose members speak the same language (Doerr 2018, 6). She argues for the benefit of involving in deliberations third party (political) translators who intentionally provide a reading of the situation which promotes the concerns of disempowered groups. Her thinking is based on a radical notion of power in communication which "assumes that playing fields require leveling before all factions can participate equally" (2018, 6).

In her study on conceptual translation in feminist communities, Geneviève Pagé actually calls on scholars to "center the notion of power" as it is expressed in both "empowerment as well as power imbalances" (chapter 6, 122). According to Pagé, conceptual translation in social movements involves "the integration of a new meaningful concept imported from 'outside' the border—[which] works to reconfigure borders, reshaping the 'us' and 'them'" (chapter 6, 129).

Finally, Pagé highlights the importance of contact zones where exchange can happen and she builds a framework identifying, "four main types of power dynamics [which] are at play to facilitate or impede the translation of concepts" from one feminist locale to another (chapter 6, 121). Pagé's four dynamics include: "(1) the strength and state of local theoretical tradition and movement", including the compatibility of a new concept with existing local theoretical tradition; "(2) the presence of bridge actors[1] with enough social capital to command a change in conceptual framings; (3) the capacity/desire of the movement to reconfigure its borders; and (4) asymmetries of power between languages" and cultures (chapter 6, 121).

I found the notions of contact zone, compatibility in theoretical traditions, and power asymmetries between languages particularly useful in my analysis of the challenges encountered by the March with integrating the concept of defense of women's bodies and territories.

Seeking to understand translocal social movement practices which facilitate or undermine solidarity-building, this paper analyzes the discursive, material, and spatial practices of a translocal social movement (the WMW) which functions as a *contact zone*—practices that may facilitate fruitful conceptual translation as a result of their capacity to level off power asymmetries. Effective conceptual translation in turn contributes to solidarity-building for movement-building. Using a translocation framework, I seek to elucidate the roots of a serious communication breakdown or "failure of translation" around the concept of "territorio," which prevented the March from crafting a unified slogan for its 2015 International Action. This failure of translation is more precisely an equivocation or "referential alterity between homonymic concepts" (Viveiros de Castro 2004, 5) where connotations of "*territorio*" and "*territoire*" are at odds. The paper then analyzes not only the practices deployed to control this equivocation but also the challenges these efforts present when taking into consideration power asymmetries among Western/ mestiza popular feminisms and Indigenous feminisms. Finally, I argue for a fully intersectional, translocal, analytical framework to resolve such issues in the face of unaligned geographies of difference and differential positionalities, in this case relative to coloniality.

The March as Contact Zone: A Solidarity Network Grounded in Local Autonomy

The WMW fits the profile of a long-lasting structured transnational "contact zone" (chapter 6, 122), whose acknowledgment of difference among women in principle bodes well for conceptual translation. For almost two decades, it has sought to build a worldwide movement across geographically distant movements, with a collective identity grounded in the acknowledgment of difference. Isabelle Giraud writes about the March:

> Diversity is the movement's foundational identity principle, as laid out by Women's Global Charter for Humanity: The World March of Women is a movement composed of women's groups of diverse ethnic, cultural, religious, political and class backgrounds, and different ages and sexual orientation. Far from dividing us, this diversity unites us in greater, more far-reaching solidarity. (2015, 96; my translation)

In fact, solidarity-building across this diversity is a crucial tool for the March, as argued by Masson and Paulos, who state that "making linkages and sustaining relations among a variety of kindred 'women's' and feminist mobilizations became one of the main organizational strategies of the March and a central component of its self-definition" (2018, 3).

Key to the March's strategy of building solidarity is its very structure as network and its grounding in the principle of granting autonomy and flexibility at the local level for input toward decisions made at the transnational level (Díaz Alba 2017).

Theoretically, this organizational form tends to generate respect for diversity because organizers need to keep a variety of actors on board (Scherer-Warren 2012). For translocal movements, networks are particularly beneficial because they facilitate the move from localized interests to a larger platform at a higher geographic level of scale (Scherer-Warren 2012, 46). This does not mean that networks cannot reproduce power dynamics from their original societal contexts. Observers of the March have found that its leadership is solidly anchored in the Global South and that the March has been effective at handling geographical diversity. However, attention to intersectional power dynamics *between women* around rurality, ethnicity/indigeneity, and class, within a given locale, has been uneven (Conway 2018). The March's international committee itself acknowledged, in 2011, the difficulties of the movement to integrate racism/colonialism in their analyses, as well as the issues faced by young people (Giraud 2015, 96).

The centrality of solidarity-building as a movement strategy for the March and the key role of conceptual translation in this dynamic are revealed most clearly in the challenges encountered in weaving local struggles into a unified, common vision/message for the whole translocal network.

LEVELING THE PLAYING FIELD IN THE CONTACT ZONE: STRUCTURE AND PRACTICES

The most crucial moment for solidarity-building in the WMW happens when choosing the theme, format, and slogan of their International Action every five years. This section analyzes the organizational, discursive, and other material and spatial practices the March deploys in this deliberative process. Many of these practices help level the playing field among member participants, which facilitates conceptual translation and helps build connections across such varied socioeconomic terrain and political histories as those of Brazil, France, Guatemala, and Quebec, to mention a few key players in these pages.

The organizational structure built by the March at the cross-border level to make decisions about the theme is guided by its desire to ensure respect for geographical diversity and a fair and balanced voice for all its member chapters. This decision is normally made by the International Meeting, a general assembly of over 150 delegates, facilitated by members of the International Committee, with the support of the International Secretariat. All three instances are designed with representativity of geographical diversity in mind. For example, each chapter sends three delegates[2] to the International Meeting every three years, where over 150 participants decide on the broad vision for the network. Each world region (Latin America, Africa, Europe, North America, etc.) chooses two delegates who sit on the International Committee, which meets every six months to guide implementation of the vision decided at the International Meeting. Emphasis is placed on rotating who sits on the committee, as well as those who attend the International Meeting, in an effort at democratizing leadership. The International Secretariat oversees the day-to-day operations of the coalition and facilitates communication across the network. This is obviously a very powerful position in the network. In this case too, the March has been concerned with geographical diversity and its attendant power dynamics. The Secretariat, originally located in Montreal, Quebec, where the March was launched, was then moved to the Global South, to São Paulo, Brazil, for seven years. Since 2014, it has been located in Maputo, Mozambique, with an eye to strengthen the African continent's participation in the March.

A translocal organizational structure geared toward the equitable distribution of power among participating members is likely to promote more open communication and negotiation of the theme among chapter members, hopefully providing a fertile terrain for effective conceptual translation among them. In other words, the March's organizational practices' strong attention to how power is distributed spatially is likely to contribute to this fertile terrain. There is, however, one important caveat, as the intersectional diversity present within national chapters is not reflected at the transnational decision-making level: for example, community-based women are rare in these instances, given the time commitment, resources, and linguistic skills needed to sit on the International Committee or attend the International Meeting (Giraud and Dufour 2010, 132–33).

CHOOSING A CAPACIOUS THEME OR RESORTING TO CONCEPTUAL TRANSLATION

The first three International Actions, in 2000, 2005, and 2010, had broad themes[3] derived from the March's already agreed-upon principles. Easing the risk of missteps in conceptual translation, these capacious themes allowed the March nonetheless to maximize the opportunity for linkages across localized grievances and aspirations under one common global theme. This strategy allows for a wide range of interpretations of a unified message, providing flexibility to adapt the message to local realities, thus facilitating linkages, without much need for new conceptual translation. These three themes articulated key overarching March principles: the struggle against poverty and violence against women, the importance of women's agency and activism in order to change the world, and a gender-class analytic: women's lives will not change until our capitalist, extractivist, and developmentalist system is changed.

Adopting a more challenging approach for the 2015 International Action, Latin American March organizers felt the need for a more specific theme. They wished to underscore the spreading and dire exploitation of natural resources, local communities, and their environment across the region, and thus also the need for access to land, and collective autonomy and control over their land by communities, especially in their struggles against agribusinesses and extractivism. In August 2013, as time came for the ninth International Meeting to choose a motto for the 2015 fourth International Action, the facilitator, a long-time feminist activist from Guatemala, introduced a few potential slogans along these lines. They included: "This is my body, this is our territory" and "We will keep on marching until our bodies and our territories are free."

The facilitator simply introduced the focus on the *cuerpo/territorio* (body/ territory) connection as originating "from the struggles in Guatemala." However, *territorio* in this case is a concept connected to Zapatismo and other forms of Indigenous quest for autonomy. This concept affirms Indigenous connections and right to the land and to self-governance denied by colonial powers. National chapters later received a text explaining the feminist meaning of connecting the exploitation of women's bodies to that of territories, which I discuss below.

The origins of the expanded concept of *territorio-cuerpo-tierra* in the diverse field of Indigenous feminisms are unclear, but it is now strongly associated with *Feminismo Comunitario* (Communitarian Feminism) and especially its elaboration by Lorena Cabnal. *Feminismo Comunitario* is a subset of Indigenous feminism which, contrary to others, "openly assert[s] its] feminism but from a radical framework (*autonoma* in Spanish)" and "theorize[s] from [its] own positionality in a permanent critique and dialogue with non-indigenous feminisms" (Gargallo 2015, 209, cited in Moore Torres 2018, 247; my translation). *Feminismo Comunitario* emerged under the leadership of two Indigenous women: Julieta Paredes in Bolivia and Lorena Cabnal in Guatemala (Cabnal 2010; Moore Torres 2018).

It is maybe *because* these Indigenous roots were not discussed early in the process that equivocation and disagreement ensued at the ninth International Meeting, as participants from various linguistic/political cultures and with various positionalities vis-à-vis coloniality engaged in an ultimately failed attempt at conceptual translation.

COMPATIBILITY CHALLENGE: EQUIVOCATION OVER *"TERRITORIO"* AND *"TERRITOIRE"*

Concerns about the proposed concept around defending women's bodies and territories emerged early, after an initial discussion in the three-language caucuses. The March has three official languages: Spanish, English, and French. The most salient concern focused on the meaning and connotations of the word *"territoire"* in a French-speaking political context. Quebec's delegation was the first to voice this concern and explained that *"territoire"* is a word used by the armed forces and the right, as well as in essentialist feminism. In the context of Quebec, they were concerned that this focus on *"territoire"* would lead to "recolonizing First Nations." Quebec's delegation received support from Greece, a delegate from the Arab world, and France. French delegates similarly argued that, in France, "territory is a word used by fascists, by the right. And slogans do matter. [Instead, they argued] Having several peoples on one territory is a blessing (*C'est une richesse d'avoir plusieurs peuples sur un territoire*)" (fieldnotes, p. 25). Note that the word "homeland" carries similar connotations in American English. Additional reservations came from colonized countries, such as New Caledonia, a French colony in the Pacific, officially considered *"Territoire d'Outre-Mer"* (Overseas Territory). As a result, for New Caledonians the term *"territoire"* is synonymous with not being able to exercise full citizenship. Palestine also had reservations (Interview by author via Skype, Miriam Nobre, August 19, 2016).

In response, other delegates argued for a re-appropriation of the word "territory." A delegate from Colombia suggested that the term should be redefined. She said: "The word 'territory' is ours. The system took it from us. We must give it meaning again, redefine it." Others searched for alternatives: Venezuela suggested finding a more capacious term, such as "it is my world." Mozambique suggested connecting "territory" and "solidarity": "regaining control over the concept of territory: linking territories and solidarities."

In sum, the fault lines here are muddled. They are not strictly along the Global North/Global South divide, otherwise, Spain and Portugal among other European countries with a colonizing history would have shared these reservations. Do note here that the Spanish chapter is not particularly strong in the March, while Galicia and Catalonia, regions with strong independence movements, are. Language/culture played a strong role in the disagreement. My notes about the language caucus reports back to the plenary include that the Spanish-speaking group stated: "We want to take up [the facilitator]'s proposal: emphasize the need for autonomy of our territory" (fieldnotes, p. 19). The Anglophone caucus also mentioned "my body, our territory" although it was not a high point of their report. Francophones mentioned autonomy of the body, autonomy at work, etc. (*autonomie des corps, dans le travail*, etc.) but they expressed an interest in a message centering on migration and solidarity. However, there is no denying that France and Quebec, the two most vocal chapters with reservations, are in the Global North, so that positionality relative to coloniality has a role to play in this scenario.

PRACTICES FOR BUILDING LINKAGES DURING DELIBERATION

In its commitment to equity and diversity, even if imperfect, the March deploys a set of material and spatial deliberation practices that can help work through this type of impasse. Exploring and perfecting such potentially power-leveling practices is essential because "[e]xperience has shown that despite the best intentions of those attempting to institute a form of democracy that is direct, grassroots-based, and fair to all, challenges arise from informal, often-hidden power differentials that can lead to inequality in the deliberative process" (Doerr 2018, 18). And all voices need to be heard for the various meanings of a given concept to be fully expressed and explored for effective conceptual translation to take place.

This section highlights how some of these practices aim to (1) build on already existing solidarities and strengths, (2) provide space for negotiation, and/or (3) alleviate tension, such as holding language caucuses, promoting informal conversations, as well as mindfulness through the use of the body and movement, and finally also prioritize consensus building. Through it all, it is also worth noting the value placed by the March on face-to-face interactions as opposed to cyber communication for this type of crucial decision-making, highlighting the spatial dimension of solidarity-building practices (see Díaz Alba 2017).

Language Caucuses for Linguistic Diversity or a North/South Cross-cutting Strategy?

Translocal movements that work across linguistic diversity generally face additional challenges for solidarity-building practices, as working through difference based on geographic distance and intersectional diversity among participants is further complicated by the presence of multiple languages and the need for linguistic translation. Thus, chances for equivocation are heightened. However, Nicole Doerr (2018) has demonstrated that, even though linguistically diverse groups are faced with greater levels of uncertainty and complexity, which can lead to the reproduction of power hierarchies, they are often more inclusive than homogeneous social movements and survive longer. This is especially the case when the presence of linguistic diversity highlights for progressive-minded activists the need for greater attention to linguistic as well as other hierarchies of power, and even more so when political translators are present in deliberation where they amplify the voices of marginalized actors.

As mentioned earlier, the three official languages of the March are Spanish, French, and English, but participants' native languages are, of course, much more diverse. Meeting organizers planned a first discussion of the theme as well as objectives, format, symbol, and motto of the fourth International Action, in the three-language caucuses. Dividing the participants in this way is interesting because it brings together, in smaller, more participatory groups, chapters from different world regions, including across the Global North and Global South divide, to hammer out differences and build consensus. These language caucuses may help level the playing field but have serious limitations.

In addition, ideally, such an approach allows participants from different parts of the world who share a language to communicate unencumbered by the mediation of a linguistic translator, in real time, and with all the nuances necessary in negotiating tense issues. Nonetheless, many delegates have to communicate and negotiate in a language which is not their first or even second language. This is especially true for delegates from Asian countries who resort to English (Díaz Alba 2017; chapter 6). This is problematic because, as Nicole Doerr argues: "civic deliberation, in order to be truly democratic and inclusive, needs to take place in people's authentic language, their local vernacular (Kymlicka 2001); otherwise public discourse reifies cultural misrecognition and linguistic colonialism (Taylor 1995)" (2018, 8).

The fact that the March's official languages are European colonial languages also obviously complicates solidarity-building processes. The language caucuses likely draw on the solidarity, cultural, and institutional commonalities resulting from a shared colonial language and history but people's mother tongues/local vernaculars are pushed aside. Also, people who are able to speak the colonial language are most likely the ones with privileged access to formal education and to learning that language. Finally, each language caucus does not only bring together participants from the (former) colonized Global South but includes participants from colonizing European countries, with all the attendant power dynamics. Direct observation of the French language caucus did not reveal any obvious dominance by French delegates at this particular meeting. However, such power dynamics need attention, along with other potential sources of influence, such as member chapters' size and resources.

"Weaving Connections": Some Material Practices of Solidarity-Building

The judicious use of time, in particular, imparting plenty of time for participants to think, share, and debate an issue, is an important practice of the March to create fertile terrain for conceptual translation. Its organizers do not blink at organizing their International Meeting over the course of a week: the ninth International Meeting lasted from August 25 to 31, 2013. Of note here too is the willingness to devote the movement's sparse resources to expensive face-to-face communication through international travel and formal professional simultaneous interpretation (highlighting the spatial dimension of solidarity-building praxis).

Once the meeting begins, on a number of occasions, reports and activities are timed so that participants can continue discussing informally in the evenings what they have heard during the meeting before making a decision. Making further judicious use of space, participants are hosted collectively to facilitate this process. Lunch is also provided on-site, which promotes conversations and intermingling of the participants.

Informal, small group discussion is also encouraged for participants during the plenary early in the process to connect with each other through "*chuchotage*" or whispering, an informal way of allowing participants to "weave connections among us," to use the phrase of the facilitator. In the case at hand, the goal was to facilitate cohesion and coalescence to see themes and slogans emerge which would weave together the various issues raised in the language caucus reports. A list of themes was generated, some including the notion of body/territory, others not.

Easing Tension and Facilitating Communication: Other Material Practices of Solidarity-Building

Organizers used other strategies to alleviate tension and facilitate the open expression of opinions and concerns, so that conceptual translation could take place and a consensus could be built. Feminist practices involving the use of the body and movement are notable here. Songs were used to set the tone at the beginning of a difficult discussion, generally with a simple positive message. Breathing and stretching exercises were used during a particularly tense discussion "to chase negative thoughts" (fieldnotes, pp. 12 and 16). Organizers seemed to draw on the rich repertoire and "other ways" of doing politics of non-Western women's groups in these efforts.

Prioritizing Linkages

The March values consensus building and its power to create connections and ensure commitment, but it also relies on voting to finalize decisions, when necessary. In the case at hand, it also demonstrates flexibility to ensure continued engagement when consensus fails, as shown below. In doing so, the March prioritizes maintaining connections, solidarity, and local autonomy over an artificial show of unity.

As consensus around the use of the notion of body/territory did not materialize after a third day of conversation, facilitators were preparing the assembly for a vote. The various options were listed on the board, then three delegations registered their opposition to a vote, highlighting the importance of building consensus for the March (fieldnotes, p. 28). A vote proceeded nonetheless, with each (national) chapter delegation entitled to one ballot. According to Michelle Spieler, a long-time March activist, votes are usually taken on paper of different colors to represent the different regions of the world to make sure that no continent is totally absent from the final choice. It means that more conversation is needed in order to deal with a problem for the missing region (fieldnotes, p. 28). However, this time the vote was not taken on paper of different colors. Granted, the problem may not appear in a continent-based identification since it was partly linguistically/culturally based. The vote demonstrated decidedly that no consensus had been reached, although the term territory was present in the first and third most voted slogans. The meeting adjourned with the prospect of further discussion the following day among national coordinating bodies and in meetings by world regions.

In the end, the various practices deployed by the March were not sufficient to elucidate the differences in meanings toward a consensus, and body/territory did not make it as the 2015 worldwide theme. Indeed, March organizers were not beholden to the vote, as a more straightforward democratic centralist model would entail. Instead, they kept the conversation going to find a solution: a query (*consulta*) with National Coordinating Bodies was organized and the slogan finally chosen for 2015 was that of the broader 2010 International Action[4] (Miriam Nobre interview, August 19, 2016). The focus on body/territory did remain in the slogans of some Central American countries.

UNDERSTANDING THE EQUIVOCATION

Contrary to what some participants said during the debate, the issue around the word "territory" was more than a simple linguistic issue. Instead, it involved navigating divergent political histories and cultures with regard to coloniality, as some of these nations have been colonized, while the others have been the colonizers. It also revealed the differential position of Indigenous peoples and migrants within national cultures and discourses on immigration. In other words, conflicting positionalities *within* national formations also mattered.

It is very different for Indigenous and peasant movements in Central America, fully involved in decolonizing struggles, to claim to defend and gain autonomy over their territory than it is for native-born citizens of colonizing European countries in the contemporary context of anti-immigrant sentiment or for non-native members of settler colonies. Indeed, defending *"notre territoire"* in the French national political culture resonates strongly with anti-immigrant rhetoric. In the Central American context, defending one's territory on the part of marginalized populations is laudable, in coherence with the March's principles of justice, equality, and solidarity (See World March of Women 2004).

Conversely, native-born European women's claim to defend the territorial integrity of "their" nation smacks of nationalist racism and anti-immigration discourse. Such claims do not align with the March's principles. They would signify the unalienable right to the land, broadly construed, of those whose ancestors were born there, thus relegating to the status of second-class citizen all those who are not considered to belong to this territory. Interestingly, this seems to point to these delegates acknowledging their own privilege, since none of them were (at least not ostensibly) members of a First Nation (Quebec) or of an immigrant community (France). The position of New Caledonia, a French Overseas Territory, also questioning the slogan, complicates this analysis even further: they certainly would claim autonomy over their island territory but it seems the very word *"territoire"* has been too irremediably tainted by its use by the colonial power.

Tensions ensued from this equivocation, as at least some March organizers judged the French position rejecting the notion of *"territoire"* as, and I quote, "imperialist" (Ceregatti, personal communication). The following section attempts to explain the source of this communication breakdown.

Pagé explains that communication in social movements breaks down "either because of a political collective decision to choose one word over the other, or because of a lack of access to theories in their complexities" (Pagé 2018, 4). Others, like Brazilian feminist literary scholar Claudia de Lima Costa (2014a), argue that there is a measure of incommensurability, or non-translatability, in all translations. Incommensurability is reflected in the fact that, according to anthropologist Viveiros de Castro: "to translate is always to betray . . . However, a good translation is one that betrays the destination language, not the source language. A good translation is one [where] the intention of the original language can be expressed within the new one" (2004, 5). Thus, "translation [is] a process of controlled equivocation— 'controlled' in the sense that walking may be said to be a controlled way of falling" (Viveiros de Castro 2004, 5).

Costa uses Viveiros de Castro's concept of controlled equivocation in her discussion of transnational feminist networks. This concept is particularly useful in illuminating the challenge experienced by the March described above. Costa writes: "The notion of equivocation, which comes from Amerindian perspectivism and theorized by Viveiros de Castro (2004), means not simply a mistake, a misconception, but the incapacity to understand that different understandings of different worlds do exist" (Costa 2014b, 285; my translation).

Controlling such equivocation means highlighting the way the two seemingly identical terms bring completely different connotations to the table. In the process, according to Viveiros de Castro, we get to understand much more deeply how the two cultural contexts are related to each other. In the case of the words *"territorio"* and *"territoire,"* the connection is through opposing experiences of colonialism (as colonized versus colonizer). Thus, it also means having to address the fact that solidarity, between women and across chapters of the March, needs to be built across the Global North/Global South divide broadly speaking, and across other multiple vectors of identity, privilege, and oppression.

Sensitive to the equivocation involved, the March could not sustain a focus on "territory" in a worldwide slogan. Slogans are especially treacherous because they require immediately recognizable words, instantaneous meaning. They leave little room for controlling equivocation. While slogans do generally benefit from being ambiguous because they can rally many under the same banner, too big a divergence in meaning, such as in this case, needs to be clarified. This is because the divergence is deeply tied to a power asymmetry among participants. The equivocation needs to be controlled for connections and solidarity to be maintained.

CONTROLLING THE EQUIVOCATION

Since 2013, March organizers have kept working at controlling the equivocation. They have sought to solidify the intended meaning of the body/territory concept—the Central American meaning rooted in Indigenous experience of land alienation—and to spread this meaning through the March, as well as through other progressive networks and fields, such as the 2016 World Social Forum held in Montreal.

In an effort to divulgate the proper context for understanding the body/territory concept, the March circulated, in spring 2014, a short conceptual paper, written by members of the WMW Guatemala and *Mesoamericanas en Resistencia*, which I translated into English for the International Secretariat (*Documento síntesis sobre Territorios y Territorialidad—Reflexiones síntesis*). The document announces its focus "on the topic of defense of territories: Body-Earth/Territory, which was approved [*sic*] as theme for the 2015 International Action" and proceeds to detail the thinking behind the connection between *cuerpo* and *territorio*, although again, no reference is made to Communitarian Feminism.

Intent on reaching a broader audience beyond its network, the March issued a declaration at the 2016 World Social Forum held in Montreal which again refers to the concept of "*cuerpo-territorio*" within the proper context. It states:

> The meeting of our WMW militants allowed us to reconfirm the linkages between the different local struggles and connect on a global level the defense of our bodies, Mother Earth and territories. (World March of Women, 2016)

In this document, efforts at controlling the equivocation rest in the fact that the reference to "*territoire*" comes only after two introductory paragraphs which (1) emphasize that territories were stolen from Indigenous people and, in this case, recognizes Montreal as non-conceded Mohawk territory (first paragraph), and (2) reject the anti-immigration policies of governments (especially those in the North, as the Spanish and French versions specify "*our* governments," although "our" was lost in the English version).[5] The text in French and Spanish also refer to "tak[ing] responsibility as non-indigenous peoples" for the colonization of indigenous territories. The English translation, which, judging from other errors, seems to have been hasty, again misses this emphasis, and should read, "this acknowledgement [of the Mohawk territory] aims to . . . take responsibility, as non-indigenous persons, collectively, for the challenges faced by indigenous peoples."

Only after these clarifications does the text of the March introduce the notion of "defense of our bodies and territories." According to Miriam Nobre, the focus on defense of bodies/territories came back at the Forum because most participants were from the Americas and this formulation comes from a construction from the Americas (Interview, August 19, 2016). However, I also wish to highlight the way the group carefully laid out the context, scaffolding the discourse in order to provide the proper context, hence clarifying the meaning of "territoire." In so doing, they controlled the equivocation for a multilingual and translocal audience, especially a French-speaking one, as well as for those native to colonizing or settler powers concerned about exclusionary discourse.

POWER, RECONFIGURATION OF MOVEMENT BORDERS, AND THE CHALLENGE OF CONTROLLING EQUIVOCATION: TRANSLATING CUERPO-TERRITORIO

For Latin American March organizers, controlling the equivocation effectively means seeking to integrate the concept of defense of our bodies and territories into the March's transnational popular feminist theoretical framework. Centering power and border policing within Latin American women's movements, this section draws on Pagé's framework, outlined earlier, to explore how power relations among various strands of feminism play out in the process of integration/conceptual translation at hand, and whose meaning ultimately prevails, especially when moving from local to higher levels of scale.

To begin, it is worth further exploring the original meaning of the body/territory concept. According to sociologist Lia Barbosa, whose work focuses on protagonism among Zapatista women, *territory-body-earth* constitutes one of the key concepts in the theoretical framework of Communitarian Feminism, as laid out by Guatemalan Maya-Xinca activist Lorena Cabnal

(Barbosa 2021). In an interview to El Pais, Cabnal states that "[its] goal was to bring to light the need to weave together struggles against extractivist projects with those against violence by men on women's bodies in these same communities in resistance" (Giménez and Sánchez 2017). However, Barbosa writes that the concept goes deeper, as it "start[s] from Indigenous cosmovision and world," as shown below (2021).

The concept of territory/body/earth, connecting struggles against patriarchy, colonial rule, capitalism, especially extractivist projects, and environmental degradation, reflects Indigenous women's need for a decolonial push, which hegemonic Latin American feminisms, including most forms of self-identified popular feminisms, have been slow in providing. The concept highlights the fact that, for Indigenous women, gender equity will not be meaningful without a challenge to colonial relations of ruling and human domination of nature. Hence, the key role of recognizing the importance of autonomy of their territory for Indigenous communities and thus for Indigenous feminist struggles. We recognize here the tensions between a counter-hegemonic and a pluriversal solidarity modality highlighted in the introduction to this book.

Considering compatibility issues, as highlighted by Pagé, I believe the WMW, a self-identified popular feminist network, welcomes this concept which resonates with its foundational critique of the interlinked oppressions of patriarchy and capitalism, including a particular focus on anti-extractivism. "Defending our body/territory" is thus compatible with the overarching Left counter-hegemonic theoretical tradition of the March. Although, this compatibility is the result of selective translation, as I discuss below. In addition, the value placed on diversity among women in the March's collective identity, described earlier, presents a fertile ground for integrating this new concept. In its quest for building a mass movement, the March also likely needs the growing mobilizing power of this concept in Central American and other Indigenous contexts.

However, this concept lacks compatibility, but not only in the way discussed earlier as due to nationalistic connotations of the word "*territoire.*" Power imbalances in Latin American women's movements present additional compatibility challenges, evident as we explore whether the March has the "capacity/desire [. . .] to reconfigure its borders" (chapter 6, 121) between its original brand of popular feminism and Indigenous/decolonial feminisms. Indeed, Indigenous feminism and indigeneity (just like Afro-*Latinidad*) have wielded little power in liberal and socialist Latin American feminisms, including popular feminisms, until very recently. The Marxist roots of the latter, where gender-class is primary, increase the risk that the decolonial critique may get lost or be presented as secondary (Giraud 2015; chapter 3, 73). In the March, we see at work the legacy of its Québécois and Francophone materialist feminist roots, as well as of its Latin American socialist and popular feminist roots (Conway 2017a, 16, 10).

I have identified three potential slippages where these differences in theoretical traditions, solidarity modalities, and power asymmetries can devolve the concept of "defending our bodies and territories" of its original meaning and political potential (chapter 6). First, *"territorio"* in Indigenous feminisms is a much fuller concept, not just related to anti-extractivism or anti-capitalism, but rather to decolonization more broadly. In an interview, Cabnal herself highlights its pluriversal solidarity logic:

> When we speak of recovering and defending land, we aren't talking about the occidental interpretation of land. We aren't referring to the geographic territory that determines a specific population, a state or country. We have used the words "land" or "territory" to get as close to what we want to express about this historic and ancestral relationship that our communities have had with the earth. (Britto Schwartz 2013; see also Cabnal 2010)

Second, others have brought attention to the fact that hegemonic Latin American feminisms, with their Western and urban roots, tend to focus on the body and the individual, while Indigenous feminists' focus is more collective and centered on both body and territory. Popular feminisms are receptive to collective demands but still within a Western cosmovision.

Finally, observers have noted "the consequence of non-Indigenous and Indigenous people inhabiting worlds of radically different ontological natures" (chapter 3, 73), which creates some incommensurability or non-translatability between these worlds. More specifically, Masson and Paulos recount the bridges built intentionally by the March Macro-Norte (Peru) with the Indigenous community of Cañaris's struggle against the extractivist project of Cañarico. They alert us to the difference in meaning this struggle holds for Indigenous women beyond the fight against extractivism (anti-capitalism) of the March activists. They write:

> Thus, when the women of Cañaris speak of defending their territory, nature, "sacred mountain" and "water as a life force," (Chambeu 2015), which de la Cadena analyzes as the irruption of sentient "earth beings" in social protest (2010, 336), the March MN ignores the excess meaning carried by their voices and reinterprets their claims under a rationale for solidarity against extractivism that makes capitalism into the "common" enemy. (chapter 3, 73–74)

Here we see how the counter-hegemonic logic behind much of the March's solidarity modality conflicts with the Indigenous pluriversal modality. In terms of translation and solidarity-building, this example brings to mind Page's reminder that "the work of bridge actors is a delicate balance between making an idea intelligible by using existing ideas and conserving its original meaning and its political potential" (chapter 6, 129).

This example also highlights the fact that equivocation or the "incapacity to understand that different understandings of different worlds do exist" (Costa 2014b, 285) may facilitate early connections and solidarity-building, but needs to be laid bare and eventually controlled for long-term solidarity ties to endure and to avoid any recolonizing. Indeed, equivocation at first may allow for differences in local meanings to be minimized, putting the emphasis on what participants from different perspectives think they have in common, without engaging in full discussion of what they agree/disagree on. Elucidating such difference seems essential to longer term solidarity-building by successfully controlling the equivocation. This last step requires, as highlighted by scholars of power in translation, understanding and counteracting the power relations among actors, which influence which version of the equivocation is going to prevail, especially as we move to a higher spatial scale in the network.

Ultimately, though, theorists of translation, such as Costa (2014a), and observers of social movement dynamics (chapter 3) call for accepting some measure of incommensurability or non-translatability in all translations. This understanding is key to the building of translocal solidarities, according to Leinius, who argues that building solidarity does not require fully understanding the Other's stance—in fact, striving for full intelligibility can actually complicate matters. Instead, political solidarity requires that we use our imagination to supplement complete intelligibility of the Other, since our understanding of the Other is always limited (chapter 5, 110). Citing Spivak, she argues that the politics of solidarity are thus a "problem of relation rather than a problem of knowledge" (Spivak 2000, 105). We see here how useful coalitional politics is, as called for by transnational feminism and highlighted in the introduction to this book.

BUILDING BONDS BEYOND GEOGRAPHICAL DIVERSITY WITH AN INTERSECTIONAL/TRANSLOCAL LENS

The reconciliation of the divergent connotations of the concept of "body/territory" discussed in these last pages illustrates the usefulness of Alvarez's translocal framework for networks such as the March, combining attention to geographical diversity with attention to localized intersectional dynamics.

While such networks may be, like the March, attentive to geographical diversity across distance, every (national) chapter is also characterized by an intersecting set of vectors of inequality *between* women, as intersectionality theory has pointed out. Of interest to us in the case at hand are power dynamics *between* women around coloniality, immigration, and ethnicity, as well as indigeneity. While Quebec activists were concerned about excluding First Nations women when using the slogan focusing on "territory," French and other European chapters with large migrant populations were concerned about an exclusionary discourse for migrants. Yet, representativity along these lines has not been a key concern of the March, although some national chapters may have been more sensitive to it than others. According to political scientist Isabelle Giraud, the March has practiced a *"politique de présence"* in its efforts to integrate feminist youth, deliberately including young women in governing bodies, whereas a *"politique des idées"* or discursive politics seem to be slowly under way in the case of racialized, migrant, and Indigenous women (Giraud 2015, 98–99, 112).

This slow change is likely related to the fact that the March's original gender-class analytic tends to obscure attention to other axes of inequality: Jennifer Nash reminds us of "the tendency of radical projects to elide critical differences *within* ostensibly marginalized subject positions" (2007, 12). The introduction to this book also helps us understand the limitations of emancipatory elaborations of solidarity as well as how "euro-modernist elaborations of solidarity elude questions of dissimilarity, marginalization and power *within* the political community that (supposedly) coalesces in, around, or thanks to solidarity" (xvi).

A further look at how the debate over "body/territory" evolved in Quebec illustrates the complexity brought about by considering intersectional dynamics and positionalities *among* women. Indeed, this debate, initiated at the transnational level, reverberated at lower levels of scale, notably at the local level. In Quebec, contrary to the position supported by this chapter's three delegates in São Paulo who feared focusing the fourth International Action on defending our *"territoire"* would mean recolonizing Canada's First Nations, Indigenous women's groups participating in the March in Quebec did express an interest in a 2015 slogan focusing on the concept of body/territory. For Quebec's dispossessed Indigenous groups, defending their *"territoire"* entailed the same progressive meaning as for Guatemalan Indigenous women, unlike for Québécoises of French descent whose ancestors colonized this part of what is now Canada. Disagreement ensued, which was later resolved, about how relevant the theme would be to mobilize Quebec women,[6] according to one observer (Díaz Alba, personal communication May 25, 2018). Conflicting positionalities *within* national formations really come into view in this case.

The key role of indigeneity and coloniality in this scenario, which others are better positioned to detail than me, nonetheless reveals the benefits of a translocal framework, attentive to unaligned geographies of difference, for cross-border feminist networks as they engage in conceptual translation to build long-lasting solidarity ties. A fully intersectional framework, which brings race/ethnicity, indigeneity, and immigration, as well as sexuality, age, ability, and religion to the table, while not an easy task, would provide powerful analytics to any given political scape (Nash 2008) and help diagnose potential equivocations and other failures of translation, and thus help build stronger solidarity it bonds.

In this context, movements need to be ready to engage in the painstakingly slow process of moving forward toward better cross-cultural understanding through controlling equivocations by laying bare the roots of conflicting preexisting localized political cultures and the differentiated positions of privilege and oppression between and among network members. I argue that a thoroughly intersectional framework is essential to such conceptual translation efforts. This means overcoming the fear of opening the Pandora's box of difference among women for movements often built on a discourse of unity.

NOTES

1. Alvarez's "*translocas*" is a good example, so is Claudia de Lima Costa's "Theory Brokers" (2014a, 25) in her work on the academy and feminist NGOs.

2. This representativity is still largely built on the primacy of the nation-state and on representative democracy.

3. 2000: "Contra la pobreza y la violencia que se hace a las mujeres" (No to poverty and violence against women).

2005: "Mujeres mudando el mundo para mudar la vida de las mujeres" (Women changing the world to change women's lives).

2010: "Estaremos en marcha hasta que todas las mujeres sean libres" (Women on the march until we are all free).

4. See note 3.

5. Original text in French, published on August 19, 2016; Spanish and English versions published on August 22, 2016.

French version: *Cette reconnaissance vise à rendre visible la colonisation des territoires sur lesquels nous sommes et à prendre responsabilité comme personnes non-autochtones, collectivement, des enjeux qui affectent les peuples autochtones aujourd'hui.*

Spanish version: *Este reconocimiento quiere hacer visible la colonización de los territorios en los cuales estamos y a tomar la responsabilidad como persona no indígena, colectivamente, de los desafíos que afectan a estos pueblos.*

English version: *This acknowledgement makes visible the colonization of these territories, as well as to take collective responsibility of the challenges faced by these peoples.*

6. First Nations women's organizations ended up participating in the 2015 action (FAQ—*Femmes Autochthones du Québec*). One of their members participated in the delegation for the Americas regional meeting in Peru (2016).

Afterword

Reflections on Cross-Border Solidarities and Transnational Feminist Analytics[1]

Manisha Desai

After a recent Nor'easter, I was excited to be the first to blaze a trail with my snowshoes on the freshly fallen snow on a rail trail near our place. But when I got there, I saw that the town had plowed it, depriving me of that possibility. Briefly disappointed, I still enjoyed the beauty and magic of an abundant snowfall, momentarily pushing to the background the reality of climate change. It led me, however, to reflect on path breaking as a metaphor that we often use to describe exciting work that provides a fresh perspective, as this book does. It was a reminder that even as we "make the path by walking" and explore new terrain, we are both guided by earlier routes, fresh or well-worn, and limited by them. It is this recognition that informs my reflections on this book that pushes us to think critically and envision boldly.

It is by combining the concrete and the abstract that the authors contribute to a feminist theorizing of cross-border solidarities in the twenty-first century, fraught as they are with the undermining of modernist certainties of progress and emancipation on the left, the neoliberal hegemonies in the center, and the ascendancy of neo-fascist and populist uprisings on the right. Yet, as the authors in this book demonstrate, cross-border solidarities continue, albeit in different registers and spaces from those evident in the heyday of contemporary transnational activism in the 1990s and the 2000s, in the context of: the fall of the Berlin Wall; the United Nations world conferences on the environment, human rights, population, social development, and women; and the rise of global justice movements[2] that coalesced around the World Social Forum gatherings and processes.

And it is in illuminating these cross-border solidarities in all their complexities that this book shines and provokes us. Informed by intersectional and transnational feminisms as well as the global justice movements of the late twentieth and early twenty-first centuries, the editors theorize the key, yet underdeveloped, problematic of solidarities as a political praxis "across political borders and spatialized differences," located in contemporary global power relations as well as histories of colonialism, imperialism, and nationalism. Moreover, solidarities are not given but have to be actively constructed and maintained through different phases of struggles. Even in a transnational context, solidarities are not free from the political and geographical realities of local communities. Thus, the editors note:

> [W]e argue and demonstrate that geographical concepts of place and scale powerfully contribute to further feminist inquiries into transnational solidarity-building in directing our attention to solidarities across space and difference as actively produced and grounded in concrete socio-spatial praxes.

Our understanding of space, scale, and place, however, has undergone a great deal of revision in the era of contemporary globalization. Massey (1994) was among those who asked us to question the binary of place as bounded versus space as flow. Indigenous feminists (e.g., Goeman 2009; Hall 2009) have provided some illuminating ways beyond such binaries. The conceptualization of place as bounded, they argue, is a specifically European formulation. In Indigenous cultures, place has been understood in more fluid ways. Place, Indigenous scholars argue, is important to the imaginary geographies of Indigenous communities but it is not bounded or static. Rather, its dynamism is articulated in varied ways. For example, Goeman (2009) notes that in the Navajo tradition, breath is the metaphor that connects all living things across boundaries. Place is thus not bound by geopolitics but rather defined by stories as continuous.

Thus, a sense of belonging can be recreated in multiple places. For example, in the United States urban Indigenous populations recreate urban clans as a way to survive in the midst of uprooting (Goeman 2009). Language brings speaker and world into existence. Similarly, Hawaiian scholar Epeli Hau'ofa's (1994) metaphor of "sea of islands" turns the concept of islands as isolated in a vast ocean on its head by suggesting instead that oceans connect people on islands and the mainland. Like breath and the sea of islands, place connects us to other humans, species, and real and imagined other spaces. Thus, these understandings of place as grounded yet fluid can be generative in how they become central to solidarities as conceptualized in this book.

Tracing a Eurocentric genealogy of solidarity from Greco-Roman, early modern Republic, Christian, and sociological origins, the editors show how BIPOC (Black, Indigenous, People of Color) activists, transnational feminists, and the global justice movement activists critiqued the white, liberal, and universal assumptions of Euro-modern models of solidarity. Instead, these critics centered difference, arising from modernity/coloniality within and across national borders that had to be confronted in any cross-border activism and solidarity. Thus, solidarities of difference become the key normative and political projects in these theorizations. Yet, as the editors note, these critical models of solidarities across difference remain normative aspirations and do not offer insights about actually existing cross-border solidarities across movements.

Hence, drawing upon insights from transnational feminisms, the global justice movements, and theoretical reflection on their own work in cross-border movements, including the World March of Women (WMW), Conway (2019) identified three modalities through which cross-border solidarities are imagined and enacted: counter-hegemonic, intersectional-feminist, and pluriversal. The first has Gramscian roots and seeks to replace the hegemony of global capitalism with an alternative socialist hegemony; the intersectional-feminist solidarities are based on multiple and intersecting systems of oppression and seek to build solidarities across difference in all domains of life to address injustice and inequality. Finally, pluriversal solidarities, emerging from Zapatista and Indigenous struggles, imagine worlds within worlds that address "cosmological, even ontological, difference in a politics of coexistence and shared or overlapping sovereignties" (introduction to this book, xxv).

These modalities led me to contemplate two interrelated issues. One, to reflect on whether *Ubuntu* and *Sarva Vishwa Kutumbh* (the whole world is a family) may be understood as modalities of solidarities from the Global South even though they may not align with the Eurocentric understanding of the concept. Two, the importance of non-colonial languages in our theorizing and praxis. I had worked with these two concepts as a way to think of belonging and citizenship beyond the Eurocentric liberal subjectivity that undergirds most modern understanding of rights and citizenship (Desai 2010). Ubuntu is a philosophy and ethics shared by many Southern African cultures, specifically the Bantu and Shona-speaking peoples. Elsewhere in Eastern and Central Africa, such as in Tanzania, Kenya, and Rwanda, there are concepts that are similar to Ubuntu. Sarva Vishwa Kutumbh is a Vedic philosophy found in many Hindu communities in India.

At the heart of Ubuntu and Sarva Vishwa Kutumbh is a sense of interconnection, a vertical one between humans, animals, and plants on earth below to gods, goddesses, and ancestors above. The horizontal connection is between people and other species that is shaped by reciprocity. These interconnections are captured in phrases like "All Our Relations" and "I am because others are and because others are I am." This ontology is distinct from the Western sense of self which is conceptualized as an autonomous individual and based on a dualism which separates the individual from the collective.

In Ubuntu and Vedic ontologies, relationships are formed and recreated by symbolic and actual relations and obligations rather than rights and nation-state borders. This sense of belonging is more explicitly reciprocal, generous, and affirms one's own humanity by the recognition of it in others. Dignity and respect for each person is the basis of humanity. Feminists everywhere, rightly so, have been wary of such collective or communitarian ontologies as they have often been the basis of marginalizing women. But as Louw notes: "True *ubuntu* . . . operates in a dialogical manner, it incorporates both 'relation and distance' . . . It preserves the other in her otherness, in her uniqueness, without letting her slip into the distance" (Louw 1998, 10–11). Shutte (2001) echoes this as well, "the community is not opposed to the individual, nor does it simply swallow the individual up; it enables each individual to become a unique centre of shared life" (2001, 9, cited in Forster 2006, 17).

Such cosmovisions may resonate with the pluriversal modality of solidarity or may suggest other hybrid modalities that include relationships across species that become even more relevant as we deal with not just the climate change but also the cyclical pandemics that result from the industrial agricultural basis of our current food system. Other modalities might also become possible if we attend to language, my second reflection related to solidarities. Despite our commitments to worlds within worlds, most scholarship is written in colonial, European languages even when writing about others whose languages are not commensurable with the colonizers' languages, as Lebon demonstrates in her chapter on the failure of translation of the concept of *territorio*, which meant different things to Indigenous, mestiza, European, and Quebecois activists, and just as intersectionality was resisted by Francophone activists in Montreal for multiple reasons as Pagé shows in her chapter. To me, this suggests the need for us to be more attentive and creative in our use of language—not just via translation and imaginative leaps as Leinius suggests in her chapter, but through learning and incorporating other languages in our theorizing and writing as poets and writers have done, for example, through the use of Spanglish. While Spanglish is a hybrid of two colonial languages, the use of cosmovisions like *ubuntu*, *sumak kawsay*, and *sarva viswa kutumbh* would not only remind us of the hegemony of colonial languages and cosmologies but also illuminate existing alternatives.

Such reminders are necessary for us to reflect on our own theoretical practices such as that evident in the transnational feminist analytic (TFA). Conway (2017a) and the editors in this book have done so in many ways, most importantly by differentiating between transnational feminism as an analytic versus actually existing transnational feminist praxis. But if TFA is to remain relevant as an example of theorizing across differences, it needs to be in conversation with other imaginings across difference. In particular, I highlight three such endeavors: decolonial feminisms that center the settler coloniality of the United States, subaltern postcolonial feminisms such as

Dalit feminism that challenge the Brahmanic supremacy of Indian *Savarna*[3] feminism, and decolonial, postsocialist feminisms that further the already recognized erasure of the erstwhile Second World from TFA.

Within Women's Studies in the United States, where transnational feminism emerged, transnational feminism has always meant feminisms elsewhere (e.g., Chowdhury 2009), hence its putative interchangeability with Third World, International, or Global/South feminisms. Even when scholars included feminisms in the Global North in considerations of transnational feminism, as for example in Naples and Desai (2002), at best it was associated with feminisms of color within the Global North. Despite this link to non-hegemonic feminisms, what remained invisible and untheorized within TFA was the settler coloniality of the United States. Although Masson and Paulos (chapter 3) note that TFA is "explicitly decolonial, anti-imperialist, anti-capitalist in the case of Mohanty; critical of the material and cultural expressions of modernity—its 'scattered hegemonies'—in the work of Grewal and Kaplan (1994, 17)," neither Grewal and Kaplan nor Mohanty explicitly read the United States as a settler colony. This is what led Bonita Lawrence to note that

> there is a very big reason that a lot of Aboriginal theorists, even women theorists who focus on Aboriginal women, don't take up transnational feminism: we are not postcolonial. We are still colonized . . . I think the reason I haven't found it useful is because of this lack of awareness of what it means to still be colonized, what it means to communities in the every day. One of the things that it means is that you are removed from being global actors, you are removed as actors on the global stage, so that decolonization stops in the Americas, and in Australia and New Zealand, it stops. (Lawrence and Thorpe 2005, 6)

Similarly, in 2017 at a workshop on "Neoliberal Spaces of Contention" at Rutgers University, a colleague from Toronto recounted how at a workshop she and her colleagues had organized to bring together Syrian refugees and BIPOC activists around issues of rights and justice, the Indigenous activists sat quietly the whole day. When asked during debriefing and evaluation the reason for their silence, one of the activists noted their frustration with the organizers and the immigrant and refugee activists for neither acknowledging nor relating refugee and immigrant rights to the history and continuing dispossession of Indigenous lands.

Likewise, even as the decolonial turn in feminism has become ubiquitous, the relationship between TFA and decolonial feminism has remained tangential at best. As Arvin, Tuck, and Morrill (2013) note, all feminisms in the United States, including transnational feminism, have to grapple with the ongoing reality of the United States as a settler-colonial nation-state and what that means for feminist theory and praxis. In particular, they highlight the heteropatriarchy and heteropaternalism of the state that is often reproduced in feminist formulations of patriarchy and gender justice in understanding the lives of Black and Indigenous Women of Color.

There are various ways in which TFA would benefit from considering the settler coloniality of the United States. One, doing so would highlight the epistemic violence that settler coloniality perpetrates. Beyond Spivak (2013), rarely cited in the genealogy of transnational feminism, most transnational feminist scholars—with exceptions like the editors and authors in this book—do not explicitly engage Indigenous ways of knowing and what that might mean for transnational feminist analytics and praxis. As Leinius indicates in her chapter, the two approaches to dealing with radical alterity have been either: translation, to turn it into mutual intelligibility à la Santos; or: apropos Lugones, to render it in subaltern language through imaginative leaps and caring disruption. Connell (2015, 61) offers a third possibility: solidarity-based epistemologies that involve mutual learning based on "active engagement and evaluation." This might avoid the impasse that radical alterity and incommensurability might suggest for theory and praxis.

Two, TFA could benefit from decolonial feminist articulations of governance beyond the nation-state. One of the strengths of the TFA is its decentering of the nation-state to highlight both historical and contemporary relations of power that construct and limit local social relations. Yet, as Arvin et al. (2013) note, most feminists have not engaged with the possibilities of what decentering the nation-state means for modes of governance beyond the nation-state.

Three, TFA needs to deal explicitly with the coloniality of the gender binary that decolonial feminisms have made visible. While Connell (2015), among others, has raised questions about the historical and empirical evidence for the ubiquity of multiple genders, most feminists today recognize that thinking beyond gender binaries and being open to a variety of relations between genders, not all of which are patriarchal, might suggest myriad pathways for gender-just worlds. Finally, decolonial feminisms like Afro Futurisms have grappled with imagining and enacting a futurity of their own making that might also contribute to TFA.

Similarly, TFA would be enriched by being attentive to subaltern feminist re-imaginings in the postcolonial world such as the formulation of Dalit feminism in India. Sharmila Rege (1998) defined Dalit feminism as a challenge both to the primarily male-defined Dalit movement and to the feminist movement which she redefined as *Savarna* for its erasure of the Dalit standpoint. More recently, in 2017, when Raya Sarkar, a twenty-four-year-old Dalit law student, released a list of prominent Indian, upper-caste male academic perpetrators of harassment, a leading Savarna, Indian feminist Nivedita Menon publicly critiqued the call out culture and its lack of due process, sidelining the role of caste and demonstrating the unexpected ways in which precolonial hegemonies become visible in postcolonial feminisms (Desai, 2021). The controversy brought fresh critiques from a new generation of Dalit and Bahujan[4] feminists, who raised a range of issues, from epistemic erasures, to the dominance of English among urban feminists, to Brahmanic supremacy, for example, Kowtal (2019). Some, for example, Paik (2014), proposed building bridges with African American women. To me, this is a call to subalternize transnational feminisms and develop more nuanced analytics that are mindful of precolonial, colonial, and postcolonial hierarchies that undermine transnational praxis. Toward that end, in my own work on subaltern feminisms in India, I am formulating an Adivasi[5]/Dalit/Bahujan feminist analytic that is in conversation with the history and erasures of feminist activism in contemporary India.

Finally, there is a growing critical literature on decolonial, postsocialist feminisms, for example, Koobak and Marling (2014) and Tlostanova (2010), that questions the earlier critique of scholars like Suchland (2011) who noted the absence of the Second World in the meta-geography of TFA. The two chapters in this book and the editors along with other scholars echo this erasure highlighting how solidarities across borders need to recognize the contributions of socialist era feminisms to transnational feminist praxis. Informed by decolonial theory, scholars like Koobak and Marling (2014) and Karkov and Valiavicharska (2018) critique the ways in which transnational feminisms incorporate Central and Eastern European feminisms via a Cold War lens, failing to recognize their specific socialist histories of collaborations with anti-colonial struggles of countries in Africa and Asia. While fraught, these collaborations led to alternative modernities that did not always converge with global capitalism and Western colonial modernity. Tlostanova (2011) focuses specifically on post-Soviet gendered imaginaries and global colonialities that raise the question, "Can the post-Soviet Think?" while Manolova, Kusic, and Lottholz (2019) focus on Southeastern Europe and the "nested orientalisms" within the postsocialist world that see it as "incomplete self of Europe."

As these new theorizations and the chapters in this book suggest, our current moment calls for deep thinking, humility, multilingual, and multi-epistemic conversations across borders so that we evolve a praxis, discursive and material, that enables our survival and flourishing. By way of inviting further reflections, I want to end with what I encountered on my walk by the Atlantic Ocean on Kiahwah Island, South Carolina, yesterday. It was an early, sunny afternoon with a mild breeze and over one hundred birds of different feathers, small sandpipers, big seagulls, and another mid-size species that I could not identify, were all sitting together on the shore. As each wave came in and receded, the sandpipers darted furiously around, I imagine to catch whatever the water brought in. The rest, however, stood silently together. Was it for warmth? For safety? For companionship? Whatever it might have been, to me it seemed an apt image for our times, the need to stand together across our differences.

NOTES

1. I would like to thank the editors for providing me the opportunity to write this afterword and for their comments on an earlier draft. I would also like to thank Dr. Rainka Roy for research assistance.

2. I use global justice movements as a shorthand for a range of anti-capitalist, anti-corporate globalization movements that emerged around the world starting with the women-led structural adjustment protests in the 1980s in the Global South, followed by the Zapatistas in 1995, and later by protests against WTO in Seattle in 1999 leading to the WSF processes in 2001 onward.

3. Savarna literally means with *Varna*. Varnas are occupation-based categories that define the fourfold stratification system in India commonly called the caste system. Castes are subgroups within each varna. The first three varnas—Brahmins (priest-scholars), Kshatriyas (warriors), and Vaishyas (merchants/traders)—are considered Savarnas, while the fourth group Shudras (peasants) and the Ati-Shudras, or Dalits, beyond the fourfold system are called *avarnas*. This system was legally abolished at independence but persists in practice in all realms of life.

4. Bahujan literally means the majority and is the term preferred by politicians and activists from the abovementioned Shudra Varna who were designated Backward Castes and Other Backward Castes in India's affirmative action policies.

5. Adivasis, or original inhabitants, is the term for Indigenous peoples in India.

References

Agnew, John. 1997. "The Dramaturgy of Horizons: Geographical Scale in the 'Reconstruction of Italy' by the New Italian Political Parties, 1992–95." *Political Geography* 16, no. 2: 99–121.

Aguiar, Vilênia Venâncio Porto. 2015. "Somos Todas Margaridas: um Estudo sobre o Processo de Constituição das Mulheres do Campo e da Floresta como Sujeito Político." PhD diss., University of Campinas.

Aguiar, Vilênia Venâncio Porto. 2016. "Mulheres Rurais, Movimento Social e Participação: Reflexões a Partir da Marcha das Margaridas." *Política & Sociedade* 15, no. 0: 261–95. https://doi.org/10.5007/2175-7984.2016v15nesp1p261.

Ahmed, Sara. 2000. *Strange Encounters: Embodied Others in Post-Coloniality.* London and New York: Routledge.

Ahmed, Sara. 2004. "Declarations of Whiteness: The Non-Performativity of Anti-Racism." *Borderlands* 3, no. 2.

Ahmed, Sara. 2012. "Diversity: Problems and Paradoxes for Black Feminists." In *Educational Diversity: The Subject of Difference and Different Subjects,* edited by Yvette Taylor, 203–18. London/New York: Palgrave.

Alexander, Jacqui, and Chandra Talpade Mohanty, eds. 1997. *Feminist Genealogies, Colonial Legacies, Democratic Futures.* New York, NY: Routledge.

Alexander, Jacqui, and Chandra Talpade Mohanty. 2010. "Cartographies of Knowledge and Power: Transnational Feminism as Radical Praxis." In *Critical Transnational Feminist Praxis,* edited by Amanda Lock Swarr and Richa Nagar, 23–45. Albany, NY: SUNY Press.

Alvarez, Sonia. 2000. "Translating the Global: Effects of Transnational Organizing on Local Feminist Discourses and Practices in Latin America." *Meridians* 1, no. 1: 29–67.

Alvarez, Sonia. 2014. "Enacting a Translocal Feminist Politics of Translation." In *Translocalities/Translocalidades: Feminist Politics of Translation in the Latin/a Américas,* edited by Sonia Alvarez et al., 1–18. Durham and London: Duke University Press.

Alvarez, Sonia, Claudia de Lima Costa, Veronica Feliu, Rebecca J. Hester, Norma Klahn, and Millie Thayer. 2014. *Translocalidades/Translocalities: Feminist Politics of Translation in the Latin/a Americas*. Durham, NC: Duke University Press.

Alvarez, Sonia, Elisabeth Friedman, Ericka Beckman, Maylei Blackwell, Norma Stoltz Chinchilla, Nathalie Lebon, Marysa Navarro, and Marcela Tobar Ríos. 2003. "Encountering Latin American and Caribbean Feminisms." *Signs: Journal of Women in Culture and Society* 28, no. 2: 537–79.

Ancelovici, Marcos, Pascale Dufour, and Heloise Nez, eds. 2016. *Street Politics in the Age of Austerity: From Indignados to Occupy*. Amsterdam: Amsterdam University Press.

Anctil Avoine, Priscyll, Anne-Marie Veillette, and Geneviève Pagé. 2019. "Le renouvellement de l'approche féministe des CALACS face à la nécessité intersectionnelle : un engagement mitigé malgré des efforts certains." *Recherches féministes* 32, no. 2: 197–215.

Anderl, Felix. 2020. "Global or Local Solidarity? That's the Wrong Question: Relationality, Aspiration and the In-between of Feminist Activism in Southeast Asia." *Globalizations*. DOI: 10.1080/14747731.2020.1838759.

Antrobus, Peggy. 2004. *The Global Women's Movement: Origins, Issues, and Strategies*. London: Zed Books.

Antrobus, Peggy. 2015. "DAWN, the Third World Feminist Network: Upturning Hierarchies." In *The Oxford Handbook of Transnational Feminist Movements*, edited by Rawwida Baksh and Wendy Harcourt, 159–87. New York: Oxford University Press.

Anzaldúa, Gloria E. 1987. *Borderlands: The New Mestiza/La Frontera*. San Francisco: Spinsters/Aunt Lute.

Anzaldúa, Gloria E. 2009. "(Un)natural Bridges, (Un)safe Spaces." In *The Gloria Anzaldúa Reader*, edited by AnaLouise Keating, 243–48. Durham and London: Duke University Press.

Aparicio, Juan Ricardo, and Mario Blaser. 2008. "The 'Lettered City' and the Insurrection of Subjugated Knowledges in Latin America." *Anthropological Quarterly* 81, no. 1: 59–94.

Arseneault, Marie-Louise. 2019. "Entretien avec Denis Veaugeois par Stéphane Savard." *Plus on est de fous, plus on lit!* Radio-Canada. February 13, 2019. https ://ici.radio-canada.ca/premiere/emissions/plus-on-est-de-fous-plus-on-lit/episod es/426816/audio-fil-du-mercredi-13-fevrier-2019/5?fbclid=IwAR2DLYapDKS l7uw0lYrNvxqcn-KXMJ6XmDMraLRmddwKFgp8fZl9TE3jV80.

Arvin, Maile, Eve Tuck, and Angie Morrill. 2013. "Decolonizing Feminism: Challenging Connections between Settler Colonialism and Heteropatriachy." *Feminist Formations* 25, no. 1: 8–34.

Aspasia: The International Yearbook of Central, Eastern, and Southeastern European Women's and Gender History 8, 2014 (theme section "Gendering the Cold War").

Ayoub, Phillip M. 2016. *When States Come Out: Europe's Sexual Minorities and the Politics of Visibility*. New York: Cambridge University Press.

Ayoub, Phillip M., and Agnès Chetaille. 2017. "Movement/Countermovement Interaction and Instrumental Framing in a Multi-level World: Rooting Polish

Lesbian and Gay Activism." *Social Movement Studies* 19, no. 1: 21–37. DOI: 14742837.2017.1338941.

Ayoub, Phillip M., and David Paternotte, eds. 2014. *LGBT Activism and the Making of Europe: A Rainbow Europe?* New York: Palgrave Macmillan.

Baer, Brian James. 2002. "Russian Gays/Western Gaze: Mapping (Homo)Sexual Desire in Post-Soviet Russia." *GLQ: A Journal of Lesbian and Gay Studies* 8, no. 4: 499–521.

Bakić-Hayden, Milica. 1995. "Nesting Orientalisms: The Case of Former Yugoslavia." *Slavic Review* 54, no. 4: 917–31.

Baksh, Rawwida, and Wendy Harcourt, eds. 2015. *The Oxford Handbook of Transnational Feminist Movements*. New York: Oxford University Press.

Barbosa, Lia Pinheiro. 2021. "*Lajan lajan 'aytik* or 'Walking in Complementary Pairs' in the Zapatista Women's Struggle." *Latin American Perspectives* 48, no. 5.

Barry, Kathleen. 1984. *Female Sexual Slavery*. New York: New York University Press.

Bassnett, Susan, and Harish Trivedi. 1999. "Introduction: Of Colonies, Cannibals, and Vernaculars." In *Post-Colonial Translation: Theory and Practice*, edited by Susan Bassnett and Harish Trivedi, 1–18. New York: Routledge.

Basu, Amrita, ed. 2010. *Women's Movements in the Global Era: The Power of Local Feminisms*. Boulder, CO: Westview Press.

Bayertz, Kurt, ed. 1999. *Solidarity*. New York, NY: Springer.

Bebbington, Anthony, et al. 2008. "Mining and Social Movements: Struggles over Livelihood and Rural Territorial Development in the Andes." *World Development* 36, no. 12: 2888–2905.

Bhambra, Gurminder. 2007. *Rethinking Modernity: Postcolonialism and the Sociological Imagination*. Palgrave-MacMillan.

Bilge, Sirma. 2010. "« ... Alors que nous, Québécois, nos femmes sont égales à nous et nous les aimons ainsi »: La patrouille des frontières au nom de l'égalité de genre dans une « Nation » en quête de souveraineté." *Sociologie et Sociétés* 42, no. 1: 197–226.

Bilge, Sirma. 2015. "Le blanchiment de l'intersectionnalité." *Recherches féministes* 28, no. 2: 9–32.

Binnie, Jon, and Christian Klesse. 2011. "Researching Transnational Activism around LGBTQ Politics in Central and Eastern Europe: Activist Solidarities and Spatial Imaginings." In *De-Centring Western Sexualities: Central and East European Perspectives*, edited by Robert Kulpa and Joanna Mizielińska, 107–29. London: Ashgate.

Binnie, Jon, and Christian Klesse. 2013. "'Like a Bomb in the Gasoline Station': East-West Migration and Transnational Activism around Lesbian, Gay, Bisexual, Transgender and Queer Politics in Poland." *Journal of Ethnic and Migration Studies* 39, no. 7: 1107–24.

Birla, Ritu. 2010. "Postcolonial Studies. Now That's History." In *Can the Subaltern Speak? Reflections on the History of an Idea*, edited by Rosalind Morris, 87–99. New York: Columbia University Press.

Blackwell, Maylei. 2014. "Translenguas: Mapping the Possibilities and Challenges of Transnational Women's Organizing Across Geographies of Difference." In *Translocalities/Translocalidades: Feminist Politics of Translation in the Latin/a Américas*, edited by Sonia Alvarez et al., 299–320. Durham and London: Duke University Press.

Blais, Marie-Claude. 2008. "La solidarité." *Le Télémaque* 33: 9–24.

Blaser, Mario. 2009. "The Threat of the Yrmo: The Political Ontology of a Sustainable Hunting Program." *American Anthropologist* 111, no. 1: 10–20.

Blaser, Mario. 2010. *Storytelling Globalization from the Chaco and Beyond.* Durham and London: Duke University Press.

Blaser, Mario. 2013. "Ontological Conflicts and the Stories of Peoples in Spite of Europe: Towards a Conversation on Political Ontology." *Current Anthropology* 54, no. 5: 547–68.

Blaser, Mario, and Marisol de la Cadena. 2018. "Pluriverse: Proposals for a World of Many Worlds." In *A World of Many Worlds*, edited by Marisol de la Cadena and Mario Blaser, 1–22. Durham and London: Duke University Press.

Bonfiglioli, Chiara, and Kristen Ghodsee. 2020. "Vanishing Act: Global Socialist Feminism as the 'Missing Other' of Transnational Feminism. Response to Tlostanova, Thapar-Björkert, and Koobak (2019)." *Feminist Review* 126, no. 1: 168–72.

Borras Jr, Saturnino M., Marc Edelman, and Cristóbal Kay. 2008. *Transnational Agrarian Movements Confronting Globalization.* Chichester: John Wiley & Sons.

Bosniak, Linda. 2006. *The Citizen and the Alien: Dilemmas of Contemporary Membership.* Princeton, NJ: Princeton University Press.

Bourdieu, Pierre. 2002. "Pour un savoir engagé." *Le Monde diplomatique* (February): 3.

Bourdieu, Pierre, and Loïc Wacquant. 1998. "Sur les ruses de la raison impériale." *Actes de la recherche en science sociales,* no. 121–122: 109–18.

Branfman, Jonathan. 2019. "Teaching for Coalition: Dismantling 'Jewish-Progressive Conflict' through Feminist and Queer Pedagogy." *Frontiers: A Journal of Women Studies* 40, no. 2: 126–66.

Britto Schwartz, Juliana. 2013. "Latinas Feministas: Lorena Cabnal." *Feministing,* December 20, 2013. http://feministing.com/2013/12/20/latinas-feministas-lorena-cabnal/.

Broqua, Christophe. 2018. "La « communauté homosexuelle » comme peuple transnational : Une fiction politique." *L'Homme & la Société* 208, no. 3: 143–67.

Brown, Gavin, and Helen Yaffe. 2013. "Non-stop Against Apartheid: Practicing Solidarity Outside the South African Embassy." *Social Movement Studies* 12, no. 2: 227–34.

Brown, Gavin, and Helen Yaffe. 2014. "Practices of Solidarity: Opposing Apartheid in the Centre of London." *Antipode* 46, no. 1: 34–52.

Bueno-Hansen, Pascha, and Sylvanna M. Falcón. 2017. "Indigenous/Campesina Embodied Knowledge, Human Rights Awards, and Lessons for Transnational Feminist Solidarity." In *Decolonizing Feminism: Transnational Feminism and Globalization*, edited by Margaret A. McLaren, 57–82. London, UK: Rowman & Littlefield International.

Bunch, Charlotte. 1987. *Passionate Politics: Feminist Theory in Action. Essays, 1968–1986.* New York: St. Martin's Press.

Bunch, Charlotte. 1990. "Women's Rights Are Human Rights: Towards a Revision of Human Rights." *Human Rights Quarterly* 12, no. 4: 486–98. DOI: 10.2307/762496.

Bunch, Charlotte, Roxanna Carrillo, and Ied Guinée. 1985. "Feminist Perspectives: Report of the Feminist Perspectives Working Group to the Closing Plenary." *Women' Studies International Forum* 8, no. 4: 243–47. https://doi.org/10.1016/0 277-5395(85)90003-2.

Bunch, Charlotte, and Niamh Reilly. 2019. "Women's Rights as Human Rights: Twenty-Five Years On." In *International Human Rights of Women*, edited by Niamh Reilly, 22–37. Singapore: Springer.

Burton, Antoinette, and Jean Allman. 2008. "Gender, Colonialism, and Feminist Collaboration." *Radical History Review* 101: 198–212.

Buyantueva, Radzhana, and Maryna Shevtsova, eds. 2020. *LGBTQ+ Activism in Central and Eastern Europe: Resistance, Representation and Identity.* Cham: Palgrave Macmillan.

Cabnal, Lorena. 2010. *Acercamiento a la construcción de la propuesta de pensamiento epistémico de las mujeres indígenas feministas comunitarias de Abya Yala.* Jalapa, Guatemala: AMISMAXAJ (Asociación de Mujeres Indígenas de Santa María Xalapán). https://www.academia.edu/7694014/Acercamiento_a_la_prop uesta_del_feminismo_comunitario_Abya_Yala.

Çağatay, Nilüfer, Caren Grown, and Aida Santiago. 1986. "The Nairobi Women's Conference: Towards a Global Feminism?" *Feminist Studies* 12, no. 2: 401–12. DOI: 10.2307/3177975.

Campbell-Fiset, Marie-Ève. 2017. *Analyse d'un backlash intramouvement : les états généraux de l'action et de l'analyse féministes (2011–2014).* MA thesis, Université du Québec à Montréal.

Caron, Chantal. 2014. "L'intervention féministe intersectionnelle—Troquer un ideal pour une idéologie trompeuse?" *Sysiphe*, April 17, 2019. http://sisyphe.org/spip .php?article4709.

Carrithers, Michael, Matei Candea, Karen Sykes, Soumhya Venkatesan, and Martin Holbraad. 2010. "Ontology Is Just Another Word for Culture: Motion Tabled at the 2008 Meeting of the Group for Debates in Anthropological Theory." *Critique of Anthropology* 30, no. 2: 152–200.

Caulier, Mathieu. 2009. "Faire le genre, défaire le féminisme : Philanthropie, politiques de population et ONG de santé reproductive au Mexique (Making Gender, Unmaking Feminism. Philanthropy, Population Policies, and Reproductive Health NGOs in Mexico)." Unpublished PhD thesis, École des Hautes Études en Sciences Sociales, Paris.

Caulier, Mathieu. 2010. "The Population Revolution: From Population Policies to Reproductive Health and Women's Rights Politics." *International Review of Sociology* 20, no. 2: 347–76. DOI: 10.1080/03906701.2010.487675.

Cerwonka, Alaine. 2008. "Traveling Feminist Thought: Difference and Transculturation in Central and Eastern European Feminism." *Signs: Journal of Women in Culture and Society* 33, no. 4: 809–32. DOI: 10.1086/528852.

Chambeu, Françoise. 2015. *Mujer del Agua—Yaku Warmi—Femme de l'eau.* Film documentary on the struggle of the women of the community of Cañaris against the Cañarico project, 34:00.

Chazan, May. 2016. "Settler Solidarities as Praxis: Understanding 'Granny Activism' Beyond the Highly-visible." *Social Movement Studies* 15, no. 5: 457–70.

Chetaille, Agnès. 2013. "Une « autre Europe » homophobe ? L'Union européenne, le nationalisme polonais et la sexualisation de la « division Est/Ouest »." (*Is the "Other Europe" Homophobic? The European Union, Polish Nationalism, and the Sexualization of the East/West Divide*). *Raisons politiques* 49, 119–40. https://www.cairn-int.info/journal-raisons-politiques-2013-1-page-119.htm.

Chowdhury, Elora Halim. 2009. "Locating Global Feminisms Elsewhere: Braiding US Women of Color and Transnational Feminisms." *Cultural Dynamics* 21, no. 1: 51–78.

Chowdhury, Elora Halim. 2015. "Development." In *The Oxford Handbook of Feminist Theory*, edited by Lisa Disch and Mary Hawkesworth. Oxford University Press.

Chowdury, Elora Halim, and Liz Philipose, eds. 2016. *Dissident Friendships: Feminism, Imperialism, and Transnational Solidarity*. Champaign, IL: University of Illinois Press.

Cîrstocea, Ioana. 2019. *La fin de la femme rouge ? Fabriques transnationales du genre après la chute du Mur (The End of the Red Woman? Making Gender Transnationally after the Cold War)*. Rennes: Presses Universitaires de Rennes.

Cîrstocea, Ioana. 2020. "Challenges and Pitfalls of Feminist Sisterhood in the Aftermath of the Cold War: The Case of the Network of East-West Women." *Aspasia: The Yearbook of Women's and Gender History in South-Eastern Europe* 14: 1–19. https://doi.org/10.3167/asp.2020.140103.

Cîrstocea, Ioana, Delphine Lacombe, and Elisabeth Marteu, eds. 2019. *Globalization of Gender, Mobilizations, Frameworks of Action, Knowledge*. London: Routledge.

Collins, Patricia Hill. [1990] 2000. *Black Feminist Thought, Knowledge, Consciousness, and the Politics of Empowerment*. New York: Routledge.

Collins, Patricia Hill, and Sirma Bilge. 2020. *Intersectionality*, 2nd ed. Cambridge: Polity.

Combahee River Collective. 1981. "A Black Feminist Statement." In *This Bridge Called My Back: Writings by Radical Women of Color*, 210–18. New York: Women of Color Press.

Comité Solidarité Cajamarca. 2015. "El Comité de Solidaridad con Cajamarca Expresa su Apoyo en la Asamblea de la Comunidad de San Juan de Kañaris." *Solidarité avec Cajamarca* (blog). August 10, 2015. http://solidaritecajamarca.blogspot.ca/2015_08_01_archive.html.

Connell, Raewyn. 2015. "Meeting at the Edge of Fear: Theory on a world scale." *Feminist Theory* 16, no. 1: 49–66.

Contag. 2000. Marcha das Margaridas: 2000 razões para marchar contra a fome, pobreza e violência sexista. Texto-Base. Brasília: Contag.

Contag. 2003. Marcha das Margaridas: 2003 razões para marchar contra a fome, pobreza e violência sexista. Texto-Base. Brasília: Contag.

Contag. 2007a. Marcha das Margaridas: 2007 Razões para marchar. Caderno de textos para estudo e debates. Brasília: Contag/Fetags/STTRs/ - MMTR-NE, MIQCB, CNS, MAMA, MMM, CUT, REDE LAC, COPROFAM.

Contag. 2007b. Pauta da Marcha das Margaridas 2007. Contra a Fome, a Pobreza e a Violência Sexista. Brasília: DF.

Contag. 2011a. Marcha das Margaridas 2011. Margaridas na Luta por desenvolvimento sustentável com justiça, autonomia, igualdade e liberdade. Caderno de textos para estudo e debates. Brasília: Contag/Fetags/STTRs/ – MMTR-NE, MIQCB, CNS, MAMA, MMM, AMB, UBM, REDELAC, COPROFAM.

Contag. 2011b. Pauta da Marcha das Margaridas 2011. Desenvolvimento Sustentável com Justiça, Autonomia, Igualdade e Liberdade. Brasília: DF.

Contag. 2015. Marcha das Margaridas 2015. Margaridas seguem em Marcha por Desenvolvimento Sustentável, com democracia, justiça, autonomia, igualdade e liberdade. Caderno de textos para estudo e debates. Brasília: Contag/Fetags/ STTRs - MMTR-NE, MIQCB, CNS, MAMA, MMM, AMB, UBM, GT Mulheres da ANA, UNICAFES, CTB, CUT, COPROFAM.

Contag. 2019. Marcha das Margaridas 2019. Margaridas na luta por um Brasil com Soberania popular, democracia, justiça, igualdade e livre de violência. Cartilha de divulgação. Brasília: Contag/Fetags/STTR's, CUT, CTB, MIQCB, MMTR-NE, CNS, MAMA, MMC, MMM, AMB, UBM, GT Mulheres da ANA, UNICAFES, CONFREM, CONAQ, CONTAR, COPROFAM.

Conway, Janet. 2004. *Identity, Place, Knowledge: Social Movements Contesting Globalization*. Halifax, NS: Fernwood Publishing Co., Ltd.

Conway, Janet M. 2006. *Praxis and Politics: Knowledge Production in Social Movements*. London & New York: Routledge.

Conway, Janet. 2008. "Geographies of Transnational Feminisms: The Politics of Place and Scale in the World March of Women." *Social Politics: International Studies in Gender, State & Society* 15, no. 2: 207–31.

Conway, Janet. 2010. "Troubling Transnational Feminism(s) at the World Social Forum." In *Solidarities without Borders: Transnationalizing Women's Movements,* edited by Dominique Masson, Pascale Dufour, and Dominique Caouette, 149–72. Vancouver: University of British Columbia Press.

Conway, Janet. 2011. "Activist Knowledges on the Anti-globalization Terrain: Transnational Feminisms at the World Social Forum." *Interface: A Journal for and about Social Movements* 3, no. 2: 33–64.

Conway, Janet. 2012. "Transnational Feminisms Building Anti-globalization Solidarities." *Globalizations* 9, no. 3: 379–93.

Conway, Janet. 2013. *Edges of Global Justice. The World Social Forum and its "Others."* New York, NY: Routledge.

Conway, Janet. 2016. *Popular Feminism—Its Past, Present and Possible Future: Considering the World March of Women*. Presented at the International Congress of the Latin American Studies Association, New York City.

Conway, Janet. 2017a. "Troubling Transnational Feminism(s): Theorising Activist Praxis." *Feminist Theory* 18, no. 2: 205–27.

Conway, Janet. 2017b. "Modernity and the Study of Social Movements: Do We Need a Paradigm Shift? Social Movements and World-System Transformation." In *Paradigm,* edited by Jackie Smith, Michael Goodhart, Patrick Manning, and John Markoff, 17–34. Routledge.

Conway, Janet. 2018. "When Food Becomes a Feminist Issue: Popular Feminism and Subaltern Agency in the World March of Women." *International Feminist Journal of Politics* 20, no. 2: 188–203. DOI: 10.1080/14616742.2017.1419822.

Conway, Janet. 2019. "The im/possibilities of border-crossing solidarities." Keynote for workshop, February 25, 2019. Kassel, Germany: University of Kassel.

Conway, Janet, and Anabel Paulos. 2017. *Popular Feminist Politics of Cross-Movement Alliances in Latin America and the Decolonial Challenge.* Presented at the International Conference on Cross Movement Mobilization, Ruhr-Universität Bochum, Bochum, Germany.

Conway, Janet, and Anabel Paulos. 2020. "Feminism, Food Sovereignty, and Cross-movement Mobilization Against Neoliberal Globalisation." *Cross-movement Alliances in the Global South and across the North-South divide* 63: 13–39. DOI: 10.13154/mts.63.2020.13-39.

Coogan-Gehr, Kelly. 2011. *The Geopolitics of the Cold War and Narratives of Inclusion. Excavating a Feminist Archive.* New York: Palgrave Macmillan.

Costa, Claudia de Lima. 2013. "Equivocation, Translation, and Performative Interseccionality: Notes on Decolonial Feminist Practices and Ethics in Latin America." *Revista Anglo Saxonica* 3, no. 6: 75–98.

Costa, Claudia de Lima. 2014a. "Lost (and Found?) in Translation: Feminisms in Hemispheric Dialogue." In *Translocalities/Translocalidades: Feminist Politics of Translation in the Latin/a Américas*, edited by Sonia Alvarez et al., 19–36. Durham and London: Duke University Press.

Costa, Claudia de Lima. 2014b. "Equivocação, tradução e interseccionalidade performativa: Observações sobre ética e prática feministas descoloniais." In *Genologías e Memorias Poscoloniales en América Latina: Escrituras Fronterizas desde el Sur,* edited by Karina Bidaseca et al., 260–93. Buenos Aires: Ediciones Godot.

Costa, Claudia de Lima. 2014c. "Feminist Theories, Transnational Translations, and Cultural Mediations." In *Translocalities/Translocalidades: Feminist Politics of Translation in the Latin/a Américas,* edited by Sonia E. Alvarez, Claudia de Lima Costa, Veronica Feliu, Rebecca Hester, Norma Klahn, and Millie Thayer, 133–48. Durham: Duke University.

Costa, Claudia de Lima, and Sonia E. Alvarez. 2014. "Dislocating the Sign: Toward a Translocal Feminist Politics of Translation." *Signs: Journal of Women in Culture and Society* 39, no. 3: 557–63.

Crenshaw, Kimberlé. 1989. "Demarginalizing the Intersection of Race and Sex: A Black Feminist Critique of Antidiscrimination Doctrine, Feminist Theory, and Anti-racist Politics." *The University of Chicago Legal Forum* no. 1: 139–67.

Curiel, Ochy. 2014. "Hacia la Construcción de un Feminismo Descolonizado." In *Tejiendo de Otro Modo: Feminismo, Epistemología y Apuestas Descoloniales en Abya Yala,* edited by Yuderkys Espinosa Miñoso, Diana Gómez Correal, and Karina Ochoa, 325–34. Popayán: Editorial Universidad del Cauca.

Daskalaki, Maria, and Marianna Fotaki. 2017. "Chapter 7: The Neoliberal Crisis. Alternative Organizing and Spaces of/for Feminist Solidarity." In *Feminists and Queer Theorists Debate the Future of Critical Management Studies: Dialogues in Critical Management Studies,* edited by Alison Pullen, Nancy Harding, and Mary Phillips, 129–53. Bingley, UK: Emerald Publishing.

Davis, Angela. 2016. *Freedom is a Constant Struggle: Ferguson, Palestine, and the Foundations of a Movement*. Chicago: Haymarket Books.

Day, Richard. 2005. *Gramsci is Dead: Anarchist Currents in the Newest Social Movements*. London: Pluto Press.

Daza, Mar, Raphael Hoetmer, Nicola Foroni, Virginia Vargas, and Luna Contreras. 2016. "Diálogos de Saberes y Movimientos en el Perú: Apuntes Sobre Una Experiencia Parecida al Tejer." In *Experiencias de Formación Política en los Movimientos Sociales*, edited by HEGOA, Joxemi Zumalabe, and Gipuzkoako Foru Aldundia, 69–128. Bilbao: HEGOA—Universidad del Páis Vasco.

de Haan, Francisca. 2010. "Continuing Cold War Paradigms in Western Historiography of Transnational Women's Organisations: The Case of Women's International Democratic Federation (WIDF)." *Women's History Review* 19, no. 4: 547–73.

de Haan, Francisca, ed. 2014. "Gendering the Cold War." Special section, *Aspasia: The International Yearbook of Central, Eastern, and Southeastern European Women's and Gender History* 8, no. 1 (March).

de Haan, Fancisca, Kristen Ghodsee, Krassimira Daskalova, Magdalena Grabowska, Jasmina Lukić, Chiara Bonfiglioli, Raluca Maria Popa, and Alexandra Ghit. 2016. "Ten Years After: Communism and Feminism Revisited." *Aspasia: The International Yearbook of Central, Eastern and South-Eastern European Women's and Gender History* 10, no.1 (March 2019): 102–68. https://doi.org/10.3167/asp.2016.100107.

de la Cadena, Marisol. 2010. "Indigenous Cosmopolitics in the Andes: Conceptual Reflections Beyond Politics." *Cultural Anthropology* 25, no. 2: 334–70.

de la Cadena, Marisol. 2015. *Earth Beings: Ecologies of Practice Across Andean Worlds*. Durham and London: Duke University Press.

de la Cadena, Marisol, and Mario Blaser, eds. 2018. *A World of Many Worlds*. Durham and London: Duke University Press.

Dean, Jodi. 1996. *Solidarity of Strangers: Feminism after Identity Politics*. Berkeley: University of California Press.

Deere, Carmen Diana, and Magdalena León. 2001. *Empowering Women: Land and Property Rights in Latin America*. Pittsburgh: University of Pittsburgh Press.

della Porta, Donatella. 2015. *Social Movements in Times of Austerity: Bringing Capitalism Back into Protest Analysis*. Cambridge, UK: Polity Press.

della Porta, Donatella, ed. 2018. *Solidarity Mobilizations in the "Refugee Crisis": Contentious Moves*. London, UK: Palgrave MacMillan.

Delphy, Christine. 1996. "L'invention du 'French Feminism': Une démarche essentielle." *Nouvelles Questions Féministes* 17, no. 1: 15–58.

Dempsey, Sarah E., Patricia S. Parker, and Kathleen J. Krone. 2011. "Navigating Socio-Spatial Difference, Constructing Counter-Space: Insights from Transnational Feminist Praxis." *Journal of International Intercultural Communication* 4, no. 3: 201–20.

Desai, Manisha. 2007. "The Messy Relationship Between Feminisms and Globalizations." *Gender & Society* 21, no. 6: 797–803. doi/pdf/10.1177/08912432 07309907.

Desai, Manisha. 2009. *Gender and the Politics of Possibilities: Rethinking Globalization*. Lanham, MD: Rowman & Littlefield.

Desai, Manisha. 2010. "Beyond Citizenship: A New Cartography and Ontology of Belonging." Paper presented at the Birkbeck Institute, University of London's Conference on Beyond Citizenship in London. June 2010.

Desai, Manisha. 2015. "Critical Cartography, Theories and Praxis of Transnational Feminisms." In *The Oxford Handbook of Transnational Feminist Movements*, edited by Rawwida Baksh and Wendy Harcourt, 117–30. Oxford University Press. DOI: 10.1093/oxfordhb/9780199943494.013.016.

Desai, Manisha. 2016. "The Gendered Geographies of Struggle: The World Social Forum and Its Sometimes Overlapping Other Worlds." *Gender and Society* 30, no. 6: 869–89.

Desai, Manisha. 2020. "Troubling the Southern Turn in Feminisms." *European Journal of Women's Studies* 27, no. 4: 381–93.

Desai, Manisha. 2021. "Dalit and Autonomous Feminisms in India." In *Producing Inclusive Feminist Knowledge: Positionalities and Discourses in the Global South*, edited by Josephine Beoku-Betts and Akosua Adomako Ampofo. Emerald Publishers.

Descarries, Francine, and Laeticia Dechaufour. 2006. "Du 'French Feminism' au 'Genre': Trajectoire politico-linguistique d'un concept." *Labrys, Études Féministes/ Estudos Feministas*, no.10 (June/December).

Dezalay, Yves, and Bryant Garth. 2002. *The Internationalization of Palace Wars: Lawyers, Economists, and the Contest to Transform Latin American States.* Chicago: University of Chicago Press.

Dhawan, Nikita. 2013. "The Empire Prays Back: Religion, Secularity, and Queer Critique." *Boundary 2* 40, no. 1: 191–222.

Diani, Mario. 2003. "'Leaders' or Brokers? Positions and Influence in Social Movement Networks." In *Social Movements and Networks: Relational Approaches to Collective Action*, edited by Doug McAdam and Mario Diani, 105–22. Oxford University Press.

Diani, Mario, and Ivano Bison. 2004. "Organizations, Coalitions, and Movements." *Theory and society* 33, no. 3: 281–309. https://doi.org/10.1023/B:RYSO.0000038610.00045.07.

Díaz Alba, Carmen Leticia. 2017. "La Marcha Mundial de las Mujeres: Feminismos transnacionales en movimiento." Ph.D. diss, Centro de Investigaciones y Estudios Superiores en Antropología Social, Guadalajara, Mexico.

Doerr, Nicole. 2018. *Political Translation: How Social Movement Democracies Survive.* Cambridge: Cambridge University Press.

DuBois, Ellen Carol, and Katie Oliviero. 2009. "Circling the Globe: International Feminism Reconsidered, 1920 to 1975." *Women's Studies International Forum* 32, no. 1: 1–3.

Dufour, Pascale. 2016. "Pour une analyse comparée de la transnationalisation des solidarités. La Marche mondiale des femmes comme 'objet' transnational complexe." *Revue internationale de politique comparée* 23, no. 2: 145–75.

Dufour, Pascale and Isabelle Giraud. 2007. "The Continuity of Transnational Solidarities in the World March of Women, 2000 and 2005: A Collective Identity-building Approach." *Mobilization: An International Quarterly* 12, no. 3: 307–22.

Dufour, Pascale, Dominique Masson, and Carmen Diaz. 2019. "La régionalisation des mouvements de femmes transnationaux." *Recherches féministes* 32, no. 2: 57–74.

Dufour, Pascale, Dominique Masson, and Dominique Caouette, eds. 2010. *Solidarities beyond Borders: Transnationalizing Women's Movements.* Toronto: University of Toronto Press.

Engerman, David. 2018. *The Price of Aid: The Economic Cold War in India.* Cambridge: Harvard University Press.

Ergun, Emek, and Olga Castro, eds. with Richa Nagar, Kathy Davis, Judith Butler, AnaLouise Keating, Claudia de Lima Costa, Sonia E. Alvarez, and Ayse Gul Altinay. 2017. "A Cross-Disciplinary Roundtable on the Feminist Politics of Translation." In *Feminist Translation Studies: Local and Transnational Perspectives,* edited by Ergun and Castro, 111–35. New York, NY: Routledge.

Estrada-Claudio, Sylvia. 2010. "The International Women and Health Meetings: Deploying Multiple Identities for Political Sustainability." In *Solidarities Beyond Borders: Transnationalizing Women's Movements,* edited by Pascale Dufour, Dominique Masson, and Dominique Caouette, 108–25. Vancouver, BC: UBC Press.

Eterovic, Ivana, and Jackie Smith. 2001. "From Altruism to a New Transnationalism? A Look at Transnational Social Movements." In *Political Altruism? Solidarity Movements in International Perspective,* edited by Marco Giugni and Florence Passy, 197–218. Lanham, MD: Rowman & Littlefield.

Evans, Sara M. 2003. *Journeys That Opened Up the World: Women, Student Christian Movements, and Social Justice, 1955–1975.* New Brunswick, NJ: Rutgers University Press.

EZLN. 1996. Fourth Declaration of the Lacandon Jungle. Accessed November 23, 2016. http://schoolsforchiapas.org/wp-content/uploads/2014/03/Fourth-Declaration-of-the-Lacandona-Jungle-.pdf.

Fábián, Katalin. 2014. "Disciplining the 'Second World': The Relationship between Transnational and Local Forces in Contemporary Hungarian Women's Social Movements." *East European Politics* 30, no. 1: 1–20. https://doi.org/10.1080/21599165.2013.856310.

Falcón, Sylvanna. 2016. *Power Interrupted: Antiracist and Feminist Activism inside the United Nations.* Seattle: University of Washington Press.

Falquet, Jules. 1999. "Un mouvement désorienté: la 8ᵉ rencontre féministe latino-américaine et des Caraïbes." *Nouvelles Questions Féministes* 20, no. 3: 5–38. https://www.jstor.org/stable/40619711.

Featherstone, David. 2012. *Solidarity: Hidden Histories and Geographies of Internationalism.* London: Zed Books.

Ferree, Myra Marx, and Aili Mari Tripp, eds. 2006. *Global Feminism: Transnational Women's Activism, Organizing and Human Rights.* New York: New York University Press.

Fidelis, Malgorzata, Renata Jambrešić Kirin, Jill Massino, and Libora Oates-Indruchova. 2014. "Gendering the Cold War in the Region: An Email Conversation between Malgorzata (Gosia) Fidelis, Renata Jambrešić Kirin, Jill Massino, and Libora Oates-Indruchova." *Aspasia: The International Yearbook of Central,*

Eastern, and Southeastern European Women's and Gender History 8: 162–90. DOI: https://doi.org/10.3167/asp.2014.080109.

Fillieule, Olivier. 2001. "Dynamics of Commitment in the Sector Known as 'Solidarity': Methodological Reflections Based on the Case of France." In *Political Altruism? Solidarity Movements in International Perspective,* edited by Marco Giugni and Florence Passy, 51–66. Lanham, MD: Rowman & Littlefield.

Fireman, Bruce, and William A. Gamson. 1979. "Utilitarian Logic in the Resource Mobilization Perspective." In *The Dynamics of Social Movements: Resource Mobilization, Social Control and Tactics,* edited by Mayer N. Zald and John D. McCarthy, 8–44. Cambridge, MA: Winthrop.

Forster, Dion. 2007. "Identity in Relationship: The Ethics of Ubuntu as an Answer to the Impasse of Individual Consciousness in Africa." In *The Impact of Knowledge Systems on Human Development,* edited by CW du Toit, 245–89. Pretoria, South Africa: Research institute for Religion and Theology, University of South Africa.

Foucault, Michel. 1977. *Language, Counter-Memory, Practice: Selected Essays and Interviews.* Ithaca, NY: Cornell University Press.

Fraser, Arvonne. 1984. *The UN Decade for Women: Developments and Dialogue.* Boulder, CO: Westview Press.

Fraser, Arvonne. 2004. "Seizing Opportunities: USAID, WID, and CEDAW." In *Developing Power: How Women Transformed International Development,* edited by Arvonne Fraser and Irene Tinker, 164–75. New York: Feminist Press.

Fraser, Arvonne. 2007. *She's No Lady: Politics, Family, and International Feminism.* Minneapolis: Nodin Press.

Fraser, Arvonne, and Irene Tinker, eds. 2004. *Developing Power: How Women Transformed International Development.* New York: Feminist Press.

Friedman, Elizabeth J. 1999. "The Effects of 'Transnationalism Reversed' in Venezuela: Assessing the Impact of UN Global Conferences on the Women's Movement." *International Feminist Journal of Politics* 1, no. 3: 357–81.

Friedman, Elisabeth J. 2003. "Gendering the Agenda: The Impact of the Transnational Women's Rights Movement at the UN Conferences of the 1990s." *Women's Studies International Forum* 26, no. 4: 313–31. https://doi.org/10.1016/S0277-5395(03)00077-3.

Fultner, Barbara. 2017. "The Dynamics of Transnational Feminist Dialogue." In *Decolonizing Feminism. Transnational Feminism and Globalization,* edited by Margaret A. McLaren, 203–30. Lanham, MD: Rowman & Littlefield.

Galerand, Elsa. 2015. "Quelle conceptualisation de l'exploitation pour quelle critique intersectionnelle?" *Recherches féministes* 28, no. 2: 179–97.

Gallegos, Sergio A. 2017. "Building Transnational Feminist Solidarity Networks." In *Decolonizing Feminism: Transnational Feminism and Globalization,* edited by Margaret A. McLaren, 231–56. London, UK: Rowman & Littlefield.

Gamson, William A. 1991. "Commitment and Agency in Social Movements." *Sociological Forum* 6: 27–50.

Garner, Karen. 2010. *Shaping a Global Women's Agenda: Women's NGOs and Global Governance, 1925–1985.* New York: Manchester University Press.

Garner, Karen. 2013. *Gender and Foreign Policy in the Clinton Administration.* Boulder, CO: First Forum Press.

Gaztambide-Fernández, Rubén A. 2012. "Decolonization and the Pedagogy of Solidarity." *Decolonization: Indigeneity, Education & Society* 1, no. 1: 41–67.

Ghodsee, Kristen. 2010. "Revisiting the International Decade for Women: Brief Reflections on Competing Definitions of Feminism and Cold War Politics from the American Perspective." *Women's Studies International Forum* 33, no. 1: 3–12. https://doi.org/10.1016/j.wsif.2009.11.008.

Ghodsee, Kristen. 2019. *Second World, Second Sex: Socialist Women's Activism and Global Solidarity during the Cold War.* Durham: Duke University Press.

Gill, Lesley. 2009. "The Limits of Solidarity: Labor and Transnational Organizing Against Coca-Cola." *American Ethnologist* 36, no. 4: 667–80.

Giménez, J., and E. Bravo Sánchez. 2017. "La indígena desterrada por feminista." *El Pais*, June 9, 2017. https://elpais.com/elpais/2017/06/06/planeta_futuro/14967566 92_101038.html.

Giraldo, Isis. 2016. "Coloniality at Work: Decolonial Critique and the Postfeminist Regime." *Feminist Theory* 17, no. 2: 157–73. https://doi.org/10.1177/146470011 6652835.

Giraud, Isabelle. 2015. "Intégrer la diversité des oppressions dans la Marche Mondiale des Femmes." *L'Homme et la Société* 4, no. 198: 95–112.

Giraud, Isabelle, and Pascale Dufour. 2010. *Dix Ans de Solidarité Planétaire: Perspectives Sociologiques sur la Marche Mondiale des Femmes.* Montréal: Éditions du Remue-ménage.

Giugni, Marco, and Florence Passy, eds. 2001. *Political Altruism? Solidarity Movements in International Perspective.* Lanham, MD: Rowman & Littlefield.

Gober, Greta, and Justyna Struzik. 2018. "Feminist Diaspora in the Making: The Case of the #BlackProtest." *Praktyka Teoretyczna* 4, no. 30: 129–52.

Goeman, Mishuana. 2009. "Notes Toward a Native Feminism's Spatial Practice." *Wicazo Sa Review* 24, no. 2: 169–87.

Gold, Tami. 2011. *Passionate Politics: The Life and Work of Charlotte Bunch. A Joyce Warshow Film.* Anderson Gold Films, Inc.

Gould, Carole C. 2007. "Transnational Solidarities." *Journal of Social Philosophy* 38, no. 1: 148–64.

Gould, Roger V., and Roberto M. Fernandez. 1989. "Structures of Mediation: A Formal Approach to Brokerage in Transaction Networks." *Sociological Methodology* 19: 89–126.

Grabowska, Magdalena. 2012. "Bringing the Second World In: Conservative Revolution(s), Socialist Legacies, and Transnational Silences in the Trajectories of Polish Feminism." *Signs: Journal of Women in Culture and Society* 37, no. 2: 385–411. DOI: 10.1086/661728.

Greene, Shane. 2006. "Getting Over the Andes: The Geo-Eco-Politics of Indigenous Movements in Peru's Twenty-First Century Inca Empire." *Journal of Latin American Studies* 38, no. 2: 327–54.

Grewal, Inderpal. 2005. *Transnational America: Feminisms, Diasporas, Neoliberalism.* Durham: Duke University Press.

Grewal, Inderpal, and Caren Kaplan, eds. 1994. *Scattered Hegemonies: Postmodernity and Transnational Feminist Practices*. Minneapolis and London: University of Minnesota Press.

Grosescu, Raluca, and Ned Richardson-Little. 2019. "Revisiting State Socialist Approaches to International Criminal and Humanitarian Law: An Introduction." *Journal of the History of International Law* 21, no. 2: 161–180. DOI: 10.1163/15718050-12340110.

Guilhot, Nicolas. 2005. *The Democracy Makers: Human Rights and the Politics of Global Order*. New York: Columbia University Press.

Hall, Lisa K. 2009. "Navigating Our Own 'Sea of Islands': Remapping a Theoretical Space for Hawaiian Women and Indigenous Feminism." *Wicazo Sa Review* 24, no. 2: 15–38.

Hallman, Ben, and Roxana Olivera. 2015. "Gold Rush: How the World Bank is Financing Environmental Destruction." *The Huffington Post*, April 15, 2015. http://projects.huffingtonpost.com/worldbank-evicted-abandoned/how-worldbank-finances-environmental-destruction-peru.

Hartmann, Susan M., 1998. *The Other Feminists: Activists in the Liberal Establishment*. New Haven: Yale University Press.

Hau'ofa, Epeli. 1994. "Our Sea of Islands." *The Contemporary Pacific* 6, no. 1: 148–61.

Hawkesworth, Mary. 2006. *Globalization and Feminist Activism*. Lanham, MD: Rowman & Littlefield.

Hayward, J.E.S. 1959. "Solidarity: The Social History of an Idea in Nineteenth Century France." *International Review of Social History* 4, no. 2: 261–84.

Henry, Alice. 1985. "Nairobi Women's Conference." *Off Our Backs* 15, no. 9: 1–6; 12–15; 26. https://www.jstor.org/stable/25775621.

Herr, Ranjoo Seodu. 2014. "Reclaiming Third World Feminism: or Why Transnational Feminism Needs Third World Feminism." *Meridians* 12, no. 1: 1–30.

Herr, Ranjoo Seodu. 2019. "Women's Rights as Human Rights and Cultural Imperialism." *Feminist Formations* 31, no. 3: 118–142. https://doi.org/10.1353/ff.2019.0033.

Heumann, Silke, Ana V. Portocarrero, Camilo Antillón Najlis, María Teresa Blandón, Geni Gómez, Athiany Larios, Ana Quirós Víquez, and Juana Urbina. 2017. "Dialogue: Transgendered Bodies as Subjects of Feminism: A Conversation and Analysis about the Inclusion of Trans Persons and Politics in the Nicaraguan Feminist Movement." In *Bodies in Resistance: Gender and Sexual Politics in the Age of Neoliberalism*, edited by Wendy Harcourt, 163–88. London: Palgrave Macmillan.

Hewitt, Lyndi. 2011. "Framing Across Differences, Building Solidarities: Lessons from Women's Rights Activism in Transnational Spaces." *Interface: A Journal for and about Social Movements* 3, no. 2: 65–99.

Hoelzl, Michael. 2004. "Recognizing the Sacrificial Victim: The Problem of Solidarity for Critical Social Theory." *Journal for Cultural and Religious Theory* 6, no. 1: 45–64.

Hooker, Juliet. 2009. *Race and the Politics of Solidarity*. Oxford, UK: Oxford University Press.

Horn, Denise. 2010. *Women, Civil Society and the Geopolitics of Democratization.* London: Routledge.

Hosken, Fran P., ed. 1981. "Symposium: Women and International Human Rights." *Human Rights Quarterly* 3, no. 2: 1–148.

Hundle, Anneeth Kaur, Ioana Szeman and Joanna Pares Hoare, eds. "Transnational Feminist Research." Special issue, *Feminist Review* 121, no. 1 (March 2019).

Hunt-Hendrix, Leah. 2014. "The Ethics of Solidarity: Republican, Marxist and Anarchist Interpretations." PhD diss., Princeton University.

Issa, Daniela. 2007. "Praxis of Empowerment: Mística and Mobilization in Brazil's Landless Rural Workers' Movement." *Latin American Perspectives* 34, no. 2: 24–38.

Jacquemond, Richard. 1992. "Translation and Cultural Hegemony: The Case of French-Arabic Translation." In *Rethinking Translation: Discourse, Subjectivity and Ideology*, edited by Lawrence Venuti, 139–58. New York: Routledge.

Jacquet, Caroline. 2017. *Représentations féministes de « la religion » et de « la laïcité » au Québec (1960–2013) : Reproductions et contestations des frontières identitaires.* PhD diss., Université du Québec à Montréal.

Jain, Devaki. 2005. *Women, Development, and the UN. A Sixty-year Quest for Equality and Justice.* Bloomington, IN: Indiana University Press.

Jenkins, Katy. 2014. "Women, Mining and Development: An Emerging Research Agenda." *The Extractive Industry and Society* 1, no. 2: 329–39.

Joachim, Jutta. 2007. *Agenda Setting, the UN and NGOs: Gender, Violence, and Reproductive Rights.* Washington, DC: Georgetown University Press.

Joachim, Jutta. 2013. "Local-Global-Local: Women's Global Organizing." In *The Oxford Handbook of Gender and Politics*, edited by Georgina Waylen, Karen Celis, Johanna Kantola, and S. Laurel Weldon, 462–84. New York: Oxford University Press.

Johnston, Josée, and Gordon Laxer. 2003. "Solidarity in the Age of Globalization: Lessons from the Anti-MAI and Zapatista Struggles." *Theory and Society* 32, no. 1: 39–91.

Juteau, Danielle. 2010. "'Nous' les femmes : sur l'indissociable homogénéité et hétérogénéité de la catégorie." *L'homme et la société* 2, no. 176–77: 65–81.

Kaplan, Caren. 1994. "The Politics of Location as Transnational Feminist Critical Practice." In *Scattered Hegemonies: Postmodernity and Transnational Feminist Practices,* edited by Inderpal Grewal and Caren Kaplan, 137–52. Minneapolis, MN: University of Minnesota Press.

Kaplan, Caren, and Inderpal Grewal. 1999. "Transnational Feminist Cultural Studies: Beyond the Marxism/Postrstructuralism/Feminism Divides." In *Between Women and Nation: Nationalism, Transnational Feminisms and the State,* edited by Kaplan et al., 349–63. Durham, NC: Duke University Press.

Karkov, Nikolay, and Zhivka Valiavicharska. 2018. "Rethinking East-European Socialism: Notes Toward an Anti-Capitalist Decolonial Methodology." *Interventions: International Journal of Postcolonial Studies* 10 : 1–29. DOI:10.10 80/1369801X.2018.1515647.

Keating, AnaLouise. 2013. *Transformation Now! Towards a Post-Oppositional Politics of Change*. Chicago: University of Illinois Press.

Keck, Margaret E., and Kathryn Sikkink. 1998. *Activists Beyond Borders: Advocacy Networks in International Politics*. Ithaca and London: Cornell University Press.

Kergoat, Danièle. 2009. "Dynamique et consubstantialité des rapports sociaux." In *Sexe, race et classe : Pour une épistémologie de la domination*, edited by Elsa Dorlin, 111–25. Paris: PUF.

Galerand, Elsa, and Danièle Kergoat, 2014. "Consubstantialité vs intersectionnalité? À propos de l'imbrication des rapports sociaux." *Nouvelles pratiques sociales* 26, no. 2: 44–61.

Kim, Hyun Sook. 2007. "The Politics of Border Crossings: Black, Post-colonial and Transnational Feminist Perspectives." In *The Handbook of Feminist Research: Theory and Praxis*, edited by Sharlene N. Hesse-Biber, 107–22. Thousand Oaks, CA: Sage Publishing.

King, Katie. 2002. "'There Are No Lesbians Here': Lesbianisms, Feminisms, and Global Gay Formations." In *Queer Globalizations: Citizenship and the Afterlife of Colonialism*, edited by Arnaldo Cruz-Malavé and Martin F. Manalansan IV, 33–45. New York and London: New York University Press.

Koobak, Redi, and Raili Marling. 2014. "The Decolonial Challenge: Framing Postsocialist Central and Eastern Europe Within Transnational Feminist Studies." *European Journal of Women Studies* 21, no. 4: 330–43.

Korey, William. 2007. *Taking on the World's Repressive Regimes: The Ford Foundation's International Human Rights Policies and Practices*. New York: Palgrave Macmillan.

Kowtal, A. 2019. "Building a Feminism That Centres the Voices of the Oppressed." *The Wire*, February 15, 2019. https://thewire.in/caste/building-a-feminism-that-centres-the-voices-of-the-oppressed.

Krunke, Helle, Hanne Petersen, and Ian Manners. 2020. *Transnational Solidarity: Concept, Challenges and Opportunities*. Cambridge, UK: Cambridge University Press.

Kubica, Grazyna. 2006. "Tęczowa Flaga Przeciwko Wawelskiemu Smokowi: Kulturowa Interpretacja Konfliktu Wokól Krakowskiego Marszu Dla Tolerancji." *Studia Socjologiczne* 4, no. 183: 69–106.

Kulawik, Teresa, and Zhanna Kravcenko, eds. 2020. *Borderlands in European Gender Studies: Beyond the East-West Frontier*. London: Routledge.

Kulpa, Robert. 2014. "Western Leveraged Pedagogy of Central and Eastern Europe: Discourses of Homophobia, Tolerance, and Nationhood." *Gender, Place and Culture* 21, no. 4: 431–48.

Kulpa, Robert, and Joanna Mizielińska, eds. 2011. *De-Centering Western Sexualities: Central and East European Perspectives*. London: Ashgate.

Kulpa, Robert, Joanna Mizielińska, and Agata Stasińska. 2012. "(Un)translatable Queer? or What Is Lost and Can Be Found in Translation. . ." In *Import - Export - Transport. Queer Theory, Queer Critique, and Activism in Motion*, edited by

Sushiula Mesquita, Maria Katharina Wiedlack, and Katrin Lasthofer, 115–46. Vienna: Zaglossus.

Kwon, Heonik. 2010. *The Other Cold War*. New York: Columbia University Press.

Laclau, Ernesto, and Chantal Mouffe. 1985. *Hegemony and Socialist Strategy*. London: Verso.

Laville, Helen. 2002. *Cold War Women: The International Activities of American Women's Organizations*. New York: Manchester University Press.

Lawrence, Bonita, and Jocelyn Thorpe. 2005. "Indigeneity and Transnationality? An Interview with Bonita Lawrence." *Women and Environments International Magazine* (Fall/Winter): 6–8. www.weimag.com.

Lebon, Nathalie. 2014. "Brazilian Popular Feminism and Its Roots and Alliances." In *Rethinking Latin American Social Movements: Radical Action from Below*, edited by Richard Stahler-Sholk, Harry Vanden, and Marc Becker, 147–66. Lanham, MD: Rowman & Littlefield.

Leinius, Johanna. 2020a. "The Postcolonial Feminist Ethics and Politics of Research Collaborations across North-South Divides." In *Beyond the Master's Tools? Decolonizing Knowledge Orders, Research Methods, and Teaching*, edited by Aram Ziai, Franziska Müller, and Daniel Bendix, 71–92. London: Palgrave.

Leinius, Johanna. 2020b. "Methodologies of Resistance: Facilitating Solidarity Across Difference in Inter-Movement Encounters." *Ephemera: Theory & Politics in Organization* 20, no. 1: 117–49.

Leite, Jose Correa. 2005. *The World Social Forum: Strategies of Resistance*. Chicago, IL: Haymarket Books.

Lépinard, Eléonore, and Sarah Mazouz. 2019. "Cartographie du surplomb : Ce que les résistances au concept d'intersectionnalité nous disent sur les sciences sociales en France." *Mouvements,* February 12, 2019. http://mouvements.info/cartographie-du-surplomb/.

Lewis, Rachel. 2010. "The Cultural Politics of Lesbian Asylum: Angelina Maccarone's Unveiled (2005) and the Case of the Lesbian Asylum-Seeker." *International Feminist Journal of Politics* 12, no. 3–4: 424–43.

Lim, Adelyn. 2015. *Transnational Feminism and Women's Movements in Post-1997 Hong King: Solidarity Beyond the State*. Hong Kong: Hong Kong University Press.

Lorde, Audre. 1982. *Zami: A New Spelling of My Name*. New York: Persephone Press.

Lorde, Audre. 1984. *Sister Outsider: Essays and Speeches*. Freedom: Crossing Press.

Loudes, Christine, ed. 2006. *Handbook on Observations of Pride Marches*. Brussels: ILGA-Europe.

Louw, Dirk J. 1998. "Ubuntu: An African Assessment of the Religious Other." Twentieth World Congress of Philosophy.

Lugones, María. 2003. *Pilgrimages/Peregrinajes: Theorizing Coalition Against Multiple Oppressions*. Lanham, MD: Rowman & Littlefield.

Mahler, Anne Garland. 2018. *From the Tricontinental to the Global South: Race, Radicalism and Transnational Solidarity*. Duke University Press.

Mahmood, Saba. 2011. "Religion, Feminism, and Empire: The New Ambassadors of Islamophobia." In *Feminism, Sexuality, and the Return of Religion,* edited by Linda

Martín Alcoff and John D. Caputo, 77–102. Bloomington: Indiana University Press.

Mahrouse, Gada. 2014. *Conflicted Commitments: Race, Privilege, and Power in Solidarity Activism.* Montreal, QC: McGill-Queen's University Press.

Mani, Lati. 1990. "Multiple Mediations: Feminist Scholarship in the Age of Multinational Reception." *Feminist Review* 35: 24–41.

Manolova, Polina, Katarina Kusic, and Phillipp Lottholz. 2019. "From Dialogue to Practice: Pathways Towards Decoloniality in Southeastern Europe." *Dversia.net* 3, no. 19: 7–30.

Massey, Doreen. 1994. *Space, Place, and Gender.* Minneapolis, MN: University of Minnesota Press.

Massey, Doreen. 2008. "Geographies of Solidarities." In *Material Geographies: A World in the Making,* edited by Nigel Clark, Doreen Massey, and Philip Sarre, 311–53. London: Sage Publications.

Masson, Dominique. 2006. "Constructing Scale/Contesting Scale: Women's Movement and Rescaling Politics in Québec." *Social Politics: International Studies in Gender, State and Society* 13, no. 4: 462–86. muse.jhu.edu/article/206834.

Masson, Dominique. 2009. "Politiques des échelles et transnationalisation : perspectives géographiques." *Politique et Sociétés* 28, no. 1: 113–33. https://doi-org.inshs.bib.cnrs.fr/10.7202/001727ar.

Masson, Dominique. 2010. "Transnationalizing Feminist and Women's Movements: Toward a Scalar Approach." In *Solidarities Beyond Borders: Transnationalizing Women's Movements,* edited by Pascale Dufour, Dominique Masson, and Dominique Caouette, 35–55. Vancouver: UBC Press.

Masson, Dominique, and Anabel Paulos. 2018. "Solidarity-building as Praxis: Anti-extractivism and the World March of Women in the Macro-Norte Region of Peru." Symposium on "Transnational Objects, Activist Solidarities, Feminist Analytics," December 5–7, 2018. University of Ottawa.

Masson, Dominique, Anabel Paulos, and Elsa Beaulieu-Bastien. 2017. "Struggling for Food Sovereignty in the World March of Women." *Journal of Peasant Studies* 44, no. 1: 56–77.

Masson, Dominique, and Elsa Beaulieu-Bastien. 2021. "The Relational Dynamics of Becoming Popular Feminist Subjects: The WMW and Rural/peasant Women's Organizing in Brazil in the 2000s." *Latin American Perspectives* 48, no. 5.

Masson, Dominique, and Janet Conway. 2017. "La Marche mondiale des femmes et la souveraineté alimentaire comme nouvel enjeu féministe." *Nouvelle questions féministes* 36, no. 1: 36–47. DOI: 10.3917/nqf.361.0032.

May, Vivian M. 2014. "'Speaking into the Void?' Intersectionality Critiques and Epistemic Backlash." *Hypatia* 29, no. 1: 94–112.

McAdam, Doug, and Dieter Rucht. 1993. "The Cross-National Diffusion of Movement Ideas." *The Annals of the American Academy of Political and Social Science* 528: 56–74.

McLaren, Margaret A., ed. 2017. *Decolonizing Feminism: Transnational Feminism and Globalization.* London, UK: Rowman & Littlefield International.

McMahon, Robert. 2013. *The Cold War in the Third World.* New York: Oxford University Press.

McMichael, Philip. 1997. "Rethinking Globalization: The Agrarian Question Revisited." *Review of International Political Economy* 4, no. 4: 630–62. https://do i.org/10.1080/09672299708565786.

McMichael, Philip. 2008. "Peasants Make Their Own History, But Not Just as They Please." *Journal of Agrarian Change* 8, no. 2–3: 205–28. https://doi.org/10.1111/j .1471-0366.2008.00168.x.

Mehrez, Samia. 1992. "Translation and the Post-colonial Experience: The Francophone North African Text." In *Rethinking Translation: Discourse, Subjectivity, Ideology*, edited by Lawrence Venuti, 120–38. London: Routledge.

Melucci, Alberto. 1988. *Challenging Codes: Collective Action in the Information Age*. Cambridge, UK: Cambridge University Press.

Melucci, Alberto. 1995. "The Process of Collective Identity." In *Social Movements and Culture,* edited by Hank Johnston and Bert Klandermans, 41–62. London, UK: Routledge.

Méndez, Luis Hallazi. 2013. "Peru: El caso de la Comunidad de Cañaris y el Derecho a la Consulta Previa." *Servindi, Servicios de Comunicacion Intercultural.* January 31, 2013. https://www.servindi.org/actualidad/81367.

Mendoza, Breny. 2002. "Transnational Feminisms in Question." *Feminist Theory* 3, no. 3: 295–314.

Mendoza, Breny. 2015. "Coloniality of Gender and Power: From Postcoloniality to Decoloniality." In *The Oxford Handbook of Feminist Theory*, edited by Lisa Disch and Mary Hawkesworth, 1–24. New York: Oxford University Press.

Michel, Sonya, ed. "Women and International Organizations in the Late 20th Century." Special issue, *Global Social Policy* 14, no. 2 (August 2014).

Mignolo, Walter. 2012. *Local Histories/Global Designs*. Princeton: Princeton University Press.

Mikkonen, Enni. 2020. "Decolonial and Transnational Feminist Solidarity: Promoting Ethically Sustainable Social Change with Women in Rural Nepalese Communities." *The International Journal of Community and Social Development* 2, no. 1: 10–28.

Mizielińska, Joanna, and Agata Stasińska. 2017. "Beyond the Western Gaze: Families of Choice in Poland." *Sexualities* 21, no. 7: 983–1001.

Moghadam, Valentine. 1995. "WID, WAD, GAD: Integration of Gender in Development." Gender & Society Working Paper #3 in series Gender and Development, Women's Studies Programme, Birzeit University: 1–30.

Moghadam, Valentine. 2000. "Transnational Feminist Networks: Collective Action in an Era of Globalization." *International Sociology* 15, no. 1: 57–85.

Moghadam, Valentine. 2005. *Globalizing Women: Transnational Feminist Networks*. Baltimore: Johns Hopkins University Press.

Mohanty, Chandra Talpade. 1984. "Under Western Eyes: Feminist Scholarship and Colonial Discourses." *Boundary 2* 12, no. 3–13, no. 1: 333–58.

Mohanty, Chandra Talpade. 1987. "Feminist Encounters: Locating the Politics of Experience." *Copyright* 1 (fall): 30–44.

Mohanty, Chandra Talpade. 1991a. "Cartographies of Struggle: Third World Women and the Politics of Feminism." In *Third World Women and the Politics of Feminism*, edited by Chandra Talpade Mohanty, Ann Russo, and Lourdes Torres, 1–48. Bloomington, IN: Indiana University Press.

Mohanty, Chandra Talpade. 1991b. "Under Western Eyes: Feminist Scholarship and Colonial Discourses." In *Third World Women and the Politics of Feminism,* edited by Chandra Talpade Mohanty, Ann Russo, and Lourdes Torres, 51–79. Bloomington, IN: Indiana University Press.

Mohanty, Chandra Talpade. 2002. "'Under Western Eyes' Revisited: Feminist Solidarity through Anticapitalist Struggles." *Signs: Journal of Women in Culture and Society* 28, no. 2: 499–535.

Mohanty, Chandra Talpade. 2003. *Feminism Without Borders: Decolonizing Theory, Practicing Solidarity.* Durham & London: Duke University Press.

Mohanty, Chandra Talpade. 2013. "Transnational Feminist Crossings: On Neoliberalism and Radical Critique." *Signs: Journal of Women in Culture and Society* 38, no. 4: 967–91.

Mohanty, Chandra Talpade, Ann Russo, and Lourdes Torres, eds. 1991. *Third World Women and the Politics of Feminism.* Bloomington, IN: Indiana University Press.

Moore Torres, Catherine. 2018. "Feminismos del Sur, abriendo horizontes de descolonización. Los feminismos indígenas y los feminismos comunitarios." *Estudios Políticos* 53: 237–59. http://doi.org/10.17533/udea.espo.n53a11.

Morgan, Robin, ed. 1984. *Sisterhood is Global: The International Women's Movement Anthology.* Garden City, NY: Anchor Press/Doubleday.

Moses, Claire Goldberg. 1998. "Made in America: 'French Feminism' in Academia." *Feminist Studies* 24, no. 2: 241–74.

Mott, Carrie. 2018. "Building Relationships Within Differences: An Anarchafeminist Approach to the Micro-politics of Solidarity." *Annals of the American Association of Geographers* 108, no. 2: 424–33.

Motta, Renata. n.d. "Feminist Solidarities and Coalitional Identity: The Popular Feminism of Marcha das Margaridas." Unpublished manuscript, *Latin American Perspectives.*

Nagar, Richa. 2014. *Muddying the Waters: Coauthoring Feminisms across Scholarship and Activism.* Urbana-Champaign, IL: University of Illinois Press.

Naples, Nancy A. 2008. "Crossing Borders: Feminism, Intersectionality and Globalisation." *Hawke Research Institute Working Paper Series*, no 36. Magill: University of South Australia.

Naples, Nancy A., and Jennifer Bickham Mendez, eds. 2014. *Border Politics: Social Movements, Collective Identities, and Globalization.* New York, NY: NYU Press.

Naples, Nancy A., and Manisha Desai. 2002. *Women's Activism and Globalization: Linking Local Struggles and Transnational Politics.* London: Routledge.

Nash, Jennifer. 2008. "Re-thinking Intersectionality." *Feminist Review* 89: 1–15.

Neier, Aryeh. 2012. *The International Human Rights Movement. A History.* Princeton: Princeton University Press.

Neufeld, Masha. 2018. "'We Will Get There, but We Have to Grow as High as That': Spinning the Narrative of Backwardness in the Russian LGBT Movement." In *Queering Paradigms VII: Contested Bodies and Spaces*, edited by Bee Scherer, 83–103. Oxford: Peter Lang.

Noiriel, Gérard. 2018. "Réflexions sur la gauche identitaire." *Le populaire dans tous ses états* (Blog). October 29, 2018. https://noiriel.wordpress.com/2018/10/29/refl exions-sur-la-gauche-identitaire/.

Nunes, Rodrigo. 2005. "Networks, Open Spaces, Horizontality: Instantiations." *Ephemera: Theory & Politics in Organization* 5, no. 2: 297–318.

O'Barr, Jean F., Irene Tinker, Tami Hultman, Rudo Gaidzanwa, Beverly Guy-Sheftall, Helen Callaway, Amrita Basu, and Alison Bernstein. 1986. "Reflections on Forum '85 in Nairobi, Kenya: Voices from the International Women's Studies Community." *Signs: Journal of Women in Culture and Society* 11, no. 3: 584–608. https://www-jstor-org.inshs.bib.cnrs.fr/stable/3174020.

Olcott, Jocelyn. 2017. *International Women's Year: The Greatest Consciousness-Raising Event in History*. New York: Oxford University Press.

Ong, Aihwa. 1996. "Strategic Sisterhood or Sisters in Solidarity? Questions of Communitarianism and Citizenship in Asia." *Indiana Journal of Global Legal Studies* 4, no. 1: 107–35.

Pagé, Geneviève. 2012. *Feminism à La Québec: Ideological Travelings of American and French Thought (1960–2010)*. PhD. diss., University of Maryland.

Pagé, Geneviève. 2014. "Sur l'indivisibilité de la justice sociale : Ou pourquoi le mouvement féministe québécois ne peut faire l'économie d'une analyse intersectionnelle." *Nouvelles Pratiques Sociales* 26, no. 2: 203–20.

Pagé, Geneviève. 2015. "'Est-ce qu'on peut être racisées nous aussi?' : Les féministes blanches et le désir de racisation." In *Le sujet du féminisme est-il blanc? Femmes racisées et recherches féministes*, edited by Naïma Hamrounie and Chantal Maillé, 133–54. Montreal: Remue-Ménage.

Pagé, Geneviève. 2018. "Power, Translation and Conceptual Border Crossing: The Stepping Stones of Transnational Feminism." Symposium on "Transnational Objects, Activist Solidarities, Feminist Analytics," December 5–7, 2018. University of Toronto.

Pagé, Geneviève, and Rosa Pires. 2015. *L'intersectionnalité en débats : Pour un renouvellement des pratiques féministes au Québec*. Montreal: Service aux collectivité, UQAM.

Paik, Shailaja. 2014. "Building Bridges: Articulating Dalit and African American Women's Solidarity." *Women's Studies Quarterly* 42, no. 3–4: 74–96.

Papanek, Hanna. 1975. "The Work of Women: Postscript from Mexico City." *Signs: Journal of Women in Culture and Society* 1, no. 1: 215–26. https://www-jstor-org.inshs.bib.cnrs.fr/stable/3172978.

Papanek, Hanna. 1977. "Development Planning for Women." *Signs: Journal of Women in Culture and Society* 3, no. 1: 14–21. https://www-jstor-org.inshs.bib.cnrs.fr/stable/3173075.

Paternotte, David. 2016. "The NGOization of LGBT Activism: ILGA-Europe and the Treaty of Amsterdam." *Social Movement Studies* 15, no. 4: 388–402.

PDTG. 2010. *Entre la Crisis y Otros Mundos Posibles: Memoria del I Taller de Diálogos de Movimientos y Saberes*. Lima: PDTG.

PDTG. 2014. *Memoria V Diálogos de Saberes y Movimientos*. Lima: PDTG.

Péloquin, Marjolaine. 2007. *En prison pour la cause des femmes : La conquête du banc des jurés*. Montréal: Remue-ménage.

Perry, Keisha-Khan Y. 2013. *Black Women against the Land Grab: The Fight for Racial Justice in Brazil*. Minneapolis, MN: University of Minnesota Press.

Perry, Keisha-Khan Y. 2016. "Geographies of Power: Black Women Mobilizing Intersectionality in Brazil." *Meridians* 14, no. 1: 94–120.

Pour le droit des femmes du Québec (PDFQ). n.d. "À propos" *Pour le droit des femmes du Québec.* Accessed October 20, 2019. http://www.pdfquebec.org/plate-forme.php.

Pratt, Mary Louise. 1991. "The Art of the Contact Zone." *Profession*: 33–40.

Puar, Jasbir. 2007. *Terrorist Assemblages: Homonationalims in Queer Times.* Durham and London: Duke University.

Quataert, Jean H. 2014. "A Knowledge Revolution: Transnational Feminist Contributions to International Development Agendas and Policies, 1965–1995." *An Interdisciplinary Journal of Public Policy and Social Development* 14, no. 2: 209–27. https://doi-org.inshs.bib.cnrs.fr/10.1177/1468018113511835.

Quataert, Jean H. and Benita Roth, eds. "Human Rights, Global Conferences, and the Making of Postwar Transnational Feminisms." Special issue, *Journal of Women's History* 24, no. 4 (Winter 2012).

Quick Hall, K. Melchor. 2019. *Naming a Transnational Black Feminist Framework: Writing in Darkness.* London, UK: Routledge.

Rai, Shirin, and Georgina Waylen. 2008. *Global Governance: Feminist Perspectives.* New York: Palgrave Macmillan.

Reagon, Bernice Johnson. 1983. "Coalition Politics: Turning the Century." In *Home Girls: A Black Feminist Anthology,* edited by Barbara Smith, 356–68. Latham, NY: Kitchen Table Press.

Rege, Sharmila. 1998. "Dalit Women Talk Differently: A Critique of 'Difference' and Towards a Dalit Feminist Standpoint Position." *Economic and Political Weekly* 33, no. 44: WS39–WS46.

Reilly, Niamh, ed. 2019. *International Human Rights of Women.* Singapore: Springer.

Reitan, Ruth. 2007. *Global Activism.* New York, NY: Routledge.

Ricci, Amanda. 2015. *There's No Place Like Home: Feminist Communities, Social Citizenship and (Un) Belonging in Montréal's Long Women's Movement, 1952–1992.* PhD diss., McGill University.

Ricci, Sandrine. 2015. "Quand le sourire de la diversité cache les rapports de domination." In *Le sujet du féminisme est-il blanc? Femmes racisées et recherches féministes,* edited by Naïma Hamrounie and Chantal Maillé, 175–93. Montréal: Remue-Ménage.

Rocheleau, Dianne, and Padini Nirmal. 2015. "Feminist Political Ecologies." In *The Oxford Handbook of Transnational Feminist Movements*, edited by Rawwida Baksh-Soodeen and Wendy Harcourt, 793–814. New-York, NY: Oxford University Press.

Rodriguez, Juana Maria. 2003. *Queer Latinidad: Identity Practices, Discursive Spaces.* New York: New York University Press.

Routledge, Paul, and Andrew Cumbers. 2009. *Global Justice Networks: Geographies of Transnational Solidarity.* Manchester: Manchester University Press.

Safuta, Anna. 2018. "Fifty Shades of White: Eastern Europeans 'peripheral whiteness' in the Context of Domestic Services Provided by Migrant Women." *Tijdschrift voor Genderstudies* 21, no. 3: 217–31.

Sandoval, Chela. 2000. *Methodology of the Oppressed.* Minneapolis and London: Minneapolis University Press.

Santos, Boaventura de Sousa. 2005. "The Future of the World Social Forum: The Work of Translation." *Development* 48, no. 2: 15–22.

Santos, Boaventura de Sousa. 2006. *The Rise of the Global Left: The World Social Forum and beyond.* London: Zed.

Santos, Boaventura de Sousa. 2018. *The End of the Cognitive Empire: The Coming of Age of Epistemologies of the South.* Durham and London: Duke University Press.

Santos, Boaventura de Sousa, Joao Arriscado Nunes, and Maria Paula Meneses. 2007. "Introduction: Opening Up the Canon of Knowledge and Recognition of Difference." In *Another Knowledge is Possible—Beyond Northern Epistemologies,* edited by Boaventura de Sousa Santos, xviii–lxii. London: Verso.

Sauer, Sérgio. 2010. *Terra e Modernidade: a Reinvenção do Campo Brasileiro.* São Paulo: Expressão Popular.

Saunier, Pierre-Yves. 2013. *Transnational History.* New York: Palgrave Macmillan.

Scherer-Warren, Ilse. 2012. *Redes Emancipatórias: Na Luta contra a Exclusão e por Direitos Humanos.* Curitiba, Brazil: Editora Appris.

Scholz, Sally J. 2007. "Political Solidarity and Violent Resistance." *Journal of Social Philosophy* 38, no. 1: 38–52.

Scholz, Sally J. 2008. *Political Solidarity.* University Park, PA: Pennsylvania State University Press.

Scott, James C., 1990. *Domination and the Arts of Resistance: Hidden Transcripts.* New Haven: Yale University Press.

Shiva, Vandana, and Maria Mies. 1993. *Ecofeminism.* Halifax, Nova Scotia: Fernwood Publishers.

Sikkink, Kathryn. 2017. *Evidence for Hope: Making Human Rights Work in the 21st Century.* Princeton: Princeton University Press.

Siméant, Johanna. 2003. "Solidarisme et solidarités dans les mobilisations transnationales." In *Les solidarités transnationales,* edited by Guillaume Devin, 75–87. Paris: L'Harmattan.

Siméant, Johanna. 2010. "La transnationalisation de l'action collective." (The Transnationalization of Collective Action). In *Penser les mouvements sociaux: Conflits sociaux et contestations dans les sociétés contemporaines* (Thinking Social Movements: Social Conflicts and Contesting in Contemporary Societies), edited by Olivier Fillieule, Eric Agrikoliansky, and Isabelle Sommier, 121–44. Paris: La Découverte.

Simon, Sherry. 1996. *Gender in Translation: Cultural Identity and the Politics of Transmission.* London and New York: Routledge.

Simon, Sherry. 1999. "Translating and Interlingual Creation in the Contact Zone: Border Writing in Quebec." In *Post-Colonial Translation: Theory and Practice,* 58–74. New York, NY: Routledge.

Slootmaeckers, Koen, Heleen Touquet, and Peter Vermeersch, eds. 2016. *The EU Enlargement and Gay Politics: The Impact of Eastern Enlargement on Rights, Activism and Prejudice.* London: Palgrave Macmillan.

Smirnova, Elena. 2020. "Could You Show Me Chechnya on the Map? The Struggle for Solidarity within the Support Campaign for Homosexual Refugees from the North Caucasus in France." In *Queering Paradigms VIII: Queer-Feminist Solidarity and the East/West Divide*, edited by Katharina Wiedlack, Saltanat Shoshanova, and Masha Godovannaya, 231–61. Oxford: Peter Lang.

Smith, Jackie, Charles Chatfield, and Ron Pagnucco, eds. 1997. *Transnational Social Movements and Global Politics: Solidarity Beyond the State*. Syracuse, NY: Syracuse University Press.

Smith, Jackie, and Dawn Wiest. 2005. "The Uneven Geography of Global Civil Society: National and Global Influences on Transnational Association." *Social Forces* 84, no. 2: 621–52.

Snyder, Sarah. 2011. *Human Rights Activism and the End of the Cold War: A Transnational History of the Helsinki Network*. New York: Cambridge University Press.

Snyder, Sarah. 2018. *From Selma to Moscow: How Human Rights Activists Transformed US Foreign Policy*. New York: Columbia University Press.

Spivak, Gayatri Chakravorty. 1988. "Can the Subaltern Speak?" In *Marxism and the Interpretation of Culture*, edited by Cary Nelson and Lawrence Grossberg, 271–313. London: Macmillan.

Spivak, Gayatri Chakravorty. 2000. "A Moral Dilemma." *Theoria: A Journal of Social and Political Theory*, no. 96: 99–120.

Spivak, Gayatri Chakravorty. 2004. "The Politics of Translation." In *The Translation Studies Reader*, edited by Lawrence Venuti, 397–416. New York: Routledge.

Spivak, Gayatri Chakravorty. 2009. "They the People: Problems of Alter-Globalization." *Radical Philosophy* 157 (Sep/Oct): 31–36.

Spivak, Gayatri Chakravorty. 2013. *An Aesthetic Education in the Era of Globalization*. Cambridge, MA: Harvard University Press.

Statistics Canada. *Language Highlight Tables, 2011 Census*. https://www12.statca n.gc.ca/census-recensement/2011/dp-pd/hlt-fst/lang/Pages/highlight.cfm?TabID =1&Lang=E&Asc=1&PRCode=01&OrderBy=1&View=1&Age=1&tableID=402 &queryID=2.

Stella, Francesca. 2015. *Lesbian Lives in Soviet and Post-Soviet Russia: Post/socialism and Gendered Sexualities*. London: Palgrave Macmillan.

Stengers, Isabelle. 2005. "The Cosmopolitical Proposal." In *Making Things Public: Atmospheres of Democracy*, edited by Peter Weibel and Bruno Latour, 994–1003. Karlsruhe, ZKM: Center for Art and Media.

Stengers, Isabelle. 2011. "Comparison as a Matter of Concern." *Common Knowledge* 17, no. 1: 48–63.

Stienstra, Deborah. 1994. *Women's Movements and International Organizations*. Basingstoke: Macmillan.

Stjernø, Steinar. 2005. *Solidarity in Europe: The History of an Idea*. Cambridge, UK: Cambridge University Press.

Stone, Diane. 1996. *Capturing the Political Imagination: Think-tanks and the Policy Process*. London: Frank Cass.

Strang, David, and Sarah A. Soule. 1998. "Diffusion in Organisations and Social Movements: From Hybrid Corn to Poison Pills." *Annual Review of Sociology* 24: 265–90.

Suchland, Jennifer. 2011. "Is Postsocialism Transnational?" *Signs: Journal of Women in Culture and Society* 36, no. 4: 837–62. DOI: 10.1086/658899.

Suchland, Jennifer. 2015. *Economies of Violence: Transnational Feminism, Postsocialism and the Politics of Sex Trafficking.* Durham: Duke University Press.

Sudbury, Julia, and Margo Okazawa-Rey, eds. 2009. *Activist Scholarship: Anti-racism, Feminism, and Social Change.* New York, NY: Paradigm Publishers.

Swarr, Amanda Lock, and Richa Nagar, eds. 2010. *Critical Transnational Feminist Praxis.* Albany, NY: SUNY Press.

Swiebel, Joke. 2009. "Lesbian, Gay, Bisexual and Transgender Human Rights: The Search for an International Strategy." *Contemporary Politics* 15, no. 1: 19–35.

Swyndegouw, Erik. 1997a. "Excluding the Other: The Production of Scale and Scaled Politics." In *Geographies of Economies*, edited by Roger Lee and Jane Wills, 167–76. London: Arnold.

Swyndegouw, Erik. 1997b. "Neither Global nor Local: 'Globalization' and the Politics of Scale." In *Spaces of Globalization: Reasserting the Power of the Local*, edited by Kevin R. Cox, 137–66. New York, NY: Guilford Press.

Tabar, Linda. 2017. "From Third World Internationalism to 'The Internationals': The Transformation of Solidarity with Palestine." *Third World Quarterly* 38, no. 2: 414–35.

Tarrow, Sidney G. 2005. *The New Transnational Activism.* Cambridge, MA: Cambridge University Press.

Teixeira, Marco Antonio, and Renata Motta. 2020. "Unionism and Feminism: Alliance Building in the Brazilian Marcha das Margaridas." *Social Movement Studies*: 1–17. https://doi.org/10.1080/14742837.2020.1770430.

Tellez, Michelle, and Cristina Sanidad. 2014. "'Giving Wings to Our Dreams' Binational Activism and Workers' Rights Struggles in the San Diego-Tijuana Border Region." In *Border Politics: Social Movements, Collective Identities, and Globalization*, edited by Nancy A. Naples and Jennifer B. Mendez, 323–54. New York, NY: NYU Press.

Thayer, Millie. 2000. "Traveling Feminism: From Embodied Women to Gendered Citizenship." In *Global Ethnography: Forces, Connections, and Imaginations in a Postmodern World,* edited by Michael Burawoy, Joseph A. Blum, Sheba George, Zsuzsa Gille, Teresa Gowan, Lynne Haney, Maren Klawiter, Steven H. Lopez, Seán Ó Riain, and Millie Thayer, 203–33. Berkeley: University of California Press.

Thayer, Millie. 2014. "Translations and Refusals: Resignifying Meanings as Feminist Political Practice." In *Translocalities/Translocalidades*, edited by Sonia E. Alvarez, Claudia De Lima Costa, Veronica Feliu, Rebecca Hester, Norma Klahn, and Millie Thayer, 401–22. Durham: Duke University.

Tinker, Irene. 1982. "Response to Comments on 'A Feminist View of Copenhagen.'" *Signs: Journal of Women in Culture and Society* 8, no. 2 (Winter): 381–82. https://www-jstor-org.inshs.bib.cnrs.fr/stable/3173914.

Tinker, Irene, ed. 1990. *Persistent Inequalities: Women and World Development.* New York, NY: Oxford University Press.

Tlostanova, Madina. 2010. *Gender Epistemologies and Eurasian Borderlands.* New York, NY: Palgrave Macmillan.

Tlostanova, Madina. 2011. *On post-Soviet Imaginary and Global Coloniality: A Gendered Perspectiv.* Unpublished manuscript.

Tlostanova, Madina, Suruchi Thapar-Björkert, and Redi Koobak. 2019. "The Postsocialist 'Missing Other' of Transnational Feminism?" *Feminist Review* 121, no. 1: 81–87. https://doi.org/10.1177/0141778918816946.

Trigg, Mary K., and Stina Soderling. 2016. "Charlotte Bunch: Leading from the Margins as a Global Activist for Women's Rights." In *Junctures in Women's Leadership: Social Movements*, edited by Mary K. Trigg and Alison R. Bernstein, 139–60. New Brunswick, NJ: Rutgers University Press.

Tripp, Aili Mari. 2006. "The Evolution of Transnational Feminism: Consensus, Conflict, and New Dynamics." In *Global Feminism: Transnational Women's Activism, Organizing, and Human Rights*, edited by Myra Marx Ferree and Aili Mari Tripp, 51–75. New York: NYU Press.

Tsing, Anna. 2012. "Unruly Edges: Mushrooms as Companion Species for Donna Haraway." *Environmental Humanities* 1, no. 1: 141–54. https://doi.org/10.1215/2 2011919-3610012.

Tudor, Alyosxa. 2017. "Dimensions of Transnationalisms." *Feminist Review* 117: 20–40.

van den Brandt, Hendrika Nella. 2015. "Feminist Practices and Solidarity in Secular Societies: Case Studies on Feminists Crossing Religious-secular Divides in Politics and Practices in Antwerp, Belgium." *Social Movement Studies* 14, no. 4: 493–508.

Van Dyke, Nella, and Bryan Amos. 2017. "Social Movement Coalitions: Formation, Longevity, and Success." *Sociology Compass* 11, no. 7: e12489. https://doi.org/10 .1111/soc4.12489.

Van Dyke, Nella, and Holly McCammon. 2010. *Strategic Alliances: Coalition Building and Social Movements.* Minneapolis, MN: University of Minnesota Press.

Vargas, Virginia. 2008. *Feminismos en América Latina: Su Aporte a la Política y a la Democracia.* Lima: PDTG/UNMSM.

Vaz, Kim Marie, and Gary L. Lemons, eds. 2013. *Feminist Solidarity at the Crossroads: Intersectional Women's Studies for Transracial Alliance.* London, UK: Routledge.

Venuti, Lawrence. 1992. *Rethinking Translation: Discourse, Subjectivity, Ideology.* London: Routledge.

Venuti, Lawrence. 2004. *The Translation Studies Reader*, 2nd ed. New York, NY: Routledge.

Viitala, Jenni. 2016. *Water, Not Gold: Campesinos Defining and Acting Citizenship in the Context of Mining Projects in Rural Cajamarca, Peru.* Unpublished Master's Thesis, University of Tampere, Finland. January 26, 2017. https://tampub.uta.fi/ handle/10024/100528.

Villa, Paula-Irene. 2012. "Embodiment is Always More: Intersectionality, Subjection and the Body." In *Framing Intersectionality: Debates on a Multi-Faceted Concept in Gender Studies*, edited by Helma Lutz, Maria Teresa Herrera Vivar, and Linda Supik, 171–86. Farnham and Burlington, VT: Ashgate.

Viveiros de Castro, Eduardo. 2004. "Perspectival Anthropology and the Method of Controlled Equivocation." *Tipití: Journal of the Society for the Anthropology of Lowland South America* 2, no. 1. http://digitalcommons.trinity.edu/tipiti/vol2/iss1/1.

Wade, Peter. 2018. "Mestizaje and Conviviality in Brazil, Colombia and Mexico." *Mecila Working Paper Series.* São Paulo: Maria Sibylla Merian International Centre for Advanced Studies in the Humanities and Social Sciences Conviviality-Inequality in Latin America.

Walby, Sylvia, ed. "Gender Mainstreaming." Special issue, *Social Politics: International Studies in Gender, State and Society* 12, no. 3 (Fall 2005).

Walker, Anne. 2004. "The International Women's Tribune Center: Expanding the Struggle for Women's Rights at the UN." In *Developing Power: How Women Transformed International Development,* edited by Arvonne Fraser and Irene Tinker, 90–102. New York: Feminist Press.

Waller, Marguerite, and Sylvia Marcos. 2005. "Introduction." In *Dialogue and Difference: Feminisms Challenge Globalization,* edited by Marguerite Waller and Sylvia Marcos, xix–xxxi. New York, NY and Houndsmills: Palgrave Macmillan.

Wallerstein, Immanuel. 1991. *Geopolitics and Geoculture: Essays on the Changing World-System.* Cambridge: Cambridge University Press.

Waterman, Peter. 2001. *Globalization, Social Movements and the New Internationalisms.* London: Continuum.

Westad, Odd Arne. 2005. *The Global Cold War: Third World Interventions and the Making of Our Times.* New York: Cambridge University Press.

Wiedlack, Katharina. 2015. "Pussy Riot and the Western Gaze: Punk Music, Solidarity and the Production of Similarity and Difference." *Popular Music and Society* 39, no. 4: 410–22.

Wiedlack, Katharina, and Masha Neufeld. 2014. "Lost in Translation? Pussy Riot Solidarity Activism and the Danger of Perpetuating North/Western Hegemonies." *Religion and Gender* 4, no. 2: 145–65.

Wiedlack, Katharina, Saltanat Shoshanova, and Masha Godovannaya, eds. 2020. *Queering Paradigms VIII: Queer-Feminist Solidarity and the East/West Divide.* Oxford: Peter Lang.

Williams, Dorothy W. 1997. *The Road to Now: A History of Blacks in Montreal.* Montreal: Vehicule Press.

Wöhrer, Veronika. 2016. "Gender Studies as a Multi-centred Field? Centres and Peripheries in Academic Gender Research." *Feminist Theory* 17, no. 3: 323–43. https://doi-org.inshs.bib.cnrs.fr/10.1177/1464700116652840.

Woodcock, Shannon. 2004. "Globalization of LGBT Identities: Containment Masquerading as Salvation, or Why Lesbians Have Less Fun." In *Gender and the (Post) East-West Divide,* edited by Mihaela Frunza and Theodora-Eliza Vacarescu, 171–188. Cluj-Napoca: Lines Publishing House.

Woodcock, Shannon. 2011. "A Short History of the Queer Time of 'Post-Socialist' Romania, or Are We There Yet? Let's Ask Madonna!" In *De-Centring Western Sexualities: Central and East European Perspectives,* edited by Robert Kulpa and Joanna Mizielińska, 63–83. London: Ashgate.

World March of Women. 2004. *Women's Global Charter for Humanity.* https://marchemondiale.org/index.php/who-we-are/key-documents/womens-global-charter-for-humanity/. Last accessed 01/08/2021.

World March of Women. 2015. *Memoria. IV Encuentro Regional de la Marcha Mundial de las Mujeres de las Américas. Construyendo Alternativas Feministas para la Vida en Defensa de Nuestros Territorios.* Cajamarca, Peru, October 23–25. [Internal document, 28 pages with photos].

World March of Women. 2016. *WMW Declaration at the World Social Forum.* 22 August. http://www.cadtm.org/WMW-Declaration-at-the-World. Last Accessed 6/9/2021.

XIII EFLAC. 2014a. *Declaración LGBTI XIII EFLAC.* Lima: 13 Encuentro Feminista de América Latina y el Caribe.

XIII EFLAC. 2014b. *Manifiesto Político: Por la Liberación de Nuestros Cuerpos.* Lima: 13 Encuentro Feminista de América Latina y el Caribe.

XIII EFLAC. 2014c. *Sistematización del 13 Encuentro Feminista Latinoamericano y del Caribe: Por la Liberación de Nuestros Cuerpos.* Unpublished Report. Lima: Movimiento Manuela Ramos y Grupo Impulsor Nacional 13eflac.

Yuval-Davis, Nira. 1993. "Beyond Difference: Women and Coalition Politics." In *Making Connections: Women's Studies, Women's Movements, Women's Lives,* edited by Mary Kennedy, Cathy Lubelska, and Val Walsh, 3–10. London: Taylor and Francis.

Yuval-Davis, Nira. 1997. *Gender and Nation.* London: Sage Publications.

Zajak, Sabrina, Giulia Gortanutti, Johanna Lauber, and Ana-Maria Nikolas. 2018. "Talking about the Same but Different? Understanding Social Movement and Trade Union Cooperation through Social Movement and Industrial Relations Theories." *Industrielle Beziehungen* 25, no. 2: 166–87. https://doi.org/10.3224/indbez.v25i2.03.

Index

activism. *See* movements; organizing
advocacy coalitions. *See* solidarity
Afro-Futurism, 164
age. *See* generation as axis of difference
agency: in solidarity, xvi; through
    language, 122; in transnational
    cooperation, 34, 43, 47; women's,
    xviii, 83, 142
Aguiar, Vilênia Venâncio Porto, 90–93
Aguyar, Neuma, 15
Ahmed, Sara, 107, 115
alliance-building, 70, 72, 102–3, 113–
    14, 152. *See also* solidarity-building
altruism and political solidarity, 42–44,
    52n32
Alvarez, Sonia, 137, 138, 154
anti-extractivism: building solidarity
    around, 64–72; Indigenous
    communities and, 66–70, 72–74,
    77n16; WMW and, 63–72. *See also*
    Cañaris project; Conga project,
    Cajamarca; *Marcha das Margaridas*
Antrobus, Peggy, 11, 15, 25n9, 26n17
Anzaldúa, Gloria, 107, 110, 111, 124
Aparicio, Juan Ricardo, 109
Arvin, Maile, 163–64
Asian and Pacific Center for Women
    and Development (APCWD), 10–11
Association for Women's Rights in
    Development (AWID), 19

Association of African Women
    for Research and Development
    (AAWORD/AFARD), 14
autonomy: Indigenous fight for, 92,
    136, 142–44, 148–49, 152; local, and
    WMW, 140–41, 147
Ayoub, Phillip, 45

Bakić-Hayden, Milica, 47
Barbosa, Lia Pinheiro, 151–52
Barroso, Carmen, 15
Beijing Platform for Action, 3, 6
Bilge, Sirma, 129
Binnie, Jon, 40, 46
Black feminists/activists:
    intersectionality and, 80, 104,
    111, 127, 160–61; in Montreal
    francophone feminism, 120, 123,
    125–28; quilombolas in *Marcha das
    Margaridas,* 93–94; translation and,
    132. *See also* Indigenous peoples
Blackwell, Maylei, 137
Blaser, Mario, 109
borders: contact zones and, 122–24;
    cultural and linguistic, 124–25,
    135–36; feminist solidarities as
    border-crossing, 113–14; networks,
    cross-, 135, 156; policing,
    within movements, 122, 151;
    reconfiguration of, 121, 129–30, 139,

151–54; solidarity across, viii–xxvi, 9, 101–3, 110, 159–65; study of, 123; transnational space and, 122–24. *See also* difference; feminism; feminist networks; global feminism; movements; organizing; power dynamics; translation; WMW
Bosniak, Linda, 123–24
Brazil, activists from, 81, 85–86, 92. *See also* International Meeting of the World March of Women (Ninth); *Marcha das Margaridas*
bridge actors, 128–29, 139
bridge-building. *See* solidarity-building
brokers. *See* bridge actors
Broqua, Christophe, 45
Bunch, Charlotte, 9–13, 15, 18–20

Cabnal, Lorena, 143, 151–52, 153
Campbell-Fiset, Marie-Ève, 126, 130
Cañaris project, 67–70, 72–74, 77n16, 153. *See also* Peru; WMW
Candente Copper mining company, 67, 70
capitalism, 97, xiv, xxiv, 161, 165. *See also* neoliberalism; patriarchy; white supremacy
Carnegie Corporation, 11, 19
Catholic Church, 29, 35, 36–38, 41, 47, 52n40
Center for Women's Global Leadership (CWGL), 9, 12, 22
Central and Eastern Europe (CEE), 29, 32, 47–48. *See also* East/West divide in Europe; Polish LGBTQ movement
Chetaille, Agnès, xxiii, xxvi–xxvii
Chiclayo. *See* Peru; WMW
Christian Michelson Institute, Norway, 15
Cîrstocea, Ioana, xxiii, xxvi
citizenship as axis of difference, 136, 138, 161
Clinton, Hillary, 22
coalition-building. *See* alliance-building; solidarity-building

Cold War: global feminism and, 4–6, 8, 14–22; politics as a tool in, 24; solidarity-building during, 5, 17, 22; Soviet Union (USSR), 4–5. *See also* intersectional modality of solidarity; women's rights
colonialism: *cuerpo-territorio* and, 148–50, 152–55; decolonial movements, 85, 152; francophone feminists of Montreal and, 133n2, 134n6; linguistic, 146, 161–62; postcolonial feminism, 80, 96, 110, 162–63; power dynamics in, 61, 81, 86, 96, 146, 155; solidarity-building and, 61, 79–80, 96, 102, 146, 159–61
Combahee River Collective, 127, 132
commonality. *See* solidarity
Comte, August, xiii
conflict: *cuerpo-territorio,* 139, 141–45, 147–56, 162; at *V Diálogos,* 105–8; mediation through bridge actors, 128; at XIII EFLAC, 114. *See also* KPH; Polish LGBTQ movement
Conga project, Cajamarca, 65–72; *Conga no va* (Conga won't happen) protest, 65. *See also* Peru; WMW
Connell, Raewyn, 164
consensus-building. *See* solidarity-building
contact zones: definition, 139; Montreal, Quebec as, 122, 125–26, 133; WMW as, 139–41. *See also* space
Contag: *Caderno de Textos,* 82, 87–92, 94. *See also Marcha das Margaridas;* National Confederation of Agricultural Workers
Convention on the Elimination of All Forms of Discrimination against Women (CEDAW), 18–19
Conway, Janet: with Masson and Dufour, viii, 97, 162; on modalities of solidarity-building, xxiv, xxvi, 161; on "time space," 123, 124; on transnational feminist organizing, 61, 74, 80

About the Contributors

Dr. Agnès Chetaille has a PhD in sociology from the School for Advanced Studies in the Social Sciences (EHESS). She wrote her dissertation on the Polish lesbian and gay movement between 1980 and 2010 in a transnational perspective. She is currently a Marie Skłodowska-Curie fellow of the European Commission at the Université libre de Bruxelles (Free University of Brussels), where she studies transnational solidarities across the East/West divide and the relationship between migration and mobilization. She has published articles and chapters in journals such as *Social Movement Studies* and *Raisons politiques*, and in collected volumes such as *The Lesbian and Gay Movement and the State*.

Ioana Cîrstocea is a sociologist, researcher at the Centre national de la recherche scientifique (French National Center for Scientific Research), and a member of the Centre européen de sociologie et de science politique CESSP (European Center for Sociology and Political Science) in Paris. Her recent publications include the following: Ioana Cîrstocea, *La fin de la femme rouge? Fabriques transnationales du genre après la chute du Mur* 2019 [English version forthcoming at Palgrave]) and Ioana Cîrstocea, Delphine Lacombe, and Elisabeth Marteu (eds.), *Globalization of Gender: Mobilizations, Frameworks of Action, Knowledge* (2019).

Dr. Janet Conway is a full professor of sociology at Brock University. She served as Canada Research Chair in Social Justice from 2008 to 2018. She held the Nancy's Chair in Women's Studies at Mount Saint Vincent University from 2019 to 2021. She is the author of over fifty published works, including *Identity, Place, Knowledge: Social Movements Contesting Globalization* (2004), *Praxis and Politics: Knowledge Production in Social*

Movements (2006), and *Edges of Global Justice: The World Social Forum and Its "Others"* (2013).

Manisha Desai is the head of the Sociology Department and professor of Sociology and Asian American Studies at the University of Connecticut. Her areas of research and teaching include transnational feminisms, gender and globalization, and contemporary Indian society. She's currently working on a book that looks at contemporary feminism in India through an Adivasi/Bahujan/Dalit analytic. Her most recent book is *Subaltern Movements in India: The Gendered Geography of Struggles against Neoliberal Development* (2016). She's been recognized for her scholarship and mentorship through national and university awards and is a committed scholar activist.

Pascale Dufour is a full professor in political science at the Université de Montréal (University of Montreal). She is directing the research team on Democracy and Political Action (www.capedmontreal.com). Her work concerns collective action and social movements in a comparative perspective. She has recently published "Pour une analyse comparée de la transnationalisation des solidarités. La Marche mondiale des femmes comme « objet » transnational complexe" (*Revue internationale de politique comparée* 23, no. 2, 2016: 145–75).

Khalil Habrih is a doctoral candidate in sociology at the University of Ottawa and a graduate of the Paris Institute of Political Studies and the School for Advanced Studies in the Social Sciences (EHESS). His research examines the topics of racism, masculinities, urbanization, and carceral geography in France through the lens of ethnography and historical sociology.

Nathalie Lebon is an anthropologist and associate professor of Women, Gender, and Sexuality Studies at Gettysburg College, USA. She is the co-editor with Elizabeth Maier of *De lo Privado a lo Público: 30 Años de Lucha Ciudadana de las Mujeres en América Latina* (2006) and of *Women's Activism in Latin America and the Caribbean: Engendering Social Justice, Democratizing Citizenship* (2010). She has coedited a thematic issue of *Latin American Perspectives* on popular feminisms (2021). Her work on professionalization and cross-class coalition dynamics in the Brazilian women's movement has been published in journals such as *Organizations, Estudos Feministas, Feminist Studies*, and *Latin American Perspectives*. Her current research focuses on the conceptual translation of "buen vivir" and its challenges in feminist and anti-racist movements in Brazil.

Johanna Leinius works as a postdoctoral researcher in the Ecologies of Social Cohesion program at the University of Kassel, Germany. She is the speaker of the Section on Gender and Politics of the German Association for Political Science (DVPW) and of the Working Group "Poststructuralist Perspectives on Social Movements" of the Institute for Social Movement Studies. Her research interests are postcolonial-feminist and decolonial theory, Latin American women's movements, post-extractivism, political ontology, and the politics of critical knowledge production.

Dominique Masson is a full professor at the Institute of Feminist and Gender Studies of the University of Ottawa. She heads a SSHRC-funded research project on solidarity building around food sovereignty in the World March of Women. With Pascale Dufour and Dominique Caouette, she coedited *Solidarities beyond Borders: Transnationalizing Women's Movements* (2010). She has also published on the usefulness of the concepts of scale and rescaling for studying movement activity, the intersectional politics of disabled women's organizing, and state funding of movement activity.

Renata Motta is a junior professor of sociology at the Institute for Latin American Studies at Freie Universität Berlin (Free University of Berlin), Germany, and project leader of the Junior Research Group Food for Justice: Power, Politics, and Food Inequalities in a Bioeconomy (2019–24), funded by the German Federal Ministry of Education and Research (BMBF).

Geneviève Pagé is an associate professor of political science at the Université du Québec à Montréal (University of Quebec in Montreal) and is the program director at the Institut d'études et de recherches féministes. Her fields of research include feminist theory, political theory, social movements, and feminist pedagogy. Her current research focuses on the creation, transformation, travels, and appropriation of theoretical concepts between feminist spaces.

Anabel Paulos is a PhD candidate in sociology at the University of Ottawa's School of Sociological and Anthropological Studies. Her doctoral dissertation is titled "Scattered Solidarities: Building Trans-local Spaces of Political Solidarity Within/By the World March of Women Peru."

Marco Antonio Teixeira is a postdoctoral researcher at the Institute for Latin American Studies at Freie Universität Berlin, Germany, and scientific coordinator of the Junior Research Group Food for Justice: Power, Politics, and Food Inequalities in a Bioeconomy (2019–2024), funded by the German Federal Ministry of Education and Research (BMBF).

www.ingramcontent.com/pod-product-compliance
Lightning Source LLC
Chambersburg PA
CBHW022308280326
41932CB00010B/1029